g, 50 high and 40 wide (capable of conveying 25 persons) made
he Car which is made of wood is 75 feet long and 7 high contain-

ix hours!

port them whilst propelling the Vessel, and moved altern-

The Story of INVENTIONS

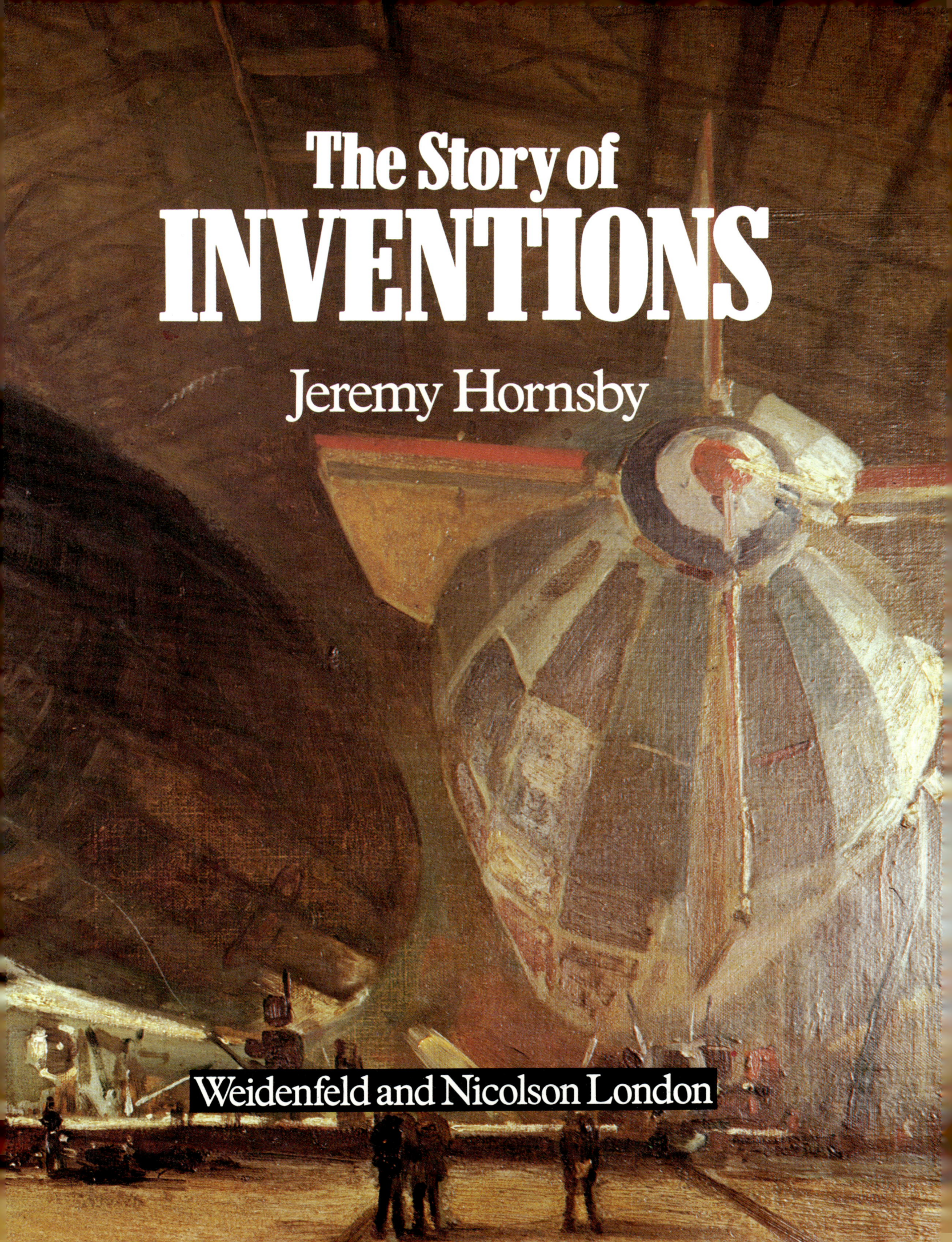

For Soapy

© Jeremy Hornsby 1977

All rights reserved. No part of this publication may be reproduced, stored in a retrieval system, or transmitted, in any form or by any means, electronic, mechanical, photocopying, recording or otherwise, without the prior written permission of the copyright owner.

Designed by Andrew Shoolbred
Layout by Janey Sugden
ISBN 0 297 77372 0

Colour Separations by Radstock Reproductions

Filmset and printed by Cox & Wyman Ltd,
London, Fakenham and Reading

Contents

Foreword 7

Foundation Stones 9

Early Civilizations 21

Greece and Rome 33

The Lull that Never Was 47

An Age of Genius 63

Industrial Evolution 83

Here Today, Where Tomorrow? 119

Acknowledgments 139

Index 141

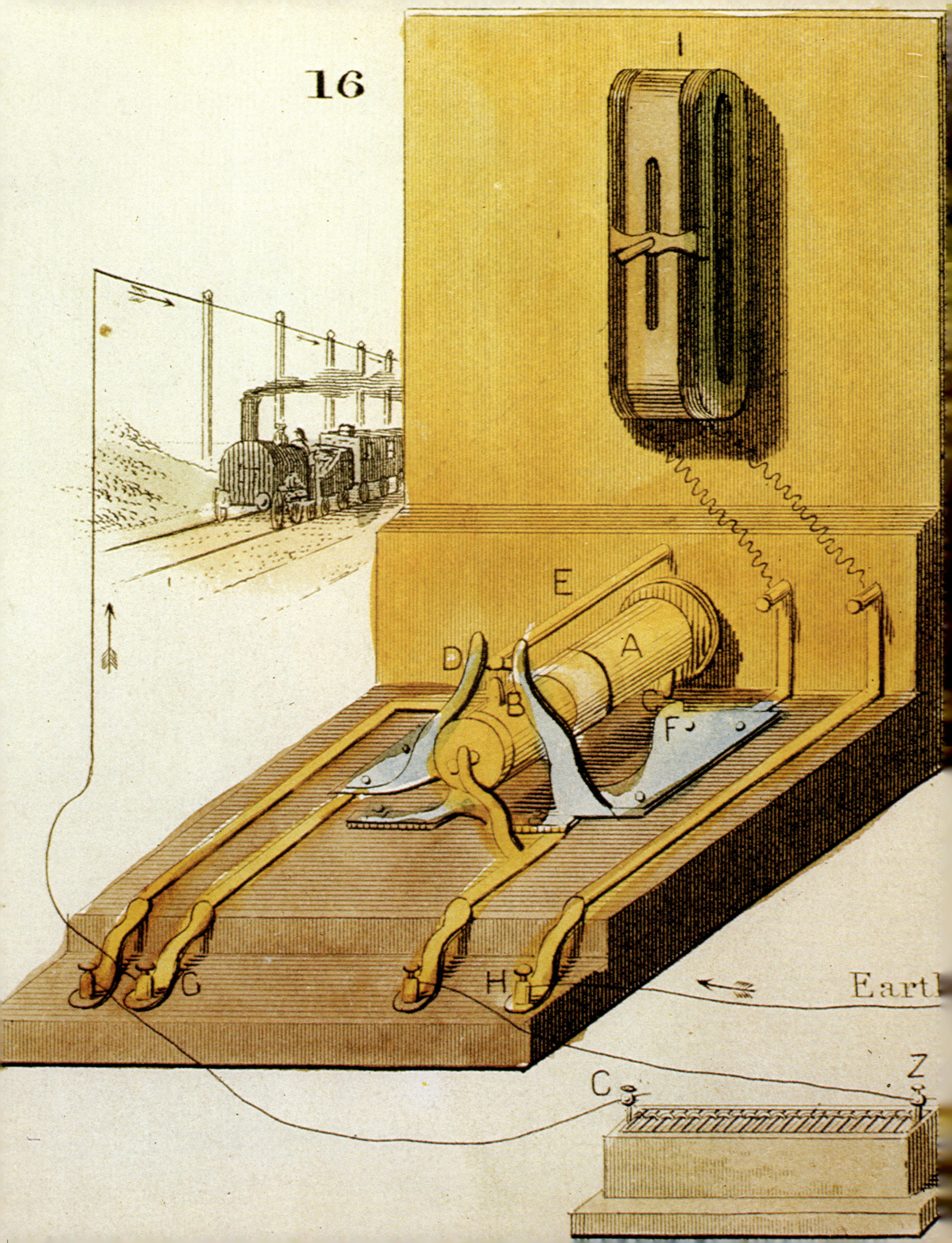

Foreword

The world of today changes so fast that most of us cannot keep up. No sooner are we accustomed to a novelty than it is made obsolete by something newer. The man-made artefacts that surround us influence every aspect of our lives: what we do, what we think, what we feel. This is why it is so important to understand *why* the world today is the way it is. Where did it all come from, and how?

This book answers these fundamental questions clearly and entertainingly. The author has spent some years writing and broadcasting on the subjects of technology and science and what they do to people. In this book he brings to bear considerable experience of communicating complex and difficult material, and the result is a fascinating look at the history of our world from a new and surprising point of view.

It is a work that can be opened at any page and enjoyed for its detail, or read from cover to cover as easily. Or both – since it is well worth reading more than once.

JAMES BURKE

A rear view of Wheatstone's telegraph; we can see how it is connected to telegraph lines running along an early railway track.

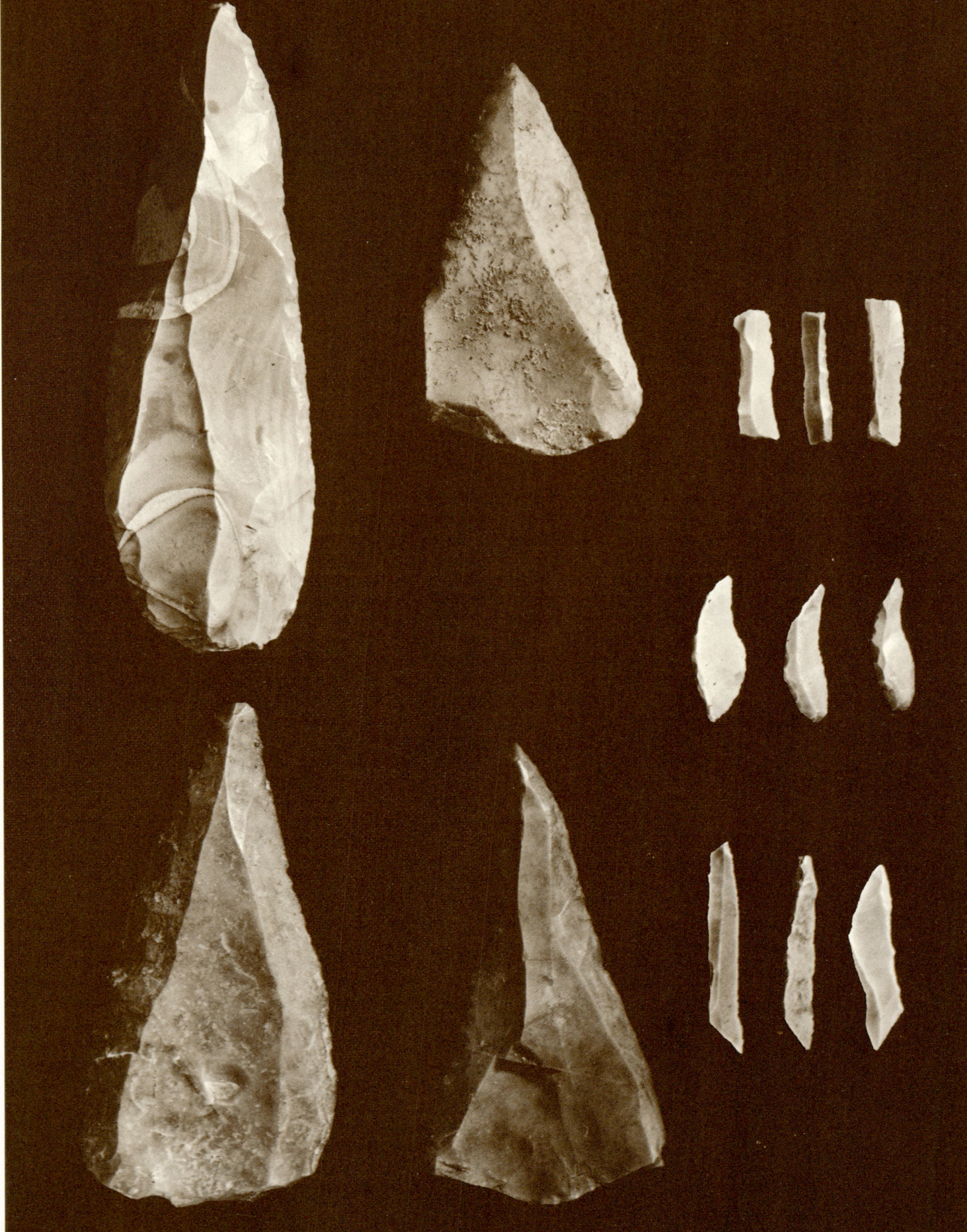

Foundation Stones

The story of man's inventions is in one very good sense the same thing as the story of man – because it is his ability to use the materials around him to shape the world for his own benefit, and the inventiveness with which he has applied this ability, that distinguishes man from the other animals. So, as an arbitrary point as good as any other for fixing the transition from ape to man, we can take that moment when man first picked up a stick or a stone and used it as a tool.

It is true that some animals are tool-users. The sea-otter uses a stone to crack open his shellfish. The chimpanzee trims a blade of grass to use as a tool for fishing tasty ants from their nest. And indeed there are types of ant who use leaves as boats for crossing rivers.

Yet these are answers to immediate problems. Once used, the stone and the grass and the leaf are discarded. There is no realization that that particular stone, or grass, or leaf, might be particularly well suited or well shaped for the purpose, and that therefore it would be worth keeping it for the next time it is needed.

For the animals, the future does not exist as an idea. For man, it is the central idea. By definition, every invention makes possible other inventions simply because there is apparently no limit to man's inventiveness. Each time an idea occurs to him, it is not for something which will work now, but for something which will work in the future once it is made.

The curiously humbling part of the study of inventions is that if one regards them as an edifice, an ever-growing tower laid stone upon stone, then one must look to the base of that tower, to its foundations, for the evidence of its strength. And the fact is that it was prehistoric man, whom we probably tend to regard as rather dim and crude, who made the truly gigantic leaps of imagination and experiment and observation upon which all our modern technology rests.

If you look up from this page, the chances are that what you will see are artefacts, many artefacts. You may see, for example,

Early flint tools. The idea of the cutting edge was one of man's first technological concepts, a key advance on the inaccuracy of breaking or ripping materials to size.

a lamp. You know that if you switch it on it will light, because you know about the concept of using electrical energy to make light. You may see a metal window catch, and you have no need to bother about the details of how it was made, because you already know, albeit roughly, that metals can be melted, and mixed, and moulded. So if you decided to invent, say, a window catch that turned on the light every time you closed the window it would not be so difficult. The basic concepts are already there and provided for you. Today, the pure and unaided leap of the imagination is rare almost to the point of non-existence.

But now consider that first prehistoric man as he sits in the grass and looks around him. He sees trees, and rocks, and water, and plants, and animals, and his own body. At that moment he has *nothing* to suggest to him that he may alter the world from that which he sees – nothing, that is, except his own intuition and genius and imagination. And there is one more, utterly important, factor: observation.

If the method of science is observation and experiment, then man has been from his very beginnings a scientist. Certainly that is the only way to account for the first, and without question the most important, of all of his technological achievements: the conquest of fire.

Fire, of course, occurs naturally all over the globe. Volcanoes produce fire. Electric storms spark forest fires. So fire was for man not an invention but an observation.

We can guess that, in the first place, man learned simply to keep fire going. He would have observed, say, that sticks near a lava flow burned; he would have picked up one of those sticks and carried it home as a brand to be kept alive by added fuel. The earliest clear evidence for fire used in this way comes from China, around 450,000 BC.

But this system has obvious disadvantages if you want to move house. And the next step was to *make* fire. Exactly when this revolutionary step took place we don't know, even to the nearest thousand years. But we do know there were two main methods. One was by what you might call the 'boy scout method' – wood friction, or rubbing two sticks together. Actually, it was not as crude as that. A common system was the 'fire-drill', in which a rod of hardwood is rotated quickly on to a

THE STORY OF INVENTIONS

piece of softwood. Eventually it wears a hole in the softwood, which then starts to smoulder. The other common method was to strike together lumps of flint, or iron pyrites. The sparks which flew off would be used to set light to dry straw or tinder.

But already, right at the bottom of man's ladder of inventions, you get the first clear sight of that cross-reference, that interaction of ideas, which runs through the whole story.

Take first the 'fire-drill'. To produce the smouldering by rubbing the stick between the hands was firstly very time-consuming and secondly very hard on the hands. But there was another invention which could be adapted to solve both problems: the bow and arrow. They took the bow and wound its string round the hardwood rod. Now, by pushing the bow backwards and forwards, the rod was spun very fast in one direction, and then in the other.

But if that is the earliest example, which it probably is, of a labour-saving device, the bow itself was an astonishing invention. It relied (though its inventors could never have known this) on two fundamental laws of mechanics.

One of these laws reflects the desire of materials to return to their point of equilibrium. The bow and the bow-string are in tension already – the string preventing the bow from returning to *its* point of equilibrium (i.e. a straight stick). So in a sense the bow is the earliest example of stored power.

Detail from a frieze showing Ashurbanipal, king of Assyria, hunting lions in the seventh century BC; *his weapon is the first 'equalizer', the bow.*

FOUNDATION STONES

In search of man's best servant, fire.
ABOVE *The blister-making method of rubbing a hardwood stick into a softwood core.*

RIGHT *The easier method of the fire-drill. By fitting a bow to the cord, it was made easier still. The humble box of matches is one of our least remembered blessings.*

The second law of mechanics concerns the fact that every lever has an optimum point at which its leverage is most effective. The lever here is the elbow. Every child knows instinctively, from playing with a bow and arrow, that once the elbow has bent back beyond the point at which it is a right angle, it becomes ever more difficult to pull. The elbow-lever has passed its optimum point. But if the bow is strung correctly, the bow and the string will, when the string is drawn back ready to fire, reach their greatest point of useful tension at exactly that point where the elbow is exerting its maximum leverage.

In its function, the bow was, of course, the first accurate long-range weapon – as an American gangster of the 'thirties would have put it, the first 'equalizer'. The small man had a chance against the wild animal (or angry, and larger, neighbour!) without needing to fight at close quarters where he would probably lose.

11

THE STORY OF INVENTIONS

The bow cross-fertilized, as we saw, into the field of fire-making, as the fire-drill, which is still used by primitive tribes in Alaska, the Kalahari, and elsewhere. Its companion fire-maker, the striking of flints, must also have come as an observed 'spin-off' from that other early technology, the making of stone tools, in the course of which sparks were produced.

As with fire, man probably started by using as tools those suitably shaped stones that happened to be lying around. Then, again probably by observation, he realized that certain stones, like flints, could be split into smaller stones, and more importantly, that he could dictate the shape by the angle and strength with which he struck one stone with another.

The idea of fire came to man with the force of exploding volcanoes.

From this most basic of materials, and equally most basic of techniques, man contrived to make an enormous variety of tools. The first was probably a crude kind of handleless axe. Then there were scrapers for removing the skins from animals. There were curved 'spokeshaves' for fashioning wooden spear-tips, daggers, exquisitely shaped arrow-heads, saws made of flint 'teeth' set into wood, and sickles for harvesting.

Now, armed with this workshop full of tools, and with fire to help him harden wooden points and pierce holes, man could make use of a whole new range of materials. Technology had started to breed technology.

From bones and antlers he started to make hammers, wedges, chisels, picks and shovels, and from wood he made handles for his stone implements. And from slivers chipped from the bone he designed a little tool that we don't think much about nowadays, but which must at the time have had a devastating effect on the whole economics of his life – the needle.

BELOW *Stone Age axes. The idea of adding a handle was to be another important breakthrough.*

BOTTOM *Fish-hooks of 1800 BC, the keys to a great larder. Like the needle, the fish-hook has remained essentially unchanged to this day.*

There are two kinds of technology. One helps man do things more efficiently, or faster, or more easily, than he could do himself. The other allows him to do things which he could *never* do himself, like sewing. A man's fingers, like the biblical camel, simply will not go through the tiny hole required for a thread.

Some forty thousand years ago, that situation was rectified. Cave-dwellings of prehistoric man have been found littered with needles made from reindeer bone and the tusks of mammoth and walrus. It was the ultimate in non-wasteful economics. Flesh was eaten, bones made tools, bone-chips made needles, and skin was worn.

Ah, yes, but *before* the needle, skins must either have been worn as they were, or torn to fit. *After* the coming of the needle, the ladies of the caves could think mink. It must have altered the whole pattern of what man would consider worth hunting.

The other fascinating thing about the needle is that its shape and its size are absolutely dictated by the job it has to do. Once it had been invented, its function decided its form, and in forty thousand years it has not changed one little bit.

Early man, as now, had three basic needs: food, shelter, and clothing. If the needle helped with the last of these, it soon gained as an ally the infant that was to grow into one of the world's greatest industries – spinning and weaving.

Very early on, man had learned the principle of weaving, using natural fibres and rushes to make baskets. But the very stiffness and inflexibility of these materials were natural limitations to the uses to which they could be put.

Early in the New Stone Age, however, man learned to use flax and wool. And in order to produce usefully long and thin threads, he learned to spin. The strands of flax or wool were attached to a long thin stick, which had a weight, made of stone or clay, attached to one end of it. This was the spindle, round which the strand was wound. By holding on to the end of the strand, and dropping the spindle (which, being unevenly balanced, spun round and round as it dropped), the strand was stretched and twisted into a thread.

Now the problem was to apply the ideas of basket-making to the interweaving of the threads – and the loom was born. The earliest form of loom consisted of a frame, at the highest point of which, usually above the head of the weaver, was a horizontal stick. The parallel rows of thread which were to form the 'skeleton' of the cloth, known as the warp, were attached at one of their ends to this stick. At the other end they were stretched and held tight by a series of weights, one weight to each thread.

Now the cross threads, known as the weft, which would 'fill out' the cloth, could be woven in and out of the warp threads. This was a fairly laborious process, and it was not long before someone realized how it could be simplified.

Another stick was brought into play, this one with a series of little loops of thread attached to it. Now every alternate warp thread could be passed through one of these loops, so that when the stick was lifted up all those alternate threads would be lifted with it, and the weft could be quickly passed through from one side to the other.

Meanwhile, prehistoric man was embarking on a series of key innovations to ensure supplies of his second great need, food.

THE STORY OF INVENTIONS

Neolithic pottery found in France.

One of these – indeed perhaps one of the half-dozen most crucial inventions in history – was the plough.

In the beginning, man had been a hunter and a collector of such vegetable foods, berries and so on, as he needed. But then he began to notice the association between the places where seeds dropped and those where plants grew the following season. He decided to select those places himself, and agriculture had begun.

In the first instance, the ground was prepared with the digging-stick and the hoe, but the trouble with this method was that it, literally, only scratched the surface, the ground quickly became exhausted – and the farmers had to move on. But the plough turned over a much deeper volume of earth, which meant that the earth had time to regenerate itself, and *that* meant that man could stay put. And *that* was absolutely fundamental.

In the first place it made it worthwhile for him to think in terms of building permanent homes. As a nomad, he had lived either in such suitable caves as he could find, or in rough tents made of sticks and hides. Now, around 6000 BC, he started to build much stronger houses, with sloping roofs sitting on vertical walls, and with the use of columns and beams as supports.

The second result of 'staying put' was very much linked with the discovery that had made it possible in the first place – the hybrid form of wild wheat called 'emmer'. Emmer was, if you like, one of Nature's great gifts to man. It was the result of a series of mutations among various forms of wild grass.

It had much plumper, protein-filled ears than the more primitive wheats, and those rich ears led to a whole new concept in society, the idea of surplus. Man still hunted, and had added the fish-hook and the barbed harpoon, both carved from bone, to his armoury. But the fields of wheat were what gave him more than he needed for himself, so that whereas it had been every

FOUNDATION STONES

man for himself, what now happened was that a group of people could afford a proportion of their number to be craftsmen.

At the start, those craftsmen specialized in the arts that man had already attained, so that there would be specialist weavers, leather-workers, and makers of stone bowls. There were even 'axe factories', whose 'professionally made' flint tools were traded for other goods over a wide area.

But to these were added two other crafts, again of absolutely fundamental importance to our subsequent technological growth and well-being. The first of these was pottery.

We can never be absolutely certain when pottery-making began, though the earliest examples have been dated around 25,000 BC. Nor can we be sure *how* it began, but the chances are that it was a matter of luck. Presumably through observation of its properties in the soil, man realized that clay had water-resisting properties. Needing containers for liquids, he used the clay to line baskets. And at some point, he put one of those baskets on the fire, perhaps to cook the contents. What he found, after removing the basket, was that the clay had hardened in the heat. Pottery was born.

Gradually the techniques for making it were improved. The potters learned to add grit or straw to help prevent it cracking. They also learned that merely putting the shaped clay out in the hot sun, or in the fire, was not enough to make it truly watertight, and by about 4000 BC the vertical kiln had been developed. Finally, they came to realize that the circumstances in which the pot is fired, a combination of the heat and the amount of air allowed into the kiln, could result in different colours.

The first actual pots were formed either by making a series of clay rings, and sitting them one on top of the other, or by making a rope of clay and winding it round and round in a spiral. In both cases it would be smoothed off before it was fired.

This laborious process was completely changed by the advent of 'the potter's wheel'. It is necessary to make a qualification, because the early potter's wheels were actually turntables, platforms which rotated back and forth. It was about two thousand five hundred years later that the true potter's wheel, which turns continually in the same direction, first appeared.

The importance of the potter's turntable was that in the first place the potter could produce much more symmetrical and elegant shapes, and secondly he had much greater control over the thickness of the finished pot. It was a further extension of that rotary motion which man had first utilized in the shape of the bow-drill for fire-making. And the continuing relevance of that idea can be gauged by a brief look around the contents of any modern household: everything from milk bottles to chair legs is based on that principle.

The second great craft which society was now able to afford was that of the metallurgist, the worker in metals, the blacksmith. Since we are talking about times before history was written, we can only guess at the early stages of metallurgy. But we do know that pure nuggets of gold and copper can be found in nature, and it seems likely that these were picked up and treasured simply because they looked nice. Then, at some time

Once the boat was established, man had a whole alternative system for transport and communications.

THE STORY OF INVENTIONS

TOP *The plough had major consequences for mankind.*

ABOVE *Settled agriculture led to the notion of surplus.*

during the sixth millennium BC, they began to be incorporated into crude pieces of jewellery.

Working, presumably, by trial and error, men discovered that by beating the metal they could change its shape, and, in the case of copper, make it harder than it was in its natural form.

The next great step was the discovery that, when heated, the metals became more malleable, and indeed when heated sufficiently, could be poured into moulds and cast. In a sense this was the true beginning of metallurgy – because whereas previously the nuggets could only be worked by using the techniques employed for wood and stone, use could now be made of the unique properties inherent in metals, and a whole new set of techniques were evolved.

Was it luck? I doubt it. For hundreds of thousands of years man had observed the several effects of fire. For some twenty thousand years he had used the reaction of fire with clay. It seems most likely that he would have put *any* new discovery to the test of fire, simply to see what happened.

And that would have been what led him to the third, crucial, step in his metallurgical education – smelting. The discovery is most generally credited to the Sumerians, in Mesopotamia, around 4300 BC.

There are two possibilities as to how it came about. The first is that copper nuggets will usually be found in an area where the attractive stones of turquoise, malachite, and lapis lazuli are found. These were already used as jewellery, and someone may simply have decided to 'try' them in the fire – which would have resulted in copper nuggets being formed after the stone had cooled.

The second possibility, and the more likely one, is that since these stones were used to make glazes for pottery, it was a potter who first realized what an important 'spin-off' he could derive from his craft.

For about fifteen hundred years copper was to stay the dominant metal, but the people of western Asia also used a great deal of gold, silver and electrum. In addition, they learned to smelt lead from its most common ore, galena, which was already used for making ornaments and as the basis for eye paint.

If one accepts the 'try it and see' explanation for a lot of early smelting, it's a strange sidelight that lead-smelting should have come nearly a thousand years later than that of copper, because whereas the melting-point of copper is 1083 degrees centigrade (2007°F.), that of lead is a mere 327 (646°F.), which is obviously far easier to achieve. The explanation may be that while smelted copper could easily be identified with the nuggets of natural copper, lead does not occur in a natural form, and for centuries it may have been regarded as simply a useless slag.

Fire, the prime mover in so much of the early history of technology, led by its very nature to the provision of yet another key development for prehistoric man: artificial light. On its own, of course, a fire gives off light, and since early man probably kept his fire going day and night, he would at least have illumination in the particular cave where the fire was burning. But a fire isn't exactly portable.

Early on, however, probably again through some accident like the observation of the effect of fat dripping on to the fire from cooking meat, man learned to make lamps – hollowed-out pieces of stone with animal fat or oil providing the fuel for a crude wick made from a twig, a piece of twisted moss, or similar fibrous material. In some areas, like the Persian Gulf, lamps of this sort have been found made from seashells, whose shape provides a natural channel for the wick.

If this should seem a fairly trivial development, one need only consider just how much of our working lives, especially during the winter months, would be impossible without artificial light, to understand its true importance.

But man, especially early man, was no stick-at-home. In the earliest days, when he was a hunter and a collector of food, he moved because he *had* to move – to where the next meal could be found. He also, undoubtedly, moved through sheer curiosity, and the perennial belief that the grass beyond the hill will be greener. And he moved because, especially once agriculture had become more settled, he started to trade. It was before written history that he made the two fundamental breakthroughs associated with movement: the boat, and the wheel.

The importance of the boat can hardly be over-emphasized. Three-quarters of the earth's surface is covered by water. Even the land is criss-crossed with the water-obstacles of rivers. On the other hand, in a pre-tarmac society, the boat allows those very rivers to be used to advantage, as the basic means of travel and transport from one point to another.

As with so much else, the concept of the boat must have arisen from observation. All sorts of wood, from twigs to tree-trunks, float on water. Experiment would soon show that a large enough tree-trunk would support not only its own weight but that of a man sitting on it. And the mere discomfort and difficulty of balance would have led man to the idea of hollowing out the trunk so that he could sit *in* it.

We don't know exactly when this was first tried, though a paddle from a dug-out canoe found in Yorkshire has been dated at about 7500 BC. Where man's true inventiveness comes in is in the observation that it is not the fact that wood floats which is important, but the shape of a receptacle which will, given that it is only carrying a certain weight, prevent the water from lapping over its edges. This observation may either have come from the trial-and-error of dug-out canoes, or from seeing what happened to a pottery bowl when it was taken to the river for a wash. If the bowl was placed level into the water, it would float.

It's true that a lot of the early boats were actually rafts, made out of reeds or logs lashed together. But there are also very early examples, from Scandinavia and Mesopotamia, of boats made of hides stretched over wooden frames.

Nor did man stick for long to the rivers. For example, a village on Cyprus, which must have been settled from the mainland around the Mediterranean, was already established by about 5700 BC, and the only way of getting there was by sea-going craft.

Finally, if we discount the use of fire (and domesticated animals for traction), the boat provides the first example of man looking outside himself for sources of power.

Early Egyptian paintings show boats made out of reeds being propelled by a sail on a mast. The reeds were covered with pitch to make them watertight, and the only means of steering was to use an oar as a rudder. But the harnessing of the wind was an idea that was to last until well into the nineteenth century AD as the best way of driving ships.

And then, on land, there was the wheel, the famous wheel, the invention that most people plump for when asked what was the most important invention of all. Well, yes, it *was* important, very important, and indeed when we look at today's cars and trains one might be tempted to say it was of paramount importance. And yet . . . in five thousand years' time, will it seem as crucial? I doubt it.

It is unlikely that the cutting laser will ever completely supersede man's first tool, the cutting edge of knife and axe. But the wheel has *already* been superseded, in its most important aspect, by the hovercraft. That aspect involves the overcoming of a basic principle of mechanics – namely, that the greater the amount of friction between two objects, the harder it is to move the one across the surface of the other, which is why it's easier to pull a load across ice than across hard ground.

In a way, the history of land transport is the history of the attempts to beat this problem. The first vehicles were simply sledges, often made from two parallel poles joined by strips of hide or bark. To these, later, were added runners, which helped to reduce the friction, especially as they could be made slippery by rubbing with grease. What was then produced was something very like the toboggan we use on the snow today.

But where heavy loads were concerned, the friction was still too great. The question is: did some genius, confronted with the problem, sit down at that point and work out ways of solving it, making use of the laws of mechanics? Undoubtedly not. In fact, it's interesting to speculate what a scientist of, say, fifty years

Stonehenge, a megalithic marvel.

Like so many inventions, the wheel was soon used in warfare.

ago, would have come up with, if he had had to work it out in abstract. I believe the chances are that he would have missed out the wheel and come up with the hovercraft, and by now we would all be driving around in hovercars.

So how *did* it happen? Well, the idea, indeed the picture, of circularity, exists throughout nature. Throw a stone into a pond, saw through a tree-trunk, gaze at the full moon, stare into the pupil of the eye, and you will see circles. Secondly, the fact that what is circular will roll more easily than that which is not could easily be discovered by the simple process of rolling stones down hills. Thirdly, the idea of using tree-trunks as *rollers* for shifting large weights had been a very early development. Together with the use of levers, that was the only way in which Stone Age man could have transported and erected the giant megaliths, or standing stones, which he left as virtually indestructible monuments to his own ingenuity.

The idea of the wheel, as such, probably developed out of these three separate notions. No one is quite sure when or where the wheel was first made, but the best guess is about 3500 BC, either in Mesopotamia, or in the central and eastern parts of Europe, or perhaps in both independently.

The first wheels were very rough affairs, made of planks joined together and chiselled into a circular shape. These planks would have been cut lengthways from the tree-trunk. Doubtless the first wheel-makers would have attempted to cut straight through the trunk, in order to make use of the natural circularity for their wheels, but they would soon have discovered that because of the way a tree grows, wheels made that way split asunder the moment any weight is put on them. (If you look at a cross-section of a tree-trunk, you will see that there are lines radiating outwards from the centre, across the lines of the rings. And these are lines of weakness.)

These, then, were the main achievements of prehistoric man. Depending on what you decide to call 'man' rather than 'ape', they had taken a long time – estimates go back as much as two million years. But if that is so, it is worthwhile repeating the fact that if the number of inventions seems small for such a long period, they *were* all utterly fundamental. If you try to imagine what sort of society we could have today without them, their importance becomes obvious.

The other key point to notice is that those early inventions typify all the subsequent history of inventions, in that all technologies are mutually dependent. Without fire you couldn't make pottery or smelt metals, and without pottery you wouldn't have containers in which to store the surplus grain which was the advantage of a settled rather than a nomadic existence. Without that settled life, you couldn't afford to employ craftsmen to work the metals. You couldn't dig the ore for those metals without tools, and the tools were made from the antlers and bones of animals, to kill which you needed weapons, which you couldn't make unless you had a cutting edge . . . and so on, and so on. It is virtually impossible to isolate any one invention and declare that it stands on its own, irrespective of any other invention.

We are still unsure of how, why and where, and when, most of these inventions 'first' occurred. Even with the increasing number of ways in which science is coming to the aid of the archaeologist, we have still only filled in the first few clues in the cro sword puzzle of early man. Most of the time we can only say that such-and-such a thing had happened *by* such-and-such a time at such-and-such a place.

All that we have to help us, apart from artefacts, houses, graves and the like, are the pictures that prehistoric man drew as evidence of the life he led. But pictures can only tell a very limited story. Luckily, man was about to change all that, with his greatest single stroke of genius.

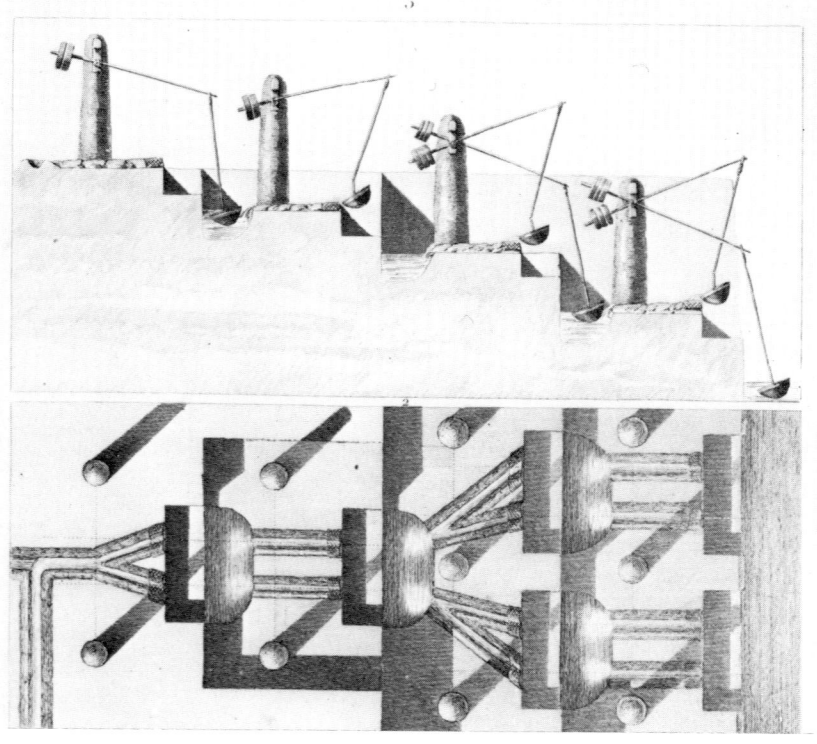

Early Civilizations

We often tend to think of the marvellous Stone-Age cave-paintings of Lascaux and Altamira as examples of prehistoric art. Yet art was not in the mind of the men who created them. Their main purpose was a religious, or mystic, one. If one could portray one's enemy or one's quarry, one would gain power over them – a belief that survives even today in voodoo rituals of sticking pins into effigies.

Doubtless, however, there was a second element to them: the desire to leave a record of existence that seems to be very basic to man, and which derives perhaps from his first awareness that he had only a short life, and not much knowledge of what happened to him after it. It is a sort of graffiti-mindedness, the manifestations of which range from the initials of lovers on trees to headstones on graves.

The tragedy lies in the scarcity of the information the picture leaves. There is the bison. There are the hunters. There are the bows and arrows. We can conclude that the bison was a prime quarry, and that it was killed with bows and arrows. But little more. We don't know if it was the bison hunted yesterday, today, or tomorrow. We don't know whether it was big or small, fast or slow, or a hundred other facts which we might find interesting, and which the artist might have wished to record.

Faced with this problem, the earliest chroniclers realized that the pictures had to be arranged into some more formal sort of order, and in Mesopotamia, round about 6000 BC, there appeared the earliest, very crude, form of 'ideographic' writing. In ideographic writing, the pictures have not only become more formalized (so that what I draw for 'bison' will be pretty much the same as what you draw for 'bison') but they are also used to stand for concepts, or ideas. For instance, a spear might also stand for the idea of hunting, or the moon for the idea of night-time.

This was to be the form of writing from which the Egyptians, by about 3100 BC, had adapted their version of 'hieroglyphic' writing. And it is the form which the Chinese had evolved, probably independently, by about 1500 BC, and which they still use today.

But there is one overwhelming disadvantage about such writing. Basically, you need a different symbol for each separate

Egyptian hieroglyphics.

Water has always been man's most precious commodity. The Egyptian shaduf, invented around 1500 BC, was still being used to raise water more than 3000 years later.

21

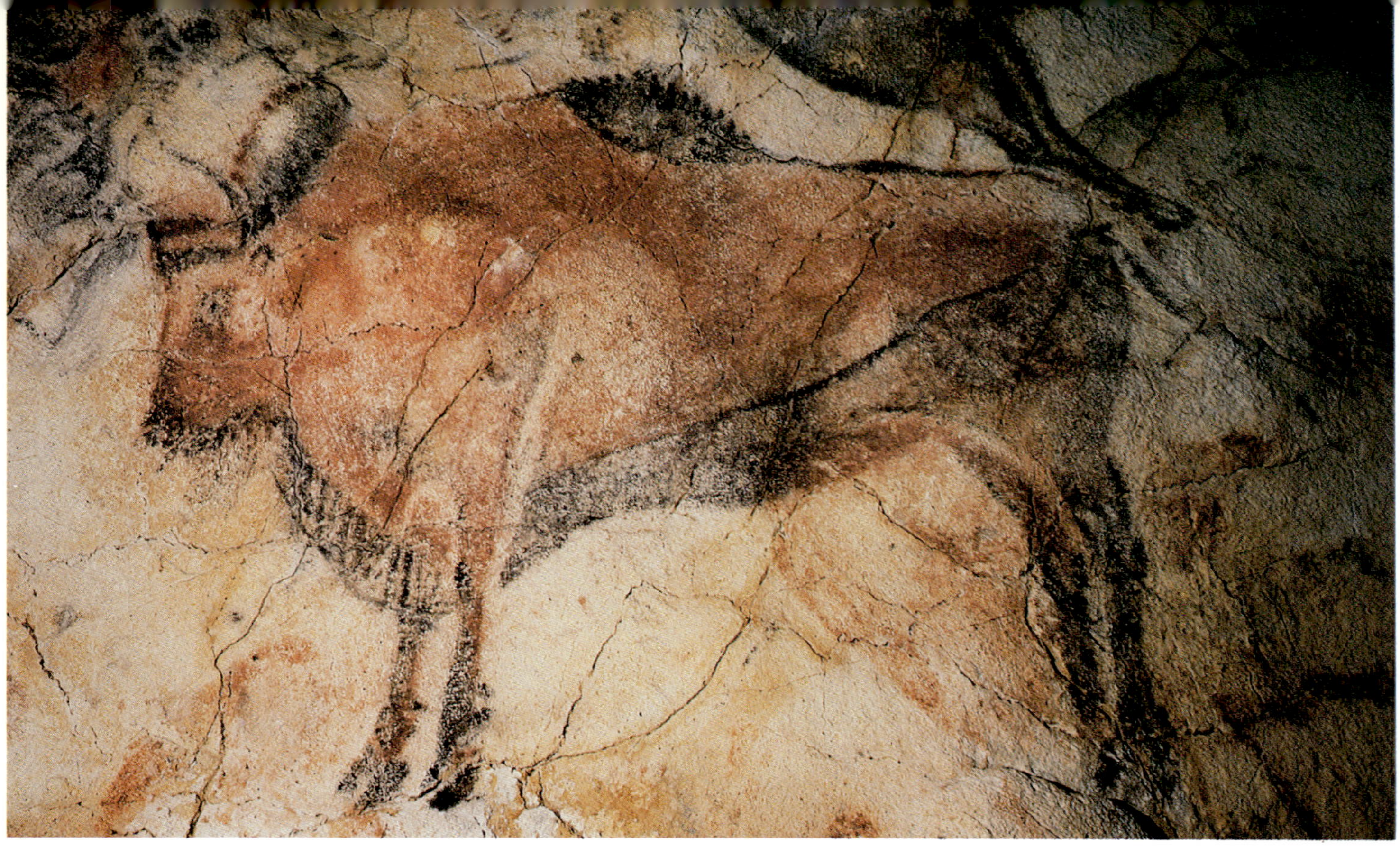

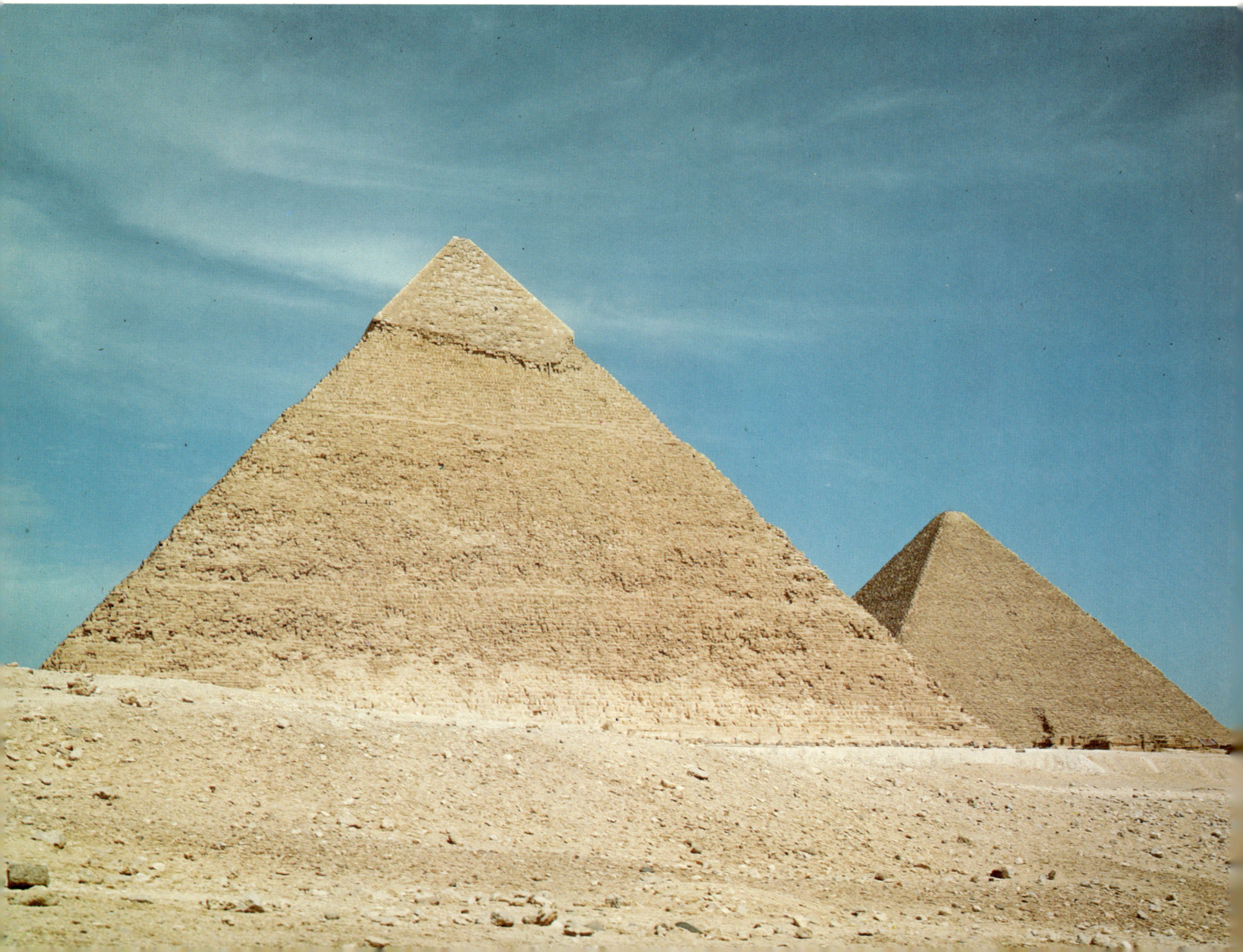

OPPOSITE ABOVE *A standing bison, one of the spectacular cave-paintings of Altamira. But if the artist wished to tell us more about the bison, he was unable to do so.*
OPPOSITE BELOW *The gigantic pyramids of Cheops and Chephren.*
ABOVE *An early Greek script from Ephesus.*

ABOVE RIGHT *This Egyptian necklace of the third millennium BC is made of glazed beads.*
BELOW *Brick-making in Egypt. The brick was the first ever standardized 'module'.*

THE STORY OF INVENTIONS

Every picture tells a story. Guess which one is pharoah!

thing that you want to say. (It has been estimated that modern Chinese has potentially about eighty thousand symbols.)

It was in answer to this problem that some one Assyrian, around 2500 BC, made what must surely be the greatest single leap of the imagination that any one person has ever achieved. I say 'some *one*', because it was not a process that could have been arrived at by committee. Nor indeed was it an idea that would have occurred in the natural evolution of ideas. It *had* to be a single, breathtaking brainwave to suggest that instead of the symbols being representations of *things*, they should be representations of the *words* used to describe those things – that the audible should be translated into the visible. Phonetic writing was born.

In its first form it was 'syllabic' – that is, each symbol stood for a whole syllable. Although a great advance, this still suffered from the disadvantage of needing a large number of symbols, ranging from about sixty in its simplest forms up to as many as three hundred or more.

It was in answer to this that the final, decisive step was taken. This was to extract from the various syllables their basic consonants, and use them as the structure of the written word. This was the first alphabet, the North Semitic alphabet, which was developed some time after 2000 BC in the area of Syria and Palestine.

The vowels in this first alphabet were shown by 'diacritical' marks – little angled strokes to indicate a variation of sound, rather like the present-day acute and grave accents in French. It was the Greeks who finally identified the vowels correctly and gave them, sometime around 850 BC, symbols of their own.

But if writing now enabled men to record their activities for posterity, they were not prepared to leave their immortality in the hands of chance readership. They began to make buildings that would last for a thousand, two thousand, five thousand years, buildings that would house their dead bodies, and therefore their souls: the pyramids of Egypt.

The earliest of these of which we know is the 'step' pyramid of Sakkara, built about 2940 BC for a Pharaoh by his Prime Minister. Within a hundred and fifty years, the greatest of them all had been built, the Great Pyramid of Cheops. Its statistics are so staggering that they are worth repeating – it was made from 2,300,000 blocks of granite, each weighing some $2\frac{1}{2}$ tons. It was 481 feet high, and its base covered 13 acres. It was also, as we would put it today, rather labour-intensive. It required a hundred thousand men working for twenty years to complete it.

Curiously, no major new inventions were attached to the building of the pyramids, although they are evidence of the first use of the plumb-line. Rollers, ropes, sledges and rafts were used, and of particular importance was the lever, a principle evolved thousands of years before, but now used to great advantage in shifting the massive blocks of masonry.

Since the early Egyptians did not have the wheel (indeed it didn't appear in Egypt until more than a thousand years after the Great Pyramid was built), it was, of course, impossible for them to have the pulley. In fact, that crucial device seems first to have appeared in Assyria in the eighth century BC.

The technological importance of the pyramids was twofold.

24

First, they incorporated the idea of using natural stone for building, which involved the development of saws which would cut stone, and wedges which would split it to the required shape. Secondly, there was the concept of prefabrication. The stone was cut from quarries in the south of Egypt and shaped to fit a particular place in the grand design. Then it was marked, to show where it was to go, and floated down the Nile on rafts.

The notion of prefabrication, of course, depends on the ability to draw up a complete plan of a building. And to do that satisfactorily depends on being certain of the size and specification of the materials from which you are going to build. That was all right in areas like Egypt where there was an abundance of natural stone. But what if there were no stone? Here man turned to one of the least applauded, but in my belief most crucial, of his inventions, the brick.

The earliest bricks known were found at one of the old cities of Jericho, and are dated about 6800 BC. They were crude affairs, made of mud, shaped by hand, and known as 'hog-backed bricks' because of their rounded tops. They were soft, and were smoothed together by hand to form the wall.

The second development in brick-making took place over the next three thousand years. Bricks began to be made from the clay which was plentiful in the river plains of Mesopotamia. They started to assume something closer to the rectangular brick we know today, and material like chopped straw was added to the clay to give it greater strength. They were dried, after shaping, by being left out in the sun. But that has the obvious disadvantage that you must be in a part of the world, or in a season, when the sun is hot enough to bake the clay, and in addition there is a limit to the hardness the sun can achieve. It seems strange that, considering the thousands of years that the potter's art had been known, it wasn't until some time shortly before 3000 BC that bricks, too, were consigned to the kiln and properly fired.

At about the same time, the brick-makers learned to use moulds, and this was a development vital to the inherent importance of brick – because *now* these basic building components could all be made exactly the same size, enabling the architect to plan *exactly* how the building should be.

The development of materials was probably the most important feature of this early historical period, and none more important than that of glass.

The first product that could really be called glass was the glaze used in Egypt and Mesopotamia, from around 4000 BC, for coating beads made of quartz and soapstone. The next stage was the pure glass bead, used for jewellery and inlays, which appears about 3400 BC in Egypt. It is to the Egyptians also that we owe the first example of glass in a really 'useful' form, the glass beaker of the Egyptian Pharaoh Thothmes III, dated around 1500 BC.

The technique used for this and other early glass artefacts was that of moulding. The glass was rolled around a core of sand and clay, and the outer surface was smoothed on a slab of stone. On to this surface, trails of coloured glass were pressed, and combed back and forth to produce a zig-zag pattern. When the glass had cooled, the core could easily be removed.

The curious thing about the development of glass was the enormous gaps between the major improvements in technique. It had, apparently, taken some seventeen hundred years since the first glass was made for it to be turned to a really useful purpose. And it was another fifteen hundred years before, at around the time of Christ, the Phoenicians invented glass-blowing. Finally, another eighteen hundred years passed before the advent of plate-glass.

It is hard to explain why man was so sluggish in the matter of glass when one looks at the number of ways in which it has become essential, from its use in microscopes and telescopes to its use in windows and light bulbs – surely it is one of the key materials of civilization.

The second vital advance in the field of materials came around 3000 BC with the first production of bronze, when the world was truly shown the importance of the family of men named Smith.

The great thing about bronze was that it was the first alloy. From the moment of its discovery, the smiths realized that they need not be content with the pure metals, which so often have natural disadvantages. In the case of copper, that disadvantage was that it was too soft for most practical purposes – for a cutting edge, or the blade of a plough, or the tip of an arrow.

Bronze is made from copper, with an addition of around ten per cent of tin. What no one knows is just how that mixture first came to be tried. One suggestion is that an ore was smelted in which there were, as can happen, elements both of copper and tin. Another, and perhaps more likely idea, is that the early smiths of Syria and eastern Turkey, where the first main mining was done, simply experimented. The chances are that they would have tried all the known metals in every possible combination in order to see what would happen. At any rate, bronze (which can be sharpened to make knives, and polished to make mirrors, and hammered when cold to give extra hardness, and which flows easily when molten, and can thus be used for pouring into moulds of exotic shape) was to be the world's main metal for two thousand years, lending its name to a whole era, the Bronze Age.

It is worth noting that, unlike the many inventions which appear to have arrived independently in various parts of the world, bronze-making spread by diffusion, by the knowledge being passed on from town to town, and from country to country. It wasn't until about 1500 BC that it was firmly established in Egypt, and at about the same time reached China, during the Shang-Yin dynasty. Astonishingly, the Chinese, without apparently going through any period of 'trial and error', began immediately to make bronze castings which were very large, technically excellent, and artistically of a very high order. How they managed to achieve this remains one of the minor technological mysteries.

Then, about 1000 BC, the Bronze Age gave way to the Iron Age, when iron, and its half-brother, steel, took over as the world's dominant metal.

OVERLEAF LEFT *An intricate casting made not long after bronze first appeared in China. The new technique had soon been turned into an art.* OVERLEAF RIGHT *A glass made by the sand-core technique.*

As with many of the early major inventions and discoveries, the *principles* upon which iron's usefulness as a material are based could not have been known to its originators. Just as the first man to use a lever had no knowledge of the laws of mechanics, so those first iron-founders knew nothing of chemistry and atomic structure. Yet that didn't prevent a mixture of luck, judgement, experiment and patience from leading them to the right result.

For a start, pure iron does not exist in the form of natural nuggets. And unlike copper, there is nothing to suggest that its dull ores are likely to yield anything useful. Furthermore, the melting-point of iron is 1535 degrees centigrade (2821°F.), which meant that the crude early furnaces were never able to get it to the point where it could be 'tapped off'. Instead, all that would be left after heating the iron ore would have been a mass of slag. And there was nothing to suggest that *that* could be useful, either. Nevertheless, at some time around 2500 BC, someone decided to try. And what he discovered was that if that spongy mass was heated and hammered, the slag particles dropped off, and wrought iron emerged.

But wrought iron, though it could be more easily beaten into shape than bronze, was a softer metal, and therefore of no great advantage. Matters stayed that way for a thousand years. Then, in about 1400 BC, a tribe living in the Armenian mountains, named the Chalybes, made a vital discovery. It was that wrought iron, frequently reheated, and hammered between the heatings, would become harder than any bronze; and the important point was that they were heating the metal by the traditional use of charcoal. What they could not know was that the heating and beating was making the iron absorb carbon particles on its surface. What the Chalybes were making was wrought iron enclosed in a casing of steel.

It didn't take them long to make a further discovery – quenching. By plunging the hot steel into cold water, a very hard steel was produced. Again, they could not have known that what they were doing was to 'freeze' an atomic structure that is only stable at high temperatures. (Not that there need be much mystery about *that* vital discovery. What could be more natural than to plunge the newly heated and hammered metal into cold water to cool it off? Once that had been done a few dozen times, the difference must have been apparent.)

The chief exponents of the new craft were the Hittites of Asia Minor and Syria, and it was from them that Tutankhamun's father got the steel dagger that was found in the boy king's tomb, where it had been placed in 1350 BC. By 1000 BC the new metal was in general use throughout the ancient world.

Apart from its inherent qualities, the beauty of iron lies in its abundance. After oxygen, silicon and aluminium, it is the fourth most abundant element found in the earth's crust, oceans and atmosphere.

As a *compound* substance, of course, the most common of all is water, and it was in his control of this most precious of fluids that man made his other great strides during this period.

There were, and are, three main areas in which water was essential: irrigation, transport, and household needs like drinking and sewage.

The need for the first became apparent at the time of, indeed went hand in hand with, the first settled agriculture, when the usefulness of drainage and irrigation ditches and dykes was realized. The Egyptians, working with the great advantage that the Nile flooded in the early autumn, at just the right time to prepare the ground for winter sowing, built great networks of dykes, which were opened to admit the water at flood time, then kept closed for a while to allow the rich silt to work its way into the soil, and finally opened again lower downstream to let the water escape back into the great river.

The Mesopotamians, on the other hand, suffered from the disadvantage that the Tigris and Euphrates rivers flooded in spring, so that they had to store the water in reservoirs, releasing it when required later in the year. This was a much more complicated process, but had the enormous advantage, born of necessity, that they were thus able to get an average of three crops every two years, and on occasion two crops in a single year.

The control of water led to three great engineering concepts: the dam, the canal, and the aqueduct. The oldest known dam, dating from around 3000 BC, was built across the valley of the Garawi river in Egypt. It was some 350 feet long. Later, but longer, was the stone dyke built in Syria in 1300 BC for conserving the waters of the Orontes valley. It stretched for a mile and a quarter.

Canals were, of course, simply ditches on a grander scale. But from very early on there were some very impressive engineering feats. In about 1875 BC, the Egyptian king Sesostris was faced with the problem of getting his ships past one of the more difficult cataracts of the Nile. To solve it, he built a detour-canal 260 feet long, 35 feet wide, and 26 feet deep.

And for those who think that the Suez Canal is an engineering marvel, it is astonishing to discover that at some time around 2000 BC the Egyptians built its ancestor – a canal that ran in two stages from the Mediterranean to the Red Sea, a distance, unbelievably, of just under a hundred miles.

For the aqueduct, we have the Persians to thank. They got water for their fields by tunnelling into the foothills of their mountain ranges, and channelling the water out to where it was needed. These tunnels, or 'qanats', are still in use in Iran.

Socially, the importance of the ideas was that settlements, towns, and cities needed no longer to be located by the side of a river or other major water source. The water could be brought to the people.

The first person to put this principle truly into effect was King Sennacherib of Assyria, in 691 BC. He dammed a mountain river, and diverted it along a stone channel thirty-five miles long to the ancient city of Nineveh, where the water was used on the fields and the palace gardens.

This search for the means of controlling water had enormous side effects. It stimulated astronomy – for the purpose of predicting the exact dates when rivers could be expected to flood. It gave a huge impetus to mathematics, as a means not of theoretical discussion but of very practical problem-solving, in working out areas, cubic quantities, and so on. And it produced the first accurate surveying: since Egyptian taxes were based on the area of irrigated land a man owned, and since the annual flood tended

EARLY CIVILIZATIONS

ABOVE *A nilometer, the ancient method of measuring the annual flooding of the Nile.* BELOW *An ox-driven wheel raises a chain of water-filled buckets.*

to wipe out border-markings, they had to be able to re-establish the boundaries as soon as possible after the flood had subsided.

In addition, the need to find ways of raising water to higher levels led to the invention of two important technological 'ancestors'. One was the adaptation of the wheel for irrigation. Around 3000 BC, we find wheels with buckets attached to their circumference. The bottom of the wheel was in the river, which, as it flowed, filled the buckets (which emptied themselves at the higher level). The wheel had to be turned by man- or animal-power, but its main importance was that it led later to the water-wheel.

The second invention was the shaduf. This consisted of an upright stake, or stone pillar, with a pole pivoting on the top of it. At one end of the pole was a bucket, and at the other a weight, which acted as a counter-balance, and made it easy for the farmer to dip the bucket into the water, then swing it up and tip the water on to a higher level. It first came into use in about 1500 BC, and can be considered the grandfather of the crane. It can also be considered the first cousin of an invention whose importance has been so underrated that many histories of technology completely ignore it – the balance.

Without the balance, of course, the regularization and expansion of trade is impossible. It's all very well to do a 'one-off' piece of bartering: 'I'll give you this sheep for that bag of grain.' But if the trade is to be a regular one, then both sides want to know that they will go on getting the same bargain. The balance is the referee of the fair deal – together with its accomplices, standard weights.

The earliest known weights come from graves at Nagada, in Egypt, and were made of limestone. They date from around 7000 BC. They were used in association with limestone balance-beams, but these were pretty crude, and only useful for giving a rough equivalence between large weights.

But the more that trade expanded, the more necessary it became for money, the medium of exchange, to become small, easily portable, indestructible, and standardized. 'Money' can, of course, be anything – cattle, hides, pieces of carved stone. It doesn't matter what it is so long as everyone concerned is agreed as to its value, in terms of goods or labour.

By about 3000 BC, it had become the practice for the standard

Watering the garden of an Egyptian sculptor with a shaduf, from an early wall-painting.

THE STORY OF INVENTIONS

ABOVE *Part of a hoard of bronze from Ein Gedi in Israel. It dates from the fourth millennium* BC.
OPPOSITE *Anubis uses scales to weigh the soul of Anhai.*

weights, inscribed with the king's name, to be kept in the major Egyptian temples. (If that seems a crude way of checking, it's worth remembering that even today, if you want to check an exact kilogram, you have to go to Sèvres, in France, and compare it with the Prototype Kilogram Number One, which is made of platinum–iridium alloy, and kept in a vault there.)

And with gold, silver, and jewels having taken the place of weightier objects as the currency medium, the balances became finer, with, by about 2500 BC, the familiar scale-pans suspended from each end.

Finally, about 700 BC, true standardization of currency was first achieved with the production of proper coins; that is to say, a coinage in which coins of the same face value had a constant weight and a constant purity of whatever metal they were made.

It is to the kings of Lydia, in Asia Minor, that we owe this invention, so universally useful in its application, yet potentially and so often so harmful when men forget that the only 'value' of 'money' or currency of any description is what other men will give for it.

The main metal used by the Lydians was electrum, which is a natural alloy of gold and silver, and it is to them that we also owe the first system of 'assay'. In Lydia were first found the stones known as 'touchstones', which, when polished and then marked with gold, will indicate the degree of purity of that gold by dint of the different shades of colour that different grades of gold will leave on the stone.

What happened with the balance was a perfect example of the way in which technology and society interact, make demands upon each other, and come to each other's support. Crude barter demanded crude balances, which allowed trade to expand, which led to the need for finer currency, which needed finer balances, which finally made possible a precise coinage.

Nothing in the world of technology happens in isolation.

Greece and Rome

One hears so often of the 'glory that was Greece and Rome' that it is a natural temptation to imagine that those two great civilizations made great leaps forward in the field of technology and inventions. Well, they didn't. By comparison with what had already been achieved, the thousand-year period from 600 BC to AD 400 saw few technical advances.

The main reason for this was the abundance of an energy source which had the advantage of human intelligence – and was known as the slave.

Most technology is devoted either to enabling man to do things which he could not otherwise do, or to helping him do what he can do more efficiently. But the supply of slaves, apparently endless, as it must have appeared to the Greeks and the Romans, made the latter purpose seem unnecessary and the former a mere intellectual pastime.

To the Greeks in particular, it was inconceivable that a citizen should 'get his hands dirty'. His role in life was that of abstract thought. Not that that was in itself a bad thing. It is roughly true to say that the more advanced and complex an invention is, the more it depends on abstract scientific principles. So the theories and proofs, in geometry and mathematics, of men like Euclid and Pythagoras, while not strictly 'inventions', nevertheless laid down the scientific basis on which thousands of subsequent inventions have depended.

To take one example: the ability to put a man on the surface of the moon requires, obviously, an exact knowledge of our planetary system. It was a Greek, Aristarchus, who first suggested that the sun, not the earth, was at the centre of the 'universe'. It was another Greek, Hipparchus, who first realized that the planets move in elliptical orbits (and, incidentally, laid down the first principles of trigonometry). And yet another, Eratosthenes, was the first to succeed in measuring the circumference of the earth (which he knew to be round, even if later generations went back to thinking it was flat!).

Without the chain of knowledge which these men began, the 'giant leap for mankind' would never have been taken.

But it was not all theory. Greece gave to the world a small

Epicurus, one of the great Greek philosophers.

band of inventors who were among the most brilliant who ever lived. The trouble was that so many of the things they invented were thought of as mere amusements, as playthings rather than objects of everyday usefulness. For this reason, historians have tended to decry their achievements. Yet the principles upon which their devices were designed were such fundamental breakthroughs that they should be given massive credit – even if in some cases a thousand years was to pass before their inventions were put to good use.

In general, these inventions can be described as 'automata', or machines that would work on their own without the agency of human or animal muscle-power. And of their inventors three stand head and shoulders above the rest: Archimedes, Ctesibius, and Hero.

Archimedes lived in Syracuse, in Sicily, from 287 to 212 BC. What most people remember about Archimedes is that he leaped out of his bath one day, and ran naked through the streets of Syracuse (a sort of early streaker!) shouting 'Eureka!', meaning, 'I have found it!' What he had discovered was the relation-

A sixteenth-century view of Archimedes' brainwave.

THE STORY OF INVENTIONS

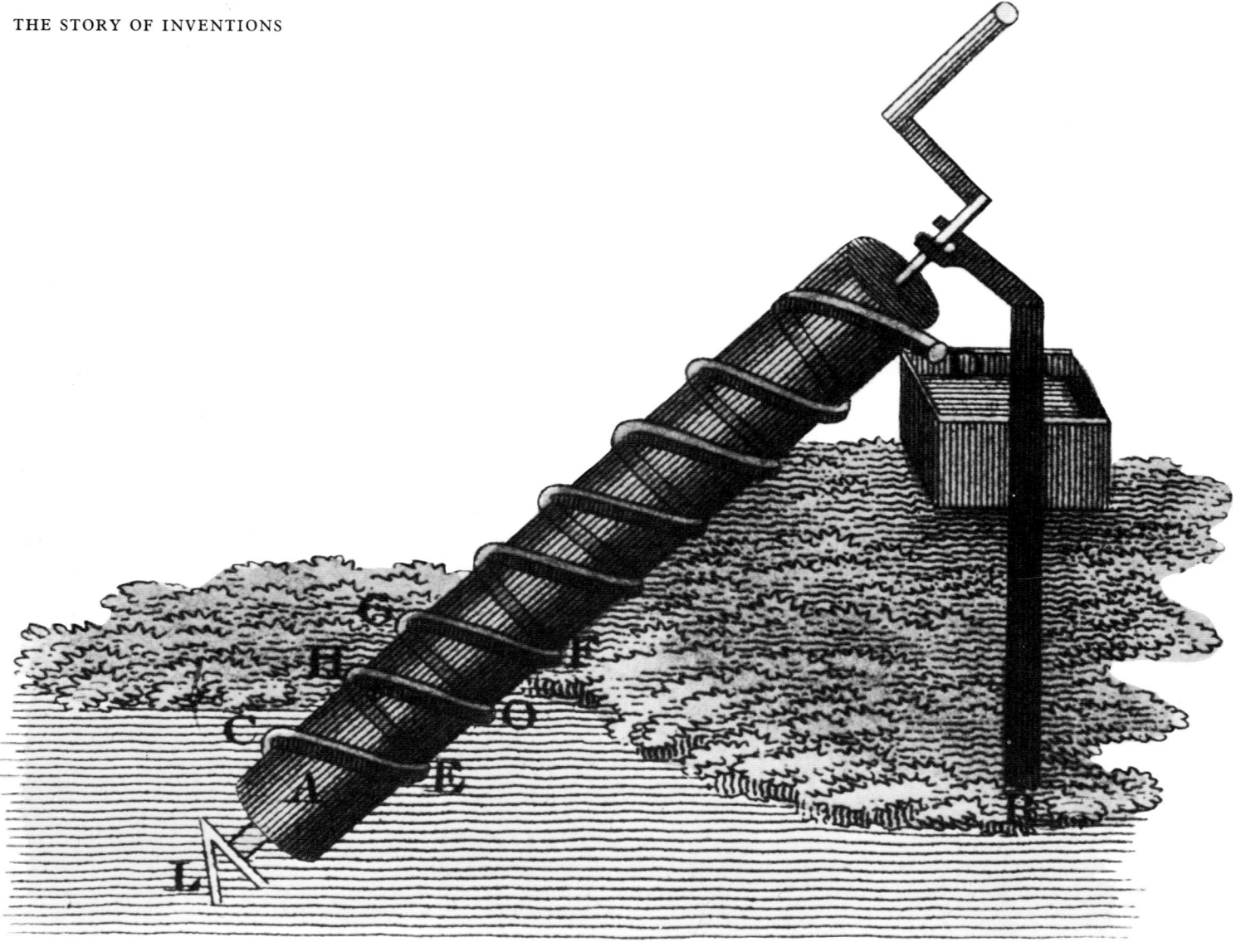

Archimedes' screw, for raising water.

ship between the weight and the volume of a body in water and the weight and volume of water that was displaced. The story goes that he used this discovery to catch out a fraudulent goldsmith, who had been commissioned to make a crown of gold for King Hieron of Syracuse, but who had added some silver to the gold in order to make a bit more profit.

But Archimedes put his knowledge of hydrostatics and the behaviour of water to more practical use than that with his invention of the hydraulic screw, otherwise known as the water-snail or Archimedes' screw. It was a cylinder which had a spiral cut into its inside wall. The bottom end of the cylinder was put into the water, and when it was turned the water rose up the cylinder (and emptied itself out at the top end) by a principle we know today as helical action.

Indeed, that invention is still in use today, as is another of Archimedes' brainchildren, the perpetual screw, also known as the worm-drive, or worm and gear. In this, the screw is located in a fixed position, with a gear-wheel intermeshing with the spirals of the screw. When the screw is turned, the gear-wheel rotates. It is one of the most powerful transmission systems ever invented, and is frequently used in, for instance, the motor industry.

The key thing about this invention was that it was an efficient way of transferring force, or energy, from one plane on to another, and it was this search for the most efficient way to use energy that led to Archimedes' third great achievement, the development of a proper theory of levers.

True, levers had been used for thousands of years, but it was Archimedes who rationalized the laws of mechanics which govern their use; namely that a given force will lift, or move, larger and larger weights if it is applied from longer and longer distances away from the fulcrum (the point around which the lever rotates, and against which it is exerting its force). Any child who wants to break a stick, or prise something open, knows this instinctively, but it was Archimedes who showed that the relationship between the weight to be lifted, the force to be applied, and the distance over which it must be applied could all be precisely quantified.

In fact the Greek historian Plutarch tells us that Archimedes wrote to King Hieron claiming that *any* weight could be moved by a given force, if that force was applied properly. He even went so far as to say: 'Give me a fixed point outside the earth to stand on, and I will move it.'

The astonished, and doubtless sceptical, king, requested a demonstration. Plutarch writes: 'Archimedes then took one of the king's merchant ships, so big that it could only be brought to land with great labour by many men, and as well as the cargo he left many people on board. He then stood a certain distance away and with the help only of a device made of ropes and tree-trunks he drew the ship up the beach as effortlessly as if it had been sailing on the sea.' What Archimedes had made was an extremely complicated winch.

Ctesibius lived across the Mediterranean, at Alexandria, at about the same time as Archimedes. Alexandria, founded by the Greek leader Alexander the Great in 332 BC, on the Nile delta, was a great centre of learning, with an academy of arts and sciences, laboratories, an observatory, a zoo, and a vast library. It was in essence the first great university campus.

Perhaps, who knows, it was the necessity for accurate time-keeping in the scientific experiments and other Alexandrian activities that led Ctesibius to his invention of the Clepsydra, or water-clock. Up till then, the only way of telling the time, other than by guesswork, was the sundial. But that depended, of course, on it being both daytime and sunny.

All that was needed was a constant flow of water. This was directed into a cylinder which had a little hole at the bottom, and an overflow hole near the top. Water trickled out of the bottom hole into another cylinder, in which there was a float. A rod stuck out of the top of the float (rather like an elongated fisherman's float) and there was a pointer attached to the top of the rod, which pointed to the hours, which were marked on a scale attached to the contrivance.

Since more water flowed into the first cylinder than trickled out into the second cylinder, the water level (and therefore pressure) was kept constant at the level of the overflow. As the water trickled into the second cylinder, the float rose, and the pointer moved up the scale; the higher the pointer, the later the hour. Although it obviously had to be emptied and restarted each day, it was an extremely accurate means of time-keeping, since there were no moving parts to wear out, and all that could affect it, eventually, would be the enlargement of the little bottom hole by the passage of the water.

'Give me a fixed point outside the earth to stand on, and I will move it.' From the Mechanics Magazine, *London, 1824.*

THE STORY OF INVENTIONS

A version of Ctesibius' Clepsydra, from a nineteenth-century French magazine.

But Ctesibius' great achievement was really three inventions in one, three key mechanical devices that we all use today.

He was the son of a barber, and the story of how he dreamed of his invention goes as follows: his father's customers, being as vain as the rest of us, liked to watch progress as they were having their shaves and haircuts. But since the chairs were of a fixed height but the customers of different heights, Ctesibius decided to build an adjustable mirror.

He hung it on a string, which had a counterpoise on the other end, like the principle of a sash window. As the mirror was pulled down, the weight was pulled up, and vice versa. The weight was hidden behind boarding, and Ctesibius noticed that if he raised the mirror quickly, so that the counterpoise descended quickly, there was a loud hiss as the air in the restricted space was compressed and escaped through the boards.

Fired by the idea, Ctesibius constructed a cylinder with a plunger in it which would not allow air to escape round its edges – the first piston. To this he added a round flap, in a pipe attached to the cylinder, which was hinged in such a way that the

36

air, or water, or whatever was being forced through the cylinder, could move in one direction, but not back again – the first valve. Using the two ideas, he constructed the first force-pump, one of whose initial uses was for fire-fighting.

Not content with this, he now adapted the pump as a whole as the provider of wind for the first organ, an instrument that would be perfectly recognizable as such today, with its pipes of differing lengths and a keyboard to admit the air to them as required.

But the most astonishing of the Greek inventors, and perhaps the only man to match Leonardo da Vinci for the range and ingenuity of his mechanical ideas, was Hero, who lived in Alexandria in the middle of the first century AD.

We know a lot about Hero's inventions, since we have a number of books written by him. Now it is true that most of the inventions described by Hero were intended only as playthings, but the ideas embodied in them were often fundamental and hundreds of years before their time.

Take his aeolipile. It was a sphere, sitting above an enclosed pan filled with water, and supported by two rods at its horizontal axis. One of the rods was hollow and connected to the pan. At the top and the bottom of the sphere were two exhaust tubes, bent at right angles and pointing in opposite directions. A fire was lit beneath the pan. The water inside turned to steam, which forced its way out through the exhaust tubes, causing the sphere to spin.

The principle involved was one which Isaac Newton was to enunciate sixteen hundred years later: that every action imposed

ABOVE *Hero's aeolipile, forerunner of the steam turbine and the jet engine.*

BELOW *Ctesibius in his study, next to the barber's shop.*

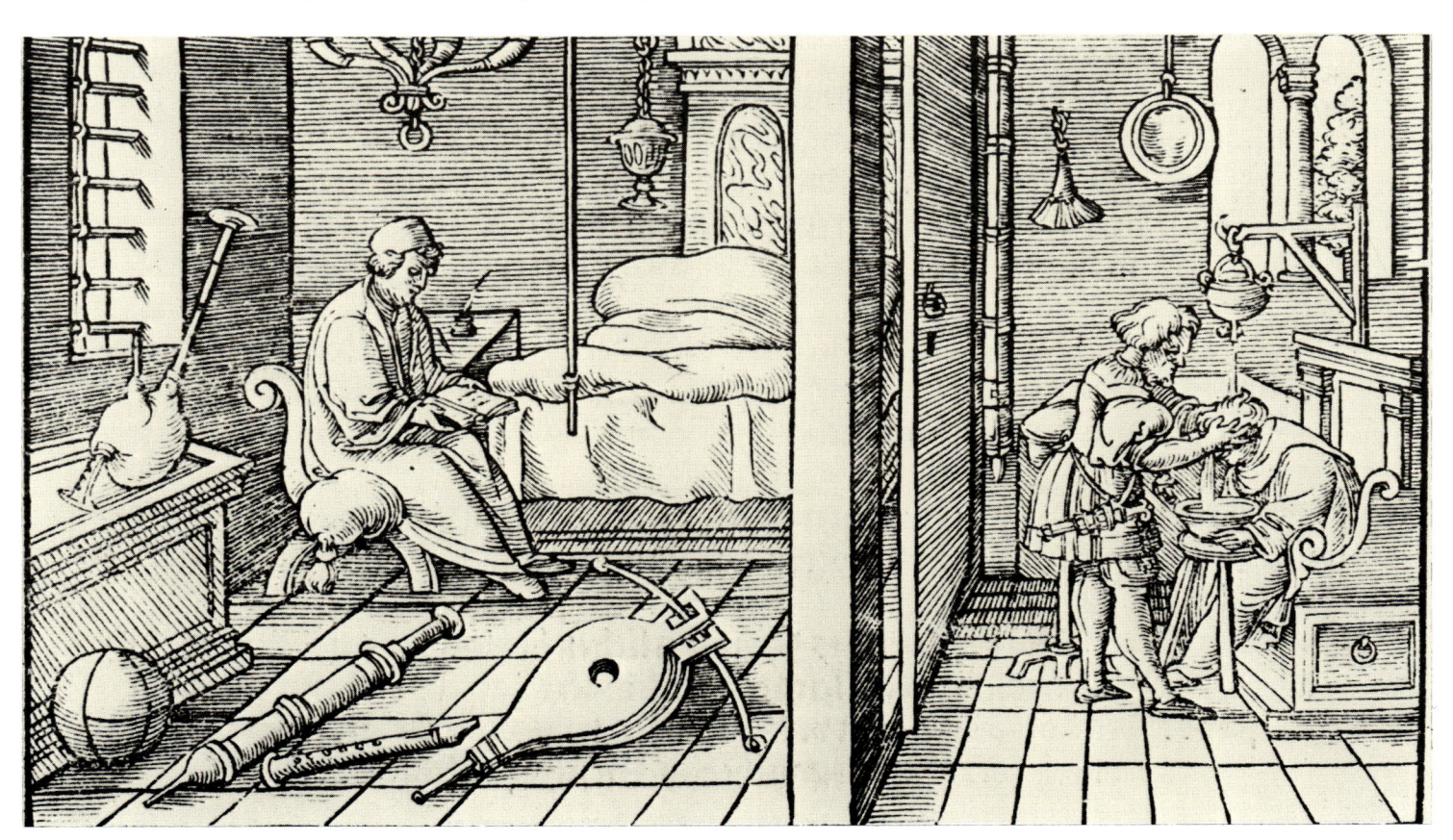

Hero demonstrates his aeolipile to his colleagues.

on a body has an equal and opposite reaction. And nineteen hundred years later it had a descendant called the jet engine.

Then there was Hero's version of the organ. Where Ctesibius had used water pressure to keep air flowing via the pump into the organ, Hero used a little windmill – again a fundamental breakthrough in the use of wind as a power-source.

He built a machine which, if a coin was put into it, would dispense a portion of holy water – the first automatic vending machine. He built a toy which was a system of communicating vessels containing water, which emptied from one to the other. When the filler tap was shut off, the vessels went on filling and emptying themselves – the first recognition of the syphon principle. He adapted the idea of a piston-plunger to design a syringe; and he built a complicated machine for the remote-control opening and shutting of a pair of doors, which depended on the knowledge that air will expand when heated.

But Hero also built practical machines and instruments. The most important was the dioptra, the first really efficient surveying instrument, which was a combined theodolite (for measuring angles) and level. Apart from its usefulness to surveyors and architects, the interesting thing about the dioptra was that each of the two instruments, the theodolite and the level, fitted separately and independently on to a common base unit. Each had three holes which fitted on to three pegs on the base unit, and it was thus the first time that the notion of interchangeable parts was used (the ancestor, if you like, of every home handyman's dream, the electric drill that will convert into anything from a saw to a sander).

Of more impact on the layman and the farmer was his development of the screw-press for making olive oil, then, as now, a basic part of the Greek diet. Earlier presses had used either weighted levers, or wedges, for crushing the olives between wooden boards. But Hero made use of a female screw (a cylinder with the screw spirals cut on the inside), which, when turned, dragged the male screw down into it. The male screw was attached to a lever which forced the wooden boards of the press together. This had the great advantage that, as more and more juice was extracted from the olives or the grapes, the screw could be tightened further and further until the last drop was squeezed out, thus ensuring the best possible return from the harvest.

And for those who could afford taxis, Hero invented the taximeter, which he called the hodometer. It was a system of reducing gears connected with a wheel of the vehicle. The gears operated a pointer, which converted the number of revolutions of the wheel into units of distance marked on a scale.

Hero, of course, was living and working during the heyday, not of the Greek, but of the Roman empire, a reminder that the two overlapped for a long period. And the greatest common denominator of the two was their striving for, and total need of, military excellence and the tools of war.

Nowadays, it has become a cocktail-party cliché that war has been responsible for many of the great innovations, in medicine, in transport, in engineering, and so on. But in no field of activity has the making of war led to greater improvements than in the making of war.

Most of the war machines of this classical period were invented by the Greeks and developed by the Romans. Many of them were ingenious but hardly great inventive breakthroughs – like the siege tower, the battering ram, the testudo (or tortoise) under cover of which soldiers could approach the walls of a besieged city, and the 'non-returnable' javelin, whose head was hinged on to the shaft and held in place by a pin which broke on impact, making it impossible for the enemy to throw it back.

But great originality was shown in the hurling of missiles over long distances, the ancestors of modern artillery. The first example of this was the gastraphetes, or stomach-bow, which was a form of crossbow invented around 400 BC. On top of the stock was a sliding board, with the bow-string fitted round its end. The archer put the bow on the ground and pushed down on

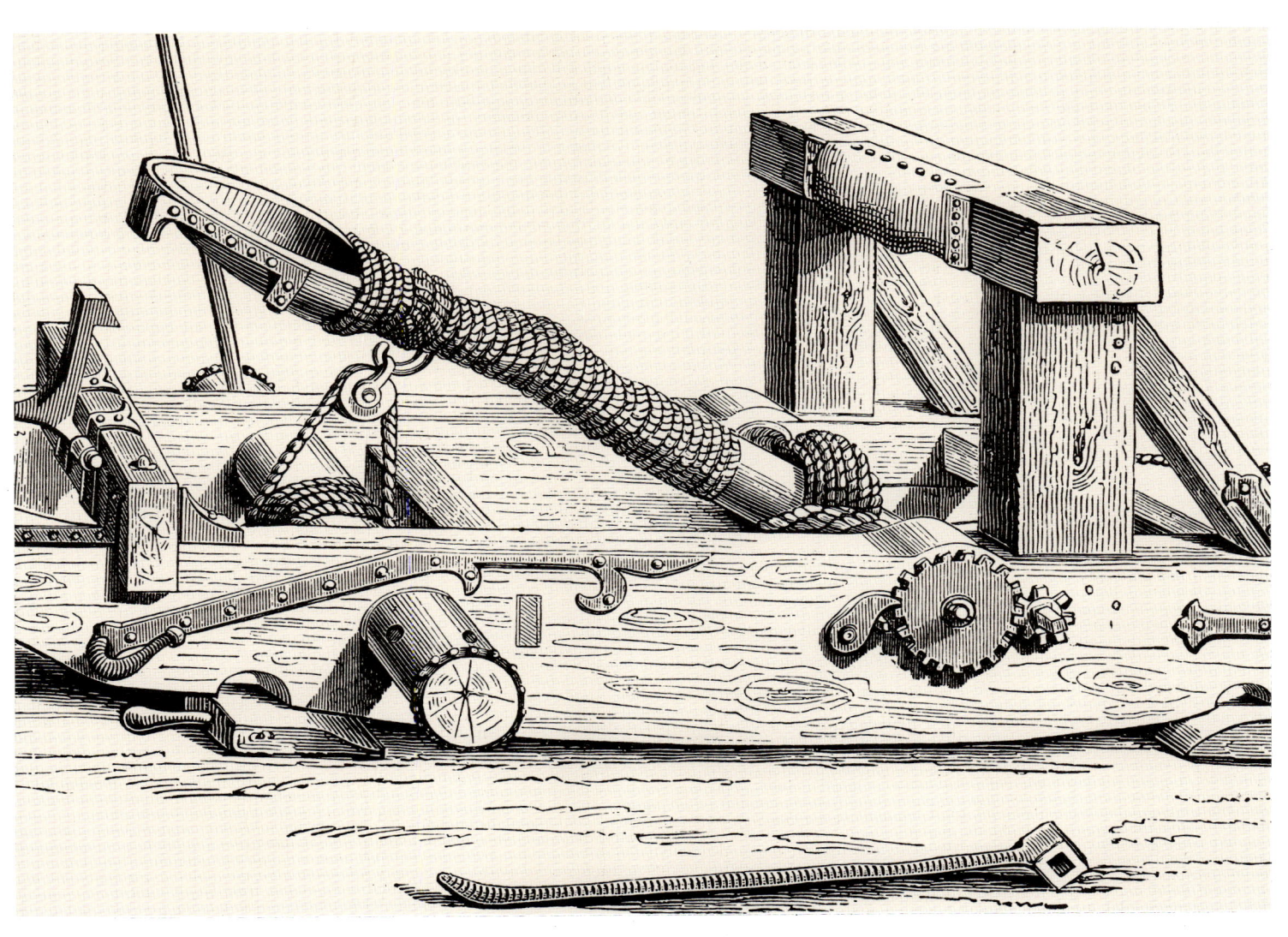

A medieval version of the giant Roman catapult.

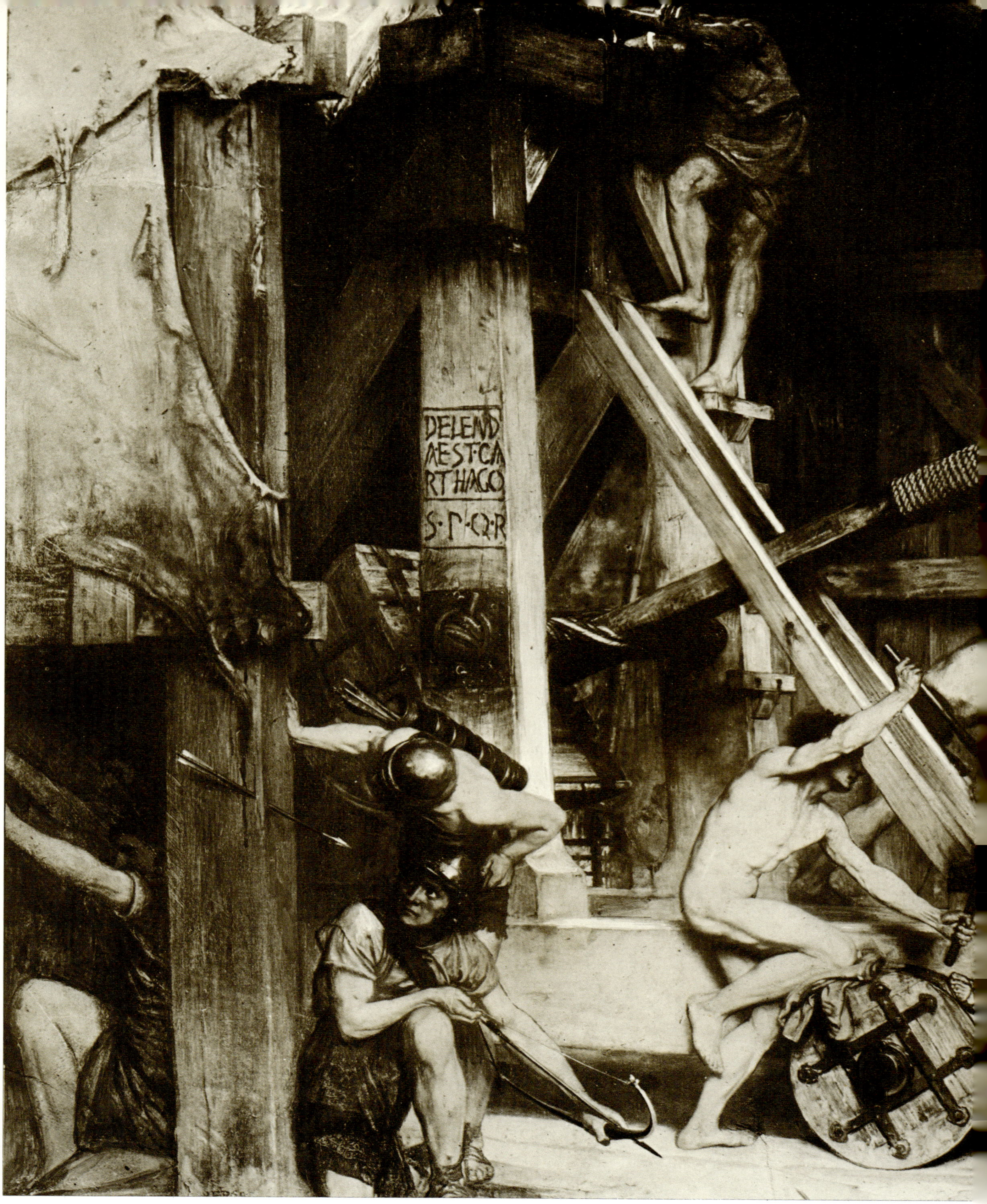
DELENDA EST CARTHAGO
S·P·Q·R

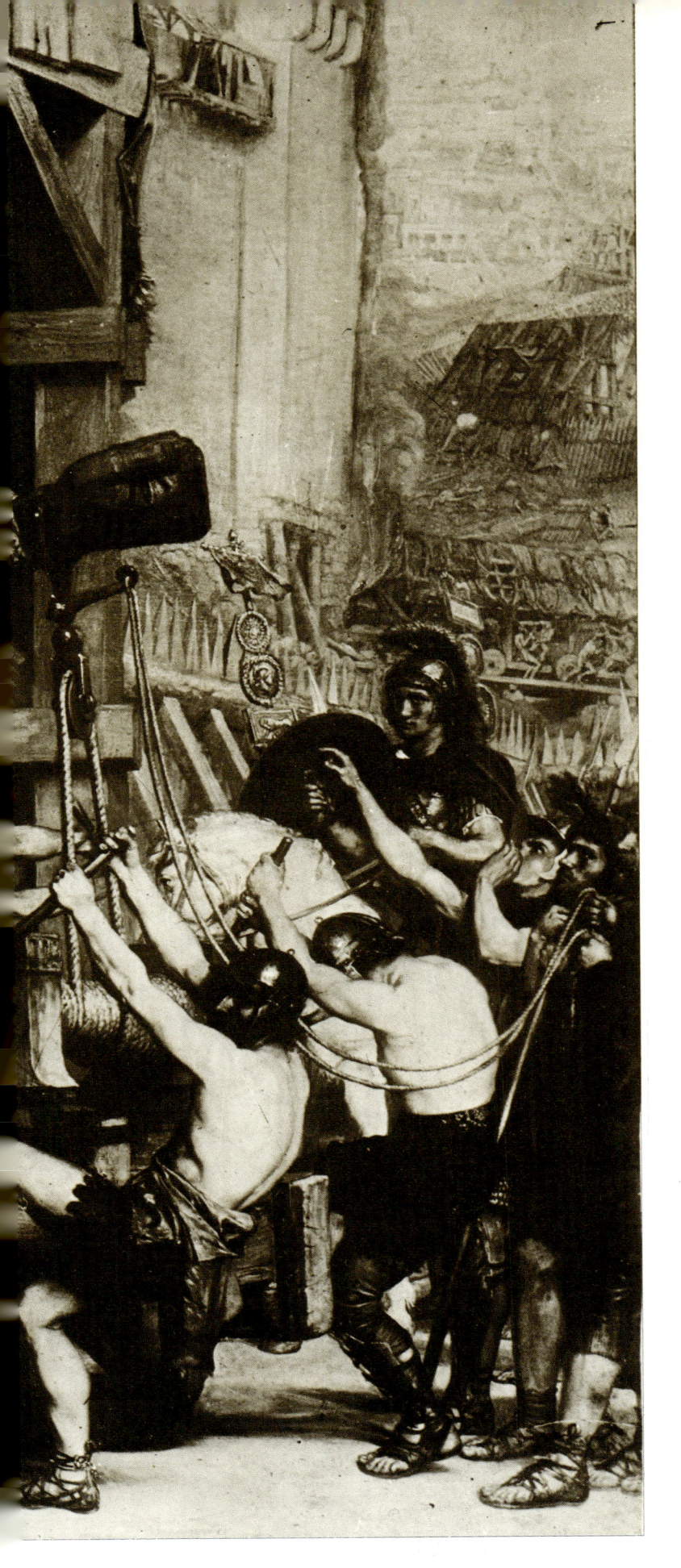

the stock, which forced the board and the string back up the stock until it engaged in a trigger.

On a larger scale was the onager, which was in effect a giant sling. The sling was attached to the top of a wooden arm, which was bent back with the use of strings made of animal entrails. When the strings were released, the arm naturally tried to snap back to its upright position. But before it could reach this it was brought to a dead halt by a pad, with the result that the sling at the top flicked forward, releasing the projectile. It could hurl a four-pound stone a distance of a thousand feet.

Mightiest of all was the giant catapult, the ballista, which gave its name to the science of ballistics (*also* concerned with putting man on the moon!). Its propulsion derived from torsion – that is, the twisting of ropes made of animal sinews. As any child knows, the more you twist a string, the faster it will rush to regain its former position. But these were no toys. The largest of them was able to throw a 500-pound stone more than five hundred yards.

If the Greeks knew that winning battles depended on weapons, the Romans realized that winning wars, and maintaining empires, depended on rapid communications. And that meant roads.

Everyone knows the saying, 'All roads lead to Rome.' In fact, this is the reverse of the truth. All roads lead *away from* Rome. As the Romans extended their dominions, their first act was always to add roads to take them to the farthest frontier. By the time they were finished, they had built 44,000 miles of them, with main highways 80 feet wide, enabling the legions to move swiftly to wherever there was trouble.

In a way, it may seem strange to regard 'roads' as an invention. After all, any route that a man takes for the simple reason that he has already tried it, and knows that it will get him from A to B, is in a sense a road, or path, or track. But what the Romans did was to recognize the importance of roads that were both straight (the shortest distance from A to B) and *permanent*, roads that would not crack apart in the hot summer, or wash away in the rains of winter. And it was in their search for this permanence that the Romans produced their greatest gift to technology, without which today's cities would not exist: concrete, and its brother, cement.

In a sense it was due to a lucky accident. In the Rome–Naples area there are thick strata of a special type of volcanic dust, called pozzolana. Around 150 BC, the Romans discovered that if they mixed this with lime and water it would set extremely hard, even under water. This made it invaluable, since previous mortars had all been very susceptible to attack by wind and rain. This *caementum* was the forerunner of what today we call Portland cement.

They didn't stop there, however, because the builders went on to realize that if they mixed the mortar with gravel, they had something which would not simply stick bricks together, but a whole new material – concrete. They used the new material for their roads, which, as the great Roman architect Vitruvius tells

The Catapult, *by the Victorian artist Edward John Poynter. The Latin declares, 'Carthage must be destroyed'. It was.*

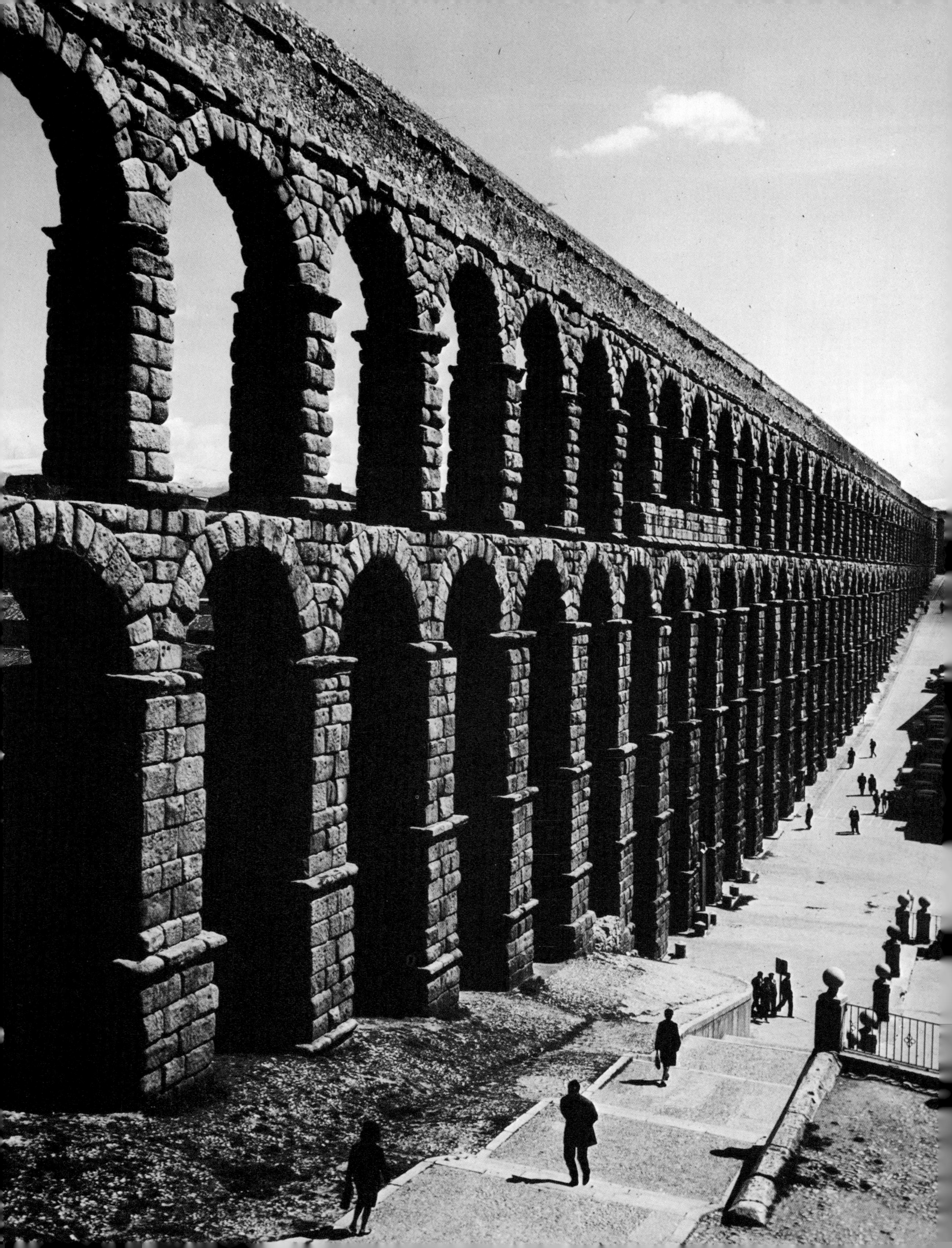

BELOW *Roman sewer in York. Built to last, and last, and ...*

ABOVE *Roman road, over Blackstone Edge in Yorkshire.*

LEFT *Roman aqueduct at Segovia, Spain, dating from the reign of Trajan (AD 96–117).*

us, were built in four layers. First there was a foundation layer of rubble called the *statumen*. Then there was a layer of small stones, mixed with mortar, called the *rudus*, which was pounded down tightly so that the bottom of it filled the cracks and bound together the foundation layer, forming at the same time a kind of damp-course. Thirdly there was the *nucleus*, a layer of powdered pottery, again mixed with lime and mortar, and finally there was the smooth surface layer, of concrete, called the *pavimentum*, or pavement. It is not surprising that such roads could be up to five feet thick, far thicker than modern motorways. Small wonder that some have lasted till today, with all the refinements, like drainage ditches, kerbstones, pedestrian walks, and a camber to drain the rain away quickly, that we would expect today.

As for the other uses of the new material, if we think that high-rise concrete apartment blocks are a curse of the twentieth century, we would be wrong. The Romans built them, the only difference being that they tended to cloak theirs with marble.

The Romans were adapters and constructors rather than inventors. Much of what they achieved was due to an attitude that anything was possible, so that developments like the under-floor central heating which they enjoyed amaze us not so

THE STORY OF INVENTIONS

much because they were great advances but because the Romans took the trouble to make them realities, and do it so thoroughly that they have lasted two thousand years. Again, their sewerage system was only an extension of the very basic idea of drainage, yet engineering and architectural feats like their *cloaca maxima*, the huge sewer built in Rome around 600 BC, are so well constructed that they are still in use today. We still marvel, too, at their gigantic aqueducts, and it was in fact in water-engineering that they produced their other great development, the water-mill, which arrived a few decades before the birth of Christ.

Three thousand years before, as mentioned in the previous chapter, the wheel had been adapted to carry buckets which raised water from rivers. And it had taken those three thousand years for someone, or possibly a group of men, whose name or names we do not know, to make what may seem to us only a small jump of the imagination, but what was an utterly fundamental advance; that is, the use of running water as motive power.

What they did was to add a series of paddles to the rim of the wheel, so that it was the flow of the river, not muscle-power, which turned the wheel, filling and emptying the buckets. Of course, that was still only using water to raise water. But it didn't take long for the next stage, the harnessing of the water-wheel as an independent power-source.

An overshot water-wheel used to drive a mill.

An early nineteenth-century version of how the Colossus of Rhodes might have looked.

44

By the use of gears attached to the horizontal axle of the turning wheel, they were able to convert the horizontal turning motion into a vertical rotation; then a millstone was attached to that axle, and the water-mill came into being. (They did realize that they could do without the need for the gearing by simply making the water-wheel horizontal and totally submerging it in the river – but this produced far less power than the vertical wheel.) The millstone, thus attached, rotated beneath the fixed grinding-stone, which had a hole in the middle of it through which the corn was fed. As it was ground, the flour passed out to the edges of the two stones, where it was collected.

The water-mill was a powerful development. At some time about AD 200, near Arles in southern France, the Romans constructed a complex of 16 water-wheels, which between them turned 32 millstones, achieving a total daily output of 30 tons.

It is curious that having harnessed water as a power-source, the Greeks and the Romans did not make more use of the wind, particularly at sea. After all, shipping was extremely important, both for trade and for war; important enough for great naval battles to be fought, and for piracy to be a going concern. The sail had already been long invented, and geniuses like Hero, with his windmill organ, were certainly aware of and considering wind in terms of energy. But the main means of propulsion remained the oar, with the great triremes driven by banks of sweating slaves.

But slaves of course have to be fed, even if they are plentiful, and the example of the water-mill should have shown that a power-source which doesn't need refuelling (even an ox or mule has to eat) is much more economic than one which does.

There was, however, one contribution which the age made to safe navigation – the lighthouse. Never were they, or have they been, more beautiful or imposing than the two lighthouses which were numbered among the seven wonders of the ancient world, the Colossus of Rhodes and the Pharos of Alexandria. Both were built around 280 BC, and both eventually perished in earthquakes, the Colossus some sixty years later, the Pharos surviving until AD 1375.

The Pharos, some five hundred feet high (compared with the one hundred and sixty-eight feet of today's Eddystone lighthouse), was built by Sostratus of Cnidus. At its top he placed a brazier, in which burned a fire which was reflected by a huge mirror. It was said to be visible thirty miles away (compared with Eddystone's eighteen).

Perhaps, in the story of inventions, it would be a fitting epitaph to the classical age to remind ourselves of what *they* considered fit for inclusion among the Seven Wonders (a list compiled and described by Philo of Byzantium around 145 BC). Apart from the two lighthouses, there were the hanging gardens of Babylon, the pyramids of Egypt, the temple of Diana at Ephesus, the statue of Jupiter by Phidias at Athens, and the mausoleum built by Artemisia at Halicarnassus.

The list speaks for itself. What they admired were great and monumental works (and beautiful ones, admittedly). But in the history of human progress, the clock, the piston, the gear, the screw, the water-mill, the lever, and concrete will stand as seven far greater monuments to the age into which they were born.

Or so I believe. But then I write from a twentieth-century point of view. It is always a healthy exercise to wonder what fortieth-century man will consider important about *our* achievements.

ET SYRIAM SOBAL · ET CONVERTIT
IOAB · ET PERCUSSIT EDOM IN VAL
LE SALINARUM · XII MILIA ·

The Lull that Never Was

In many people's minds the thousand-year period between the end of the Roman empire and the beginning of the Renaissance was what Raymond Chandler would have called 'The Big Sleep'. After all, the word Renaissance, or rebirth, itself implies that with the end of Rome all knowledge, inventiveness, culture and progress were snuffed out. Civilization is thought of as the Sleeping Princess, waiting for the kiss of awakening from Leonardo da Vinci.

This picture of what went on is totally untrue. What is more, it is astonishing that anyone should ever have thought it possible for it to be true – because technology and society move hand in hand. The way society is moving at any one time demands a particular set of innovations. And those innovations in turn alter society.

Society, made up of people, doesn't 'unlearn' things. Of course, important books and treatises get lost, stolen or burned. But you can't destroy *all* the water-mills; you can't forget the notion of the plough, once it is there; and the crafts, like that of the smith, are handed down from father to son, and are continually being improved. If one has any doubt about this, one need only look around at the world today and then imagine, even if one has no technical knowledge at all, what a mountain of useful information one could pass on if one were suddenly transported back to 2000 BC.

And there's another reason why the notion of the Middle Ages as a void is foolish. Part of it is that inventions don't just stand still. They are continually being worked on, and made better and better, until suddenly they are at a stage where a further invention becomes possible. And that leads to the second part, which is that inventions interact with each other. An invention in one field makes possible an invention in another. So that they are like an inverse pyramid – the more that is invented, the more it is possible to invent. So far from being a period when technology stood still, it can truly be said of the Middle Ages that they were the time when technology, and inventions, entered with enthusiasm into the essential processes of interbreeding and cross-fertilization. Perhaps they should be renamed 'The Melting Pot'.

Finally, it was a period when regular trade and communications had brought together disparate civilizations, from Ireland to China, from Norway to those south of the Sahara. Societies which had had to develop their own ideas independently were able to compare and exchange information. And even wars and invasions inevitably brought non-warlike technology in their train.

Nowhere did the techniques of war and peace overlap more startlingly than in the case of one of man's best friends, the horse. And few inventions have had a more profound effect than that little hoop of metal called the stirrup. The harmless stirrup? The deadly stirrup.

The first crude stirrups had appeared in India in the second century BC. From there the idea had spread out, reaching China by the fifth century AD, then back through Korea, Turkestan and northern Persia to the great city of Byzantium (later Constantinople, now Istanbul).

But the first man to realize its full potential was Charles Martel, leader of the Franks and grandfather of Charlemagne. He knew that the great disadvantage of the cavalry was that, since the rider's only way of staying on the horse was to grip with his knees, he was extremely vulnerable to any blow from the ground. In other words, he would fall off. On top of that, the reverse was true: if the rider struck too hard with his weapon, he would knock himself off.

The stirrup changed all that. It was assisted by the development of a saddle with a high pommel at the front and a high cantle at the back, so that the rider was really 'slotted' into it. Now the rider and the horse became as one. The lance could be tucked beneath the rider's arm, and when it struck, it struck with the full impetus of horse and rider.

Charles Martel saw this as the basis of a whole new form of warfare, mounted shock-combat, the medieval blitzkrieg, and in AD 732 he put it to the test when he defeated the Muslim army at Poitiers.

But when the sword was turned into the ploughshare, the horse was at a disadvantage. The old way of pulling a plough had

A contemporary picture of Charlemagne's cavalry. The stirrup had made possible the blitzkrieg.

47

Forging horseshoes. A lucky invention for the horse!

been with the use of yoked oxen. But an ox is built differently from a horse, and when the yoke was applied to the horse, the only way of keeping it in place was by a strap round its neck. This had the unfortunate effect that the harder a horse pulled, the more it was in danger of strangling itself.

In about AD 800, this was answered by the invention of a hard, padded collar, which fitted over the horse's neck and down until it rested against its shoulders. Now the traces, or the shafts, could be attached to the collar, and the horse could put its whole weight against the collar without hurting itself.

It was a development vital to agriculture. Whereas the old scratch plough had been perfectly adequate for the light soils of the Mediterranean area, it was quite unable to turn over the heavier soils in the fertile river plains of northern Europe. In answer to this, the Slavs and the Germans had during the sixth and seventh centuries developed a new kind of plough, which was composed of three elements: a vertical blade to cut through the surface, a horizontal blade to cut the furrow, and an angled board which turned over the sods as they were cut.

At first, oxen continued to be used for pulling the revolutionary new plough. They were strong, but slow, so during the ninth century the Norwegians started using the much quicker horse, harnessed with the new collar. Within two centuries most of Europe's ploughmen had switched from the ox to the horse.

There was one problem with the horse. In wet climates, its feet tended to grow soft. This was especially tricky if the horse were used for pulling carts along roads, because its feet would quickly get worn. Around 890 the problem was solved by an invention of startling simplicity, though again of great importance, the horseshoe, which could be nailed into the sole of the horse's foot.

We don't know exactly who invented the horseshoe, the emblem of luck (well, certainly lucky for the horse!). It first appeared at roughly the same time in three widely separated places: Siberia, Germany, and Byzantium. True, the problem was glaringly there to be solved, but it's hard to imagine that *three* men came up with the answer, independently, at the same time.

At any rate, horses could now be considered for heavy haulage on roads, but once again, technology had provided society with an invention (the horseshoe) which made possible an idea (horse-haulage) which in turn demanded another invention before it could be made to work. The problem was that of turning. If a pair of horses, pulling side by side, turned right, all the pulling would be done by the horse on the left, and vice versa, because the traces were joined directly to the rigid frame of the cart.

The answer, which came during the eleventh century, was the whippletree, or swingletree. It was a crossbar, with a pivot in the middle to which was attached the beam leading back to the cart. The traces leading to the horses' collars were attached to each end of the crossbar. As the horses turned, the whippletree would pivot, so that it was always at right angles to the direction of pull, and thus the labour was equally divided (the idea could also, of course, be applied to a single horse).

In war the system of cavalry established by Charles Martel was to rule the world's battlefields, as the main arm of attack, for a thousand years, which is surprising, since a horse presents such a large target. As the English longbowmen under Edward III proved when they destroyed the French at Crécy in 1346, it's a hard target to miss, and the rider of a wounded animal runs the additional risks of falling off and then getting trampled on.

At the same time that the horse was emerging supreme, other weapons were being developed. Without doubt the nastiest was 'Greek fire', the ancestor of napalm. It was invented by a Syrian architect named Callinicus, who had fled to Byzantium to escape the invading armies of Islam. In AD 673, the Muslim navy arrived off Byzantium itself, and the secret weapon was used against it, setting the ships ablaze.

The process for making this devastating weapon was such a close secret that the formula was kept under guard in Byzantium's arsenal, and it has remained a secret to this day. What we do know is that it was either thrown in pots, like fire bombs, or projected through nozzles which worked like flame-throwers.

There have been many suggestions as to what it was. Some have thought that it must have been a form of quick-lime, which does get hot when it comes into contact with water. Most recently, it has been suggested that the basic ingredient was a fraction of distilled petroleum.

If that is true, it is ironic that it should first have been used

THE LULL THAT NEVER WAS

against the forces of Islam, which from AD 610, when Mohammed first received the 'call' at the age of forty-one, was to carry the main torch of civilization for more than six hundred years. Ironic, because one of the greatest of the Arab contributions to technology was in the field of chemistry, and among the techniques they perfected was that of distillation. A thousand years before oil once again put the world at Arab feet, they knew how to distil it to get gasoline.

For the mass production of chemicals by distillation they invented the alembic. This had three elements. First, the vessel which contained the original material before it was heated. Then a second vessel, into which the vapour from the heated material passed, and where it was condensed. And finally a third vessel, connected to the second by a pipe, where the distilled material was collected.

Between roughly 800 and 1200, the Arabs were the world's foremost scientists. We know from the writings of Jabir (now thought to be the pen-name of a number of scholar–scientists) that by the tenth century they knew, apart from distillation, a great deal about techniques like filtration, evaporation, crystallization, melting, and purification.

If these are techniques rather than 'inventions' as such, the Arabs nevertheless laid the groundwork for a mass of subsequent technology. In the process they improved and developed many scientific instruments. One example is the pycnometer invented by Al-Biruni, one of the greatest Arab scholar–scientists, who lived from 973 to 1048. It was an instrument for measuring a given material's specific gravity, and with it he pronounced, with astonishing accuracy, the specific gravity of eighteen different minerals and precious stones.

Meanwhile, the Chinese were doing their own chemical experiments, and putting them to the uses of war. Possibly for want of any better suggestion, most historians seem to agree that

ABOVE *Greek fire in use. Napalm was to come later.*

BELOW *Medieval traders with horse and cart. The padded collar had made horsepower possible.*

THE STORY OF INVENTIONS

ABOVE *Firing an early rocket.*

A fourteenth-century gun – could be traversed or depressed.

the first known use of rockets was by the Chinese in 1232, when they defended the city of Kai-feng Fu against the invading Mongols. The evidence for this view is based on the contemporary description of their having used 'arrows of flying fire'. This, of course, may well have been a variation in the method of hurling Callinicus' much earlier 'Greek fire', and if they *were* rockets, no one knows what the propellant was.

But one suggestion is that this was one of the most significant inventions in the history of war (and peace) – the combination of saltpetre, charcoal and sulphur known as gunpowder. Again, no one is sure who first invented gunpowder. Suggestions include, apart from the Chinese: the Arabs, the Hindus, the Greeks, the Germans, and the English philosopher–scientist Roger Bacon. What is certain is that it was being used by the middle of the thirteenth century, and what is significant about the various candidates for title of inventor is that they should have come from such widely spread communities which all by that time possessed the technology which would have made the invention possible.

It had, of course, many potential uses for peace – in excavation, quarrying, mining, tunnelling, and the like. But men being what they are, its first main use was for the mighty 'equalizer' that was to change the face of warfare – the cannon.

Although it must obviously be included in any story of inventions, the cannon is actually not so much an invention as a development. Anyone who knew of the dart-firing blowpipe would be provided with the basic notion. Indeed, anyone familiar with the idea of the piston, as used by the earlier Greeks in pumps, would realize that just as the piston can compress the air in the cylinder, so an expansion of the air in the cylinder would drive the piston back up. All that was needed was a substance which would do that rapidly enough to make the 'piston' retreat fast enough to become a projectile. That substance was gunpowder.

As in the case of gunpowder, no one seems sure who made the first cannon, or when. The Mongols are said to have used cannon in Java in 1293. One account claims that the first European town to be bombarded was Amberg in 1301; another says that it was Facchio in 1261. There is even a suggestion that in 1216 the walls of Sant'Arcangelo were breached by the cannon of the army of Bologna.

Whatever the truth, the fact is that cannon came into something approaching general use midway through the fourteenth century. The earliest guns, which were quite small, were cast of bronze. But this of course was a comparatively expensive alloy. The obvious metal to use was iron, which was still only known in the form of wrought-iron.

The system used was to get a number of wrought-iron rods and weld them together along their lengths so that their ends made a circle. This 'cylinder' of rods (formed like a barrel, which is where the term 'gun barrel' originates) was then encircled from end to end by a series of wrought-iron rings, which gave it greater strength.

But there were two problems. One was that wrought-iron contained a number of impurities. The other was that the method of manufacture meant that the breech had to be a

Gunners aligning an artillery piece, the mighty equalizer.

separate entity; and engineering was still far too primitive to allow the perfectly machined fitting required of a breech-loading gun. The result of both these factors was that guns were continually going off in the wrong direction, and were as dangerous to the firer as to his target.

Once again, technology, having posed a problem, came up with the answer: cast-iron, that is, iron melted until it reached its liquid form, at which point it could be poured into moulds, an obviously enormous advantage, both from the point of view of the size of object that could be made, and of the speed in making it; in addition, the greater purity of the metal gave it far greater strength than wrought-iron.

The reason cast-iron had not been made much earlier was the problem encountered in heating iron. Its melting-point is 1535 degrees centigrade (2821 °F), and to achieve this it was necessary to be able to force large quantities of (oxygen-laden) air into the furnace to make it burn hotter; in other words, to build the blast-furnace.

The question was: how could *that* be done? Perhaps this is a suitable point at which to observe that while this book deals only with the pinnacles of *innovation* in technology, it must always be borne in mind that inventions, once they had arrived, didn't just stand still. They were always, or nearly always, being improved and adapted.

So it was with the water-wheel. At first used for milling, it was adapted during the thirteenth and fourteenth centuries to move

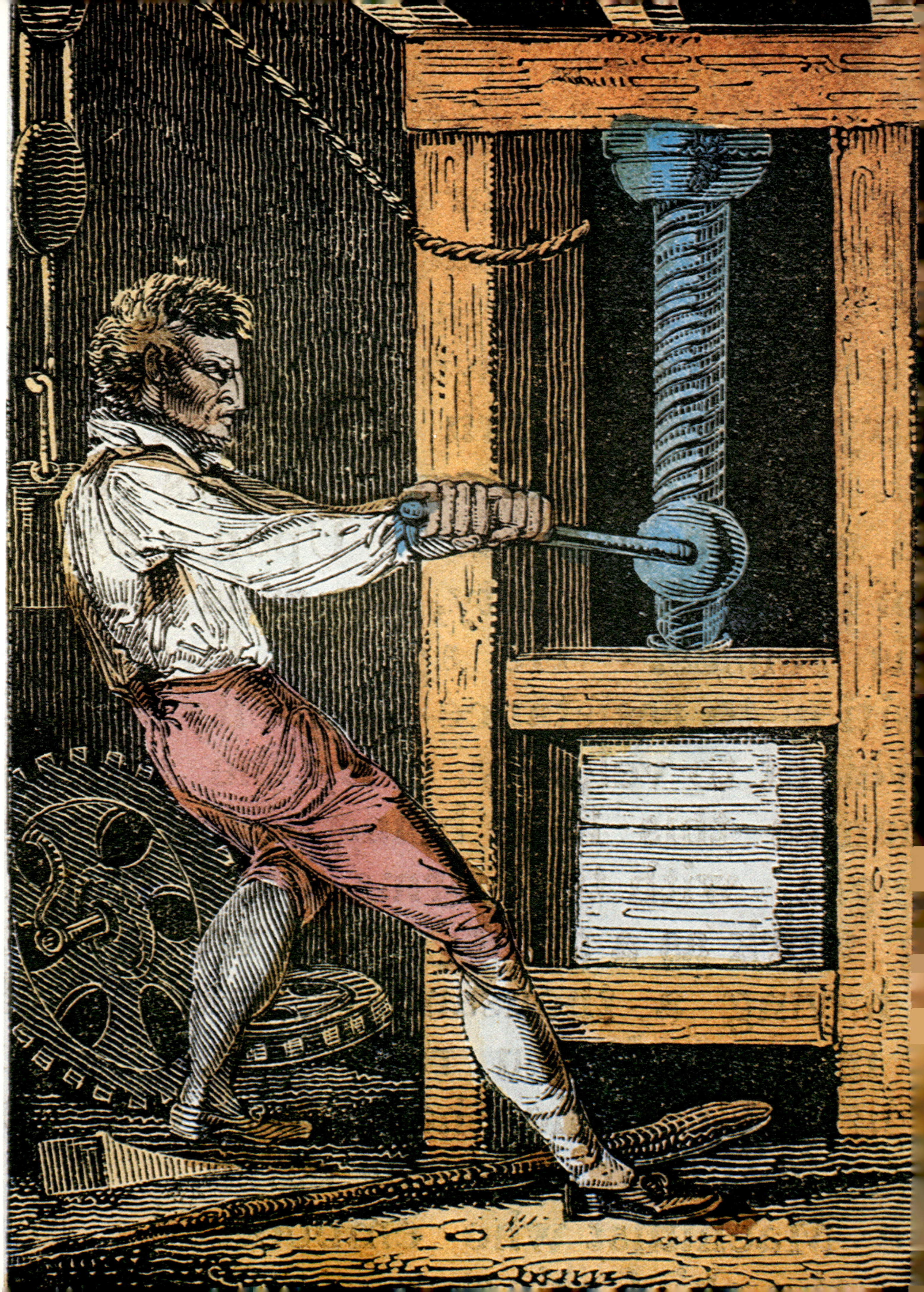

LEFT *A screw-press being used in paper production, the Chinese secret that escaped to the West.*

ABOVE *The first page of Gutenberg's 42-line Bible.*

THE STORY OF INVENTIONS

ABOVE *An 'undershot' water-wheel drives bellows and a trip-hammer. Note the cam (C), the crank, and the connecting rod.*
RIGHT *The Chinese, too, put the trip-hammer to work.*

vast bellows, which blasted air into the furnaces of the iron-founders. By the middle of the fifteenth century cast-iron was being made widely throughout Europe, and the cannon were being made of it; and the separate breech could disappear, because the breech was now cast as an integral part of the cannon, which became a muzzle-loader. More than four centuries were to pass before the problem of breech-loading was successfully solved.

But the power of the water-wheel was being allied to other vital mechanical ideas. One of the most brilliant of these was the crank, the device that could turn a rotating motion into an up-and-down (or reciprocal) motion – or vice versa. It had been known in Europe as early as the ninth century (and in China since the time of Christ), but lay little used until the fourteenth century. Then, in 1335, the simple crank (like the brace we use in the workshop today) was given the vital addition of a connecting-rod, which attached to, and swivelled around, the bent part of the crank. Now, if the outer arms of the crank were attached as an extension of the water-wheel's axle, the connecting-rod moved forward and back, enabling it to power not only the bellows of the furnace, but also, in wood-mills, a saw attached to the end of the connecting-rod. And so the saw-mill was born.

The other brilliant idea that was applied to the axle-shaft of the water-wheel was one of extreme simplicity, but one which we can see in the modern motor-car, for instance, as a part as essential as the crankshaft. That idea was the cam. It wasn't a new idea, but it wasn't until around AD 1000 that it was put to practical purpose.

Basically, the cam is simply a 'blip' or 'pimple' on the surface of an otherwise round shaft. But of course it can be shaped in any number of ways, and in particular with a shallow gradient on the side towards which the shaft is turning, and a steep or even vertical drop on the other side. That means that anything which is in contact with the shaft will be slowly raised as the cam starts to meet it, and then dropped suddenly when it loses contact with the cam.

What the cam, attached to the water-wheel's shaft, had made

possible was the trip-hammer – raised, then allowed to fall suddenly and with its full weight each time the shaft rotated.

Again, it was a vital invention. First, it was of enormous help to the smith, especially when he was forging larger pieces of metal. Secondly, it was applied to the medieval textile industry, for the process of fulling, in the course of which the newly woven cloth was put in water and beaten.

This process has two advantages. First, the cloth shrinks, giving it greater 'body' for a given area. Secondly, it entangles the fibres of the woven yarn, giving it a much more homogeneous effect and a smoother finish.

Previously, this had always been a job for human labour, either stamping by foot or beating by hand. Now, a series of trip-hammers could do the work of several fullers. What's more, they could be attended by just one man – an early example of the need for economic production conflicting with the need of men to work.

But there was a third application of the trip-hammer, in the manufacture of one of the Everests in the mountain range of inventions: what you are looking at now, paper.

The credit for the invention of paper, in AD 105, goes to a Chinese court official named Ts'ai Lun, who was honoured by the Emperor for his achievement, which rapidly superseded the woven cloth, and strips of bamboo, which the Chinese had previously used. What he did was to take a mixture of rags, hemp, the bark of the mulberry tree, old fishing nets, and even grass, add water to them, and beat them into a pulp, the point being that they were all fibrous materials. This 'soup' was then ladled on to a fine wire sieve, through the holes of which the water drained off. The residual sheet of pulp was then peeled off, dried, made smooth by treating with various forms of size, and then used for writing.

For five hundred years the secret remained with the Chinese. In the seventh century it crossed to Japan. Then, in 751, the Chinese attacked the legendary city of Samarkand, midway between Tashkent and the northern border of Afghanistan. It was then under the rule of Islam, and when the Arabs drove off the attackers they took some of the Chinese prisoner. It just happened that a few of them knew how to make paper, and thus the secret reached the West.

It was one of those incredibly lucky chances that the technique should have been passed on to a people who were reaching the height of their powers as cultural leaders of the world. And the degree to which they made use of it can be judged by the fact that in AD 900, the library in the Arab-ruled university town of Cordoba, in Spain, contained an astonishing six hundred thousand books.

If anyone has any doubt about the importance of books, or about the adage that the pen is mightier than the sword, it's worth considering that Plato's *Republic*, the Bible, the Koran, Darwin's *Origin of Species*, Marx's *Das Kapital*, Hitler's *Mein Kampf*, and *The Thoughts of Mao Tse-tung* have probably changed the course of history as much as any process or event, any individual or any nation.

But of course, the vast majority of those books in Cordoba, as elsewhere at that time, were written by hand – a long-winded

Gutenberg reads proofs. His assistant works the press.
OVERLEAF *The map of the world, from the first edition of Ptolemy's* Geography *printed at Ulm in 1482.*

process, and one which necessarily made a severe limitation on the number of books which could be produced, and thus made literacy and learning the sole preserve of the rich. Until, that is, literature gained its greatest servant – printing.

In a sense, printing is one of the first ideas ever used by man. When he hunted his prey, the tracks he followed would tell him whether the animal was young or old, wounded or fit. From there he moved to the notion of the personal seal, which would stand for a person's unique signature when pressed into wax, or inked and stamped on parchment – an idea that is still used throughout the world, by common men and by great heads of state.

Then, in AD 770, the Japanese, who had inherited the secret of paper a century before, invented block-printing. The Empress Shotoku ordered a million prayer-sheets to be printed, and it took the printers six years to do it. A century later, in 868, the Chinese produced the first block-printed book, called the *Diamond Sutra*. It had six pages of text and one woodcut illustration.

But it was still a lengthy process to prepare the blocks, and of course they could only be used for that particular book. And then came the great breakthrough, movable type, which at last allowed the idea of the alphabet, as standing for the components of an infinity of words, to be allied to printing. Again, we are indebted to a Chinaman, Pi Sheng, for the idea. He made the characters of earthenware, which was then fitted into an iron frame.

The trouble was Pi Sheng's type tended to be much too brittle and fragile to be truly reusable, and in addition there was difficulty in finding a suitable ink, since earthenware is porous. That was around 1045, and it wasn't until two hundred years later, 1241, that a Korean, Yi Kyo-bo, who was in the last year of

CAVRVS·CHORVS·VEL·IAPIX·SIVE·ARGESTES
CIRCTVS
VEL·TRESIIAS
FAVONIVS·ZEPHIRVS
mare glaciale
EVROPA
Pontus euxinus
ARABIA
Sinus hesperus
LIBIA INTERIOR
AFFRICA
Circulus equinoctialis
ETHIOPIA INTERIOR
Terra incognita secundum ptholomeum
AFRICVS·VEL·LIBS
LIBONOTVS·EVROAV·STER

nzer de Arnßheim
AQVILO VEL BOREAS
CECIAS APELIOTES
SVBSOLANVS
ASIA
ARIA
Sinus gangeticus
Sinus magnus
MARE INDICVM
MARE INDICVM
PRASODVM
MARE
Terra incognita secūdū ptholomeū
Gradus longitudinis ab occidente in orientem
VVLTVRNVS EVRVS
EVRNOTVS

his life, made a wooden movable type that would work. He published twenty-eight books, which was a bold start to the new industry. Since then, publishers have been content with more modest beginnings!

By the end of the following century, the Koreans were casting movable type in the much more suitable bronze, and then in 1439 the West finally started to make its contribution. There lived in Strasbourg a goldsmith in his early forties, who had earlier been exiled from his native city of Mainz. Working quite independently of the Chinese and Koreans, of whose ideas he had almost certainly never heard, he started to experiment with printing. His name was Johann Gensfleisch zum Gutenberg, whose name we give to the first printed Bible of 1456.

His achievement involved many important new elements – like the development of a new alloy that could easily be cast into type, and the ability to engrave the hardened steel punches used to form the characters. But above all his greatest importance lay in the fact that he was the first to realize that printing had to be considered as a whole – that the papers and the inks were as much the concern of the printer as the type and the presses.

One of the first uses of the new printing was for the production of maps – suitably, since the world was about to embark on a brilliant period of exploration by sea. The first printed map, of 1477, was produced from copperplates at Bologna. It consisted of a world map and twenty-six regional maps, based on the world map drawn by the great Alexandrian astronomer and mathematician Ptolemy in his eight-volume *Geography* of AD 150. It was a brilliant map, in view of the meagre supply of facts he had to go on, and for nearly fifteen hundred years after its creation was regarded as *the* authoritative world map.

Both the navigators, and therefore also the map-makers, were during this period given two vital instruments to help them on their way. One was the compass. It is not clear who invented it; a case has been made for the Chinese, the Italians, the Arabs, and the Scandinavians. But it was in general use by the middle of the thirteenth century.

It was based on the principle, known to every good Boy Scout, that a free-floating magnetized needle will swing until it points to the (magnetic) North. At first the compass was simply a needle, floating in a bowl of water with the support of a splinter of wood. The needle was magnetized by touching it with a loadstone, or lump of magnetic iron oxide. But by 1250 this had been greatly improved. Instead of floating, the needle was balanced on a pivot. The pivot stood at the centre of a circular card, marked off at its edge in three hundred and sixty degrees, and the whole thing was housed in a box with a glass top. Now, by aligning the needle with the north on the graduated card, the mariner could determine exactly in which direction he was travelling.

The other great aid to navigation was one of the most beautiful instruments ever devised, the astrolabe, forerunner of the sextant. It had first been invented by the Greek Hipparchus in about 150 BC, but it had to wait for the Arab scholars, astronomers and delicate metal-workers to bring it to its peak.

It was an astonishingly intricate instrument, and was said to be able to answer a thousand different questions. Two of the

THE LULL THAT NEVER WAS

most important of these were: 'What latitude am I at?' and 'What time is it?' So many were its functions that it is virtually impossible to explain in words, without holding one in the hand. But it was a combination of a sighting apparatus; a circle graduated in degrees for noting the altitude of the sun or stars with the help of the sighting apparatus; a zodiacal circle which showed the position of the sun for every day of the year; and a circular map of the stars which could rotate, to imitate the way in which the stars appear to rotate around the North Pole.

A Viennese astrolabe of 1457. The most beautiful instrument in the world?

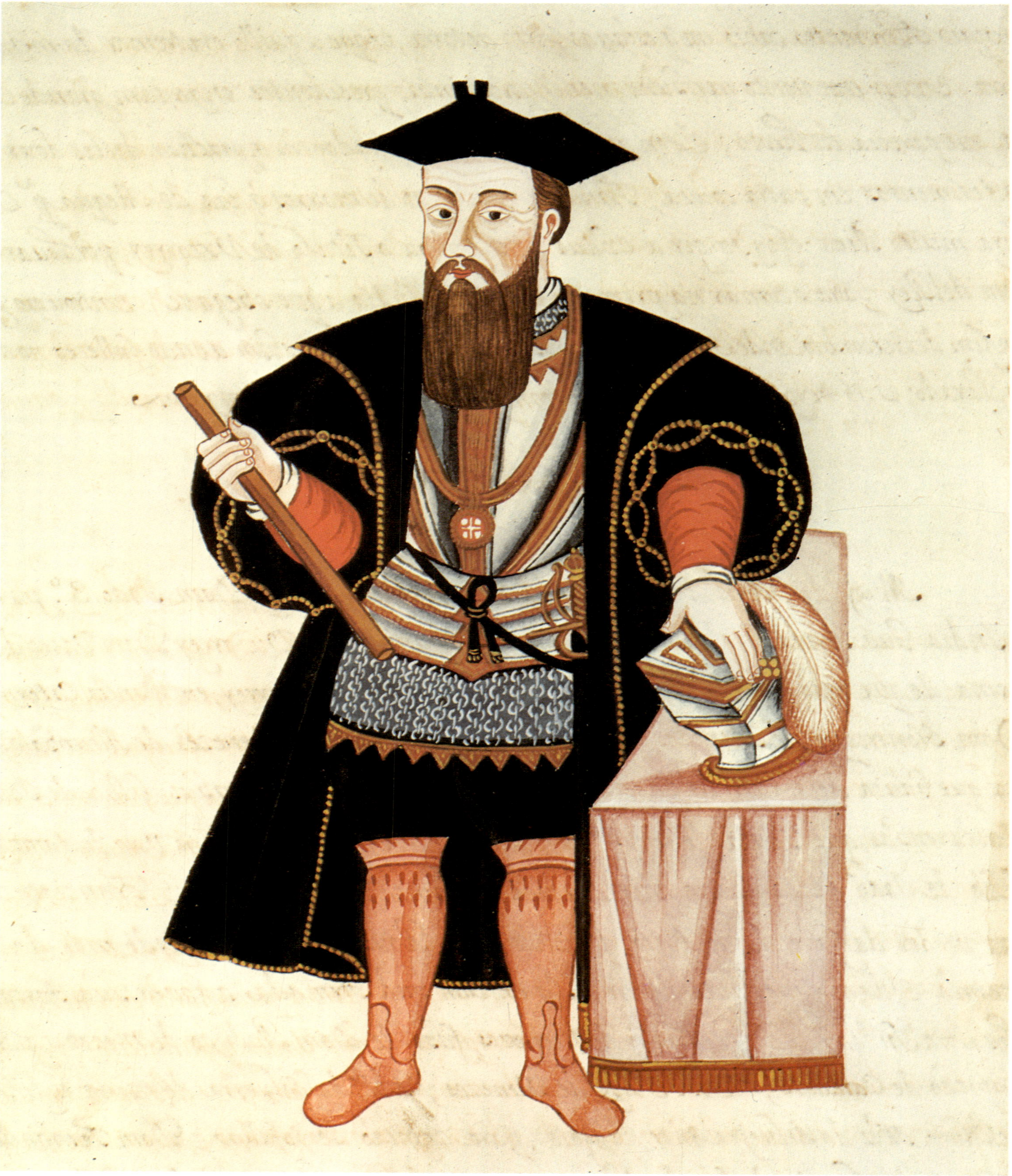

THE LULL THAT NEVER WAS

The Santa Maria, *flagship of Columbus. Note the lateen sail and the stern-post rudder.*

If these helped mariners to know where they were going, they also gained two valuable aids in getting there at all.

The first was the lateen sail. Ships had previously been equipped only with square sails. These are fine for running before the wind, but travelling sideways across the wind is difficult, and sailing *into* the wind virtually impossible. The lateen sail, developed by the Arab sailors, was a completely different concept. It was a triangular sail, whose leading edge was attached to a long yard-arm (attached to the mast and rising from deck level to way above the mast). Like the jib sail of a modern yacht, the rear part of the sail could be moved from side to side, allowing the wind to catch either side of the sail, and allowing the ship itself to sail as close as possible into the wind.

But the additional versatility and accuracy of sailing which this new sail promised could not be brought to its fullest realization without a strong rudder. Until about 1200, the rudder had been a long oar held out over one or other of the stern sides of the ship (rather in the way a canoeist steers his craft). Then there appeared, probably first in the Netherlands, one of the most significant inventions in the history of ships – the stern rudder.

It is astonishing that it took so long to be invented. First, the

Vasco da Gama, the Portugese navigator who, in 1498, found the sea route to India round the Cape of Good Hope.

problem was so obviously, and for so long, waiting to be solved. The use of the oar for steering puts an enormous strain both on the man using it and on the oar itself. Secondly, man has come to so many of his important inventions through an observation of nature that one would have thought that *someone* would much earlier have taken a look at a fish and see how *it* steers.

At any rate, the problem was now solved, with the rudder itself below water, attached to a long beam hinged to the stern of the ship. To the top of this another beam was attached, at right angles – the tiller. It was indeed a form of lever, and as Archimedes had shown, the longer the tiller, the easier it was for the helmsman to move it.

Together, the stern rudder and the triangular sail revolutionized the manœuvrability of sailing ships, and the way was paved for the epic voyages of Columbus, Magellan and Vasco da Gama.

It is fitting that their explorations should mark the passage from the Middle Ages to the centuries of genius that were to follow, because they constituted the final proof that the Middle Ages had not been some useless blank in history, but an essential transition period, following the high theory of Greece and Rome, which allowed the world to cope with, and take best advantage of, the amazing discoveries with which the travellers were to return. In a sense, they prepared the world to see itself, for the first time, as it really was.

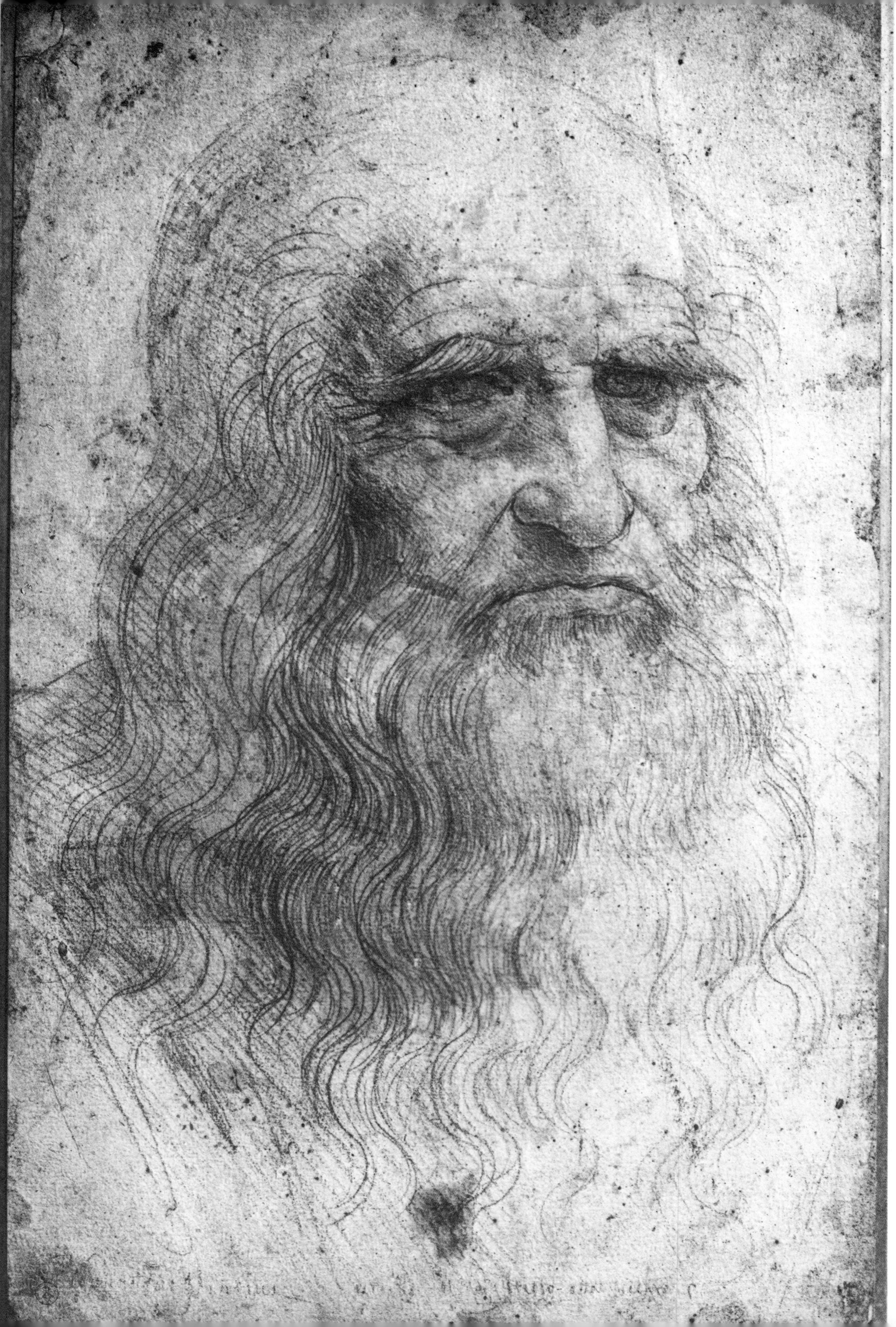

An Age of Genius

This book is about the story of inventions; or rather, it is an attempt to skim across the surface of inventions, at a constant height, touching only those masterpieces of inventive thought which rise above the others by virtue of being completely new ideas – side-steps away from the preceding technological ladder of improvement and adaptation. So it's funny that the most important date in the book, *as* a book, should not be the date of an invention at all. The date is 1421. It was in that year that the Republic of Florence issued the first patent of which we know. It was given to one Filippo Brunelleschi for his design of a cargo boat; and in 1474 the Republic of Venice passed the first law which formalized the idea of protecting the inventor and allowing him to enjoy the benefits of his creative ability, benefits which had never been denied to the artist, whose works are essentially unique, and can therefore be copied but not reproduced. (I know pictures are 'reproduced', but I prefer to call that 'copying'. The original is not re-produced as is, for instance, a car engine.)

After its adoption in Venice, the idea of patents quickly spread throughout Europe. Perhaps it was eminently suitable that this should have happened at a time when the artist and the inventor were frequently embodied in the same person – like Michelangelo, who was as important an architect as he was a painter and sculptor.

The Renaissance, or rebirth, was so named because it saw a revival of interest in the ideas and the designs of the classical era of Greece and Rome. But there was one profound difference. Whereas the classical philosophers had for the most part been content to deal in theory and theorem, the men of the Renaissance, centred in Italy, realized that the only true way to find out about nature was to observe it, dissect it, and experiment upon it. What's more, the period provided them with the instruments with which to do it.

The explosion of inventive thought which now began grew and grew and has never stopped growing, until today something like sixty thousand patent applications are made every year in Britain alone. Nothing begets inventions so much as inventions.

Leonardo da Vinci, by Leonardo da Vinci.

So from this point onwards, it becomes increasingly difficult to select those that are true 'highlights'. And it becomes increasingly important to know and understand the background against which the inventors worked.

One of the most crucial elements in this background was the growth of the monetary system. The explorers of the New World brought back not only the key new products like tobacco and the potato, but enormous quantities of gold and silver. This resulted in a vast increase in the supply of money, which in turn led to the development of the banking system.

Because it was cumbersome (and dangerous) to transport large sums of money for long-distance transactions, the bill of exchange (roughly equivalent to today's cheque) came into use, together with the idea of credit. Inherent in that was the idea of interest, and finally, therefore, the growth of capitalism.

Many of the new inventions were either so large, or so difficult to develop and produce, that they had to be financed by the bankers. Nowhere was this more true than in war. Battles were starting to be won by cannon, and lost for the lack of them. They were extremely costly, and for the most part could only be afforded by the richest rulers. The feudal lords, whose great castles had previously made them immune to punishment for acts of rebellion, could now be literally blown out of them.

This led to the rise of the nation-state, as we see it today; and since, economically, a larger grouping tends to be richer and more powerful than the sum of its parts, the rulers (four hundred years before 'nationalization' and the welfare state) began to think in terms of public works, not for their own glorification alone, but because they bore that responsibility towards their subjects.

The application of this to tasks like the provision of sewerage and public water-supplies, the drainage of fens and marshes, and the building of harbours and canals, meant a constant demand on the ingenuity of the inventor-engineers. And nowhere was it more necessary than in the cities, which were expanding rapidly in size.

One of the main reasons for this was the enclosure system. Previously the peasants had been allowed to farm strips of land for their own food. Now the landowners were fencing in great

63

THE STORY OF INVENTIONS

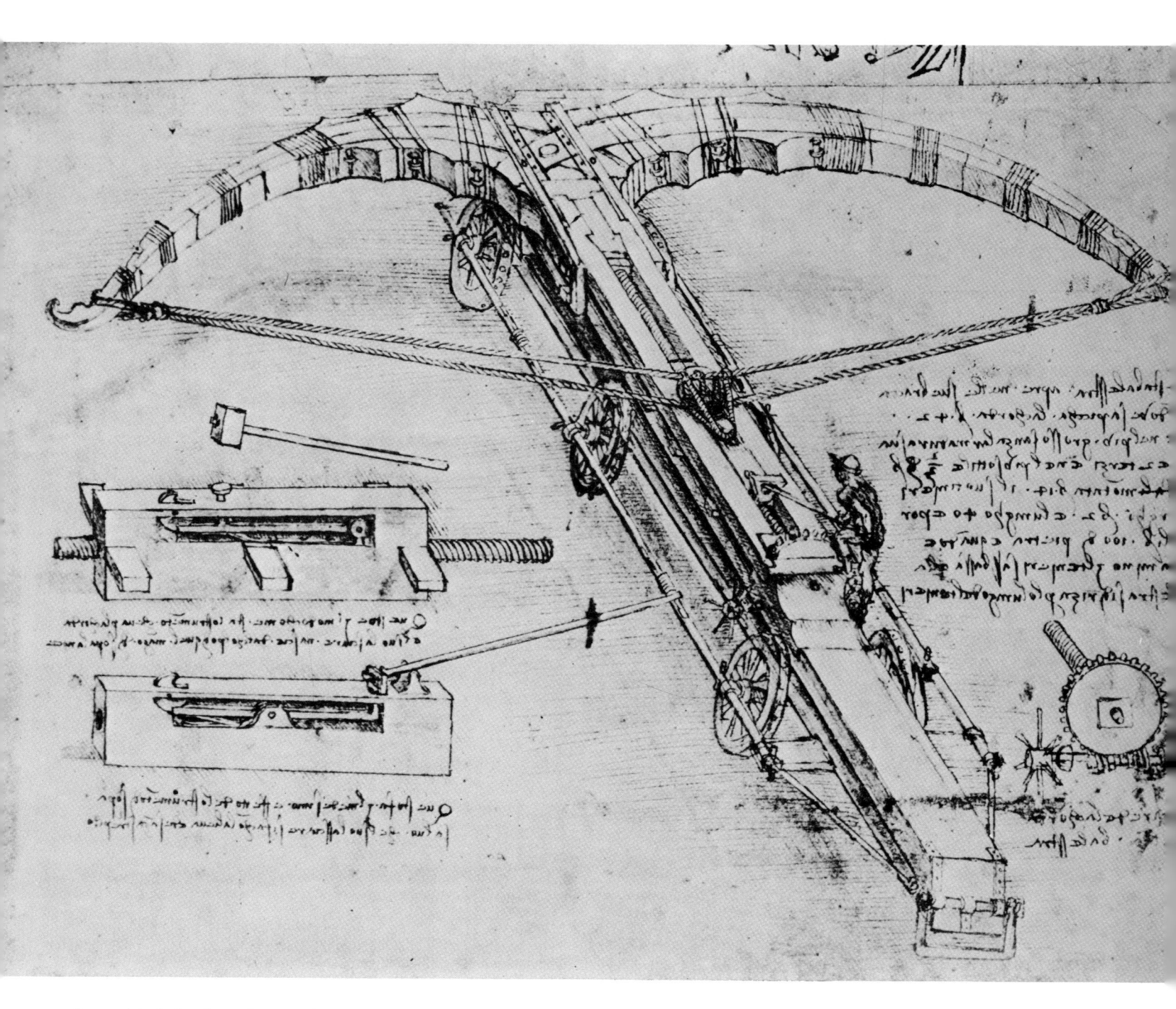

Leonardo's design for a giant crossbow.

areas of the countryside and turning to sheep-farming, which again meant less work on the land, since one shepherd can care for a lot of sheep.

The flight to the cities focused attention on the problems of public health. It meant that there was no shortage of labour for the city-based workshops and foundries. And the rapid growth of these itself had a profound effect. By 1500, Europe was producing some sixty thousand tons of iron a year, which displaced copper, and its alloys like bronze, as the most used metal.

But the only known way of making iron was by smelting it with charcoal. To make charcoal you need wood – several tons of it for each ton of iron. Wood had been the traditional fuel for heating the home. Now there was a frantic demand for an alternative – and that alternative was coal. More coal meant more, and deeper, coal-mines, and that in itself demanded a whole new technology.

Improvements in the techniques of sailing and the construction of ships led to much larger vessels. Together with the new banking system, this in turn led to a vast expansion of trade, and the growth of a whole new class of entrepreneurs, or middlemen, who were the link between the producers and the consumers – an absolutely profound development, since every person who turned to *distributing* goods meant one less body available for *making* them.

That, too, had a series of consequences. The more middlemen there were, the more the men *making* things had to produce per head to satisfy the demand. This inevitably led to the search for more and more efficient machines, with the corresponding need for less and less men in those areas where machines replaced them. Throughout Europe there were instances of clashes with the inventors of the new technology, and the destruction of their brainchildren.

But the demand of the consumers had to be met, and more and more men started to turn their hands to the old crafts. The reaction by the guilds that controlled key areas of production and commerce was to become even more restrictive – in other words, to establish 'closed shops'.

This didn't prevent the new technologies from spreading more rapidly than ever before – for two good reasons. One was that, through a combination of better transport, religious persecutions, and often simply the offer of better wages, there was a huge increase in the migration of labour. And the craftsmen who found shelter or better reward in other countries took their skills with them.

The second reason was printing. During the late fifteenth century and the sixteenth century, great numbers of technical books started to be printed. One of the best-known examples is the *De Re Metallica*, published in 1556. It was written by the German scholar Georg Bauer, better known as Agricola. (Bauer means 'farmer' in German, and it was a nice affectation, worthy of an age which worshipped the classics, that he should adopt the Latin word which means the same thing.) It was an astonishing book, full of detailed drawings and descriptions of processes in the metal and mining industries. So advanced and practical was it that it was still being reprinted a hundred and fifty years later.

It was against this complex social and economic background that the new age of technology was to develop. Fittingly, it was ushered in by the man who was not only unquestionably the greatest of his time, but who would be an excellent candidate for the title of the most extraordinary genius who has ever lived: Leonardo da Vinci.

He lived from 1452 until 1519, and was a native of Florence. Any census of the world's best-known and admired paintings would almost certainly contain the 'Mona Lisa' and 'The Last Supper' among the top half-dozen. Both, of course, were by

A model made from Leonardo's design for an armoured car, or tank.

Leonardo's flying machine.

Leonardo. Yet they are but a fragment of his total achievement. Indeed, he earned most of his income as an architect and military engineer.

The major reason for our celebration of Leonardo nowadays should be the series of 'Notebooks' in which he recorded descriptions, drawings, and diagrams of a host of 'inventions'. I put the word in inverted commas because of the dispute that continues about these 'inventions'. It springs from the fact that almost nothing he designed was ever actually made. He was so secretive about his ideas that few of his contemporaries saw them – besides, some would have been thought so heretical that he would have been risking his life to have made them public. It wasn't until the nineteenth century that people began to realize just how much his mind had encompassed.

There are two other factors to be taken into account. One was that Leonardo was probably more interested in the process of problem-solving, than in pushing the answers into practical application. True, there were some, like his machine for polishing sewing-needles, that he tried to get constructed, and from which he hoped to make a lot of money. But so many were his ideas that there would simply have been no time to 'push' more than a small percentage of them.

The second factor was simply that Leonardo's ideas were *centuries* before their time. Even if people had known of them, and had wanted to put them into practice, the technology didn't exist to have done it.

But in spite of all this, I believe it is crazy to claim, as some writers have done, that Leonardo was not the inventor of the majority of his designs, just because they don't happen to have been made. *Of course* he invented them, and if anyone has any doubt, they need only look at his notebooks and the conclusion will be obvious. So let me list just a few of the more startling of them: the universal joint, the friction-reducing roller bearing, bevel and spiral gears, the conical screw, link chains (as on a modern bicycle), the power loom, machines for making rope, spinning wool and winding silk, clockwork turnspit and clockwork fan, the wheelbarrow, the parachute, the ship's log, the pendulum-driven pump and the centrifugal pump, water dredgers, the hydraulic press, the wheel-lock pistol, rifling in firearms, a continuous-motion lathe worked by a treadle crank, and an automatic file-cutting machine. To these we may add, if we feel generous, because he *did* draw them in detail: the tank, the machine-gun, the helicopter – and the aeroplane.

One cannot overpraise his achievement. It was, simply, incredible. And although some of these devices will necessarily have to appear later in our story, with other names attached, it was Leonardo who thought of them first.

Happily, there was one major invention which he did live to see – the double-mitring lock-gate for canals, which were becoming increasingly important for heavy transport. Previously, lock-gates had either been lifted vertically, or had been single swinging gates, which needed great effort to open them, and which were also likely to split, standing as they did at right angles to the flow and pressure of water. Leonardo saw that if he split the gate into two gates, which met in the middle at an angle, like an arrow-head pointing upstream, then they would be much stronger, since the water pressure would force them together to form a tight fit. In addition, once the water-level inside the lock was equalized with the level of the stream beyond whichever gate was to be opened or shut, the fact that it was made of two half-gates would make it much easier to operate. We still use them today.

On top of everything else, Leonardo made a whole series of amazingly accurate anatomical drawings, assisted by the fact that, as he tells us, he dissected some thirty bodies. It was a fair reflection of the new feeling that one had to look at nature in order to find out about it. And it was of enormous importance at a time when there was a growing movement to put some order into the art of medicine.

A key figure in this movement was the Frenchman Ambroise Paré, regarded as one of the founders of modern surgery. Starting from a poor background, he rose to become the chief surgeon to the French King Charles IX in 1562.

One of the worst features of war had always been the agonies of the wounded – for many, death would have been infinitely preferable, and for no reason more strongly so than the most common remedy, amputation. If a limb were badly damaged, the only way to avoid gangrene, and death, was to cut it off. Once that had been done, the bleeding at the point of amputation would be stopped by the application of a red-hot iron – a procedure known as 'cauterizing'. Paré realized that the bleeding could equally well be stopped by binding a tight ligature around the limb.

Thereafter, of course, the wounded had to go around armless, or on crutches. All that was changed by Paré, who founded the whole new field of medicine known as prosthetics, which is another way of saying 'artificial parts of the body'. Paré designed a whole series of limbs which he successfully fitted to wounded soldiers, including an ingenious artificial hand which was equipped with a pen-holder.

He was also noted for his, at the time revolutionary, method of treating gunshot wounds with a soothing dressing rather than by the established practice of pouring boiling oil on to them. And he remained one of the most endearingly modest of the great inventors – when someone congratulated him on a successful case, he replied: 'I treated him. God cured him.'

But there was another treatment for human disabilities that was to have far wider ramifications: the improvement of poor eyesight with spectacles, and most crucially, the lenses in them.

No one is sure who invented spectacles, though the first mention of the use of optical lenses was made by Roger Bacon in 1268. The first picture we have of eyeglasses as such is dated 1352. They had convex lenses, and it isn't until 1517, in Raphael's portrait of Pope Leo X, that we first see a definitely concave lens.

At first, optical lenses had been made of quartz and beryl, but as with all natural stones, there was always the risk of fractures, and it was hard to obtain real clarity. But by one of those lucky coincidences that keep occurring in the story of inventions, the right industry happened to be in the right place at the right time.

In the early sixteenth century there was an increasing demand for spectacles in the West, particularly by the men of Italy's Renaissance. And it was in Italy, in Murano, that the Venetian glass-makers had established the world's centre in that industry. Now, they began to make the lenses of glass – and it was *that* which made possible the dramatic series of instruments that were about to be invented.

But it was obviously *no* coincidence that the first of these, the microscope, should have been invented by a spectacle-maker, Zacharias Janssen, a Dutchman. It was a compound microscope, which is to say that it had two lenses. The objective (the lens nearest the object to be observed) was convex, and the eye-piece lens was concave.

In 1611, the great German astronomer Johannes Kepler, who was the first to prove that the sun, not the earth, was at the centre of the solar system, and that planets move in elliptical paths (thus supporting the earlier theory of the Polish astronomer Copernicus), suggested an improvement. It was simply that both lenses should be convex. This gave a larger field of view, and produced the forerunner of the modern optical microscope.

Yet the man who made the first dramatic impact on the new science of microscopy was the Dutchman Anton van Leeuwenhoek. He lived in the pottery town of Delft, and his great skill lay in the careful and painstaking grinding of very

Leeuwenhoek's microscope – 'a glorified magnifying-glass'.

THE STORY OF INVENTIONS

powerful, clear and optically accurate lenses. The actual instrument he built, in the mid-seventeenth century, had only a single lens, and was in effect no more than a glorified magnifying glass – but one that could magnify up to three hundred times.

That was, however, much better than the compound microscopes could yet achieve, and with it he opened up the whole new inner universe of micro-organisms. By the time he died, just short of his ninety-first birthday, he had given accurate descriptions of the life-cycles of, among other things, the ant and the flea; he had described blood corpuscles and spermatozoa; and most important of all, he had made the momentous discovery of bacteria, revolutionizing scientific thought in areas like health and agriculture.

Meanwhile, Kepler had not been the only astronomer to interest himself in the microscope. The instrument had been improved and used by the great Italian astronomer–mathematician Galileo Galilei. But *his* great contribution, of course, was the instrument that enabled the human eye to examine not the inner, but the outer universe – the telescope.

In Middelburg, in Holland, where Janssen worked, there was another spectacle-maker named Hans Lippershey. The story goes that one day in 1608 Lippershey chanced to look at a near-by church tower through a pair of spectacle lenses he was holding. He was astounded to discover that if he held the two lenses in line, the weathercock on top of the tower seemed to be both nearer and larger. The telescope was born.

In the following year Galileo visited Venice, where he heard about the new instrument. Returning to Padua, where he was professor of mathematics, he immediately built his own telescope. It was a lead tube, with a concave lens at one end and a convex lens at the other. It only magnified three times, but he quickly improved it until finally he obtained a magnification of thirty-two times. Using this instrument, he made a series of remarkable discoveries, from the satellites of Jupiter, to sunspots and the valleys of the moon.

The disadvantage of Galileo's telescope was that it had a concave eye-piece lens. In 1611, Kepler showed why a convex lens would be better, and a telescope incorporating one was finally built by a Jesuit named Christoph Scheiner.

The problem still remained of making any measurements, as opposed to mere observations. The solution was provided in 1638 by an Englishman, a Yorkshire squire-turned-astronomer named William Gascoigne, with the invention of the micrometer. In his original version, it was a pair of parallel pointers, which could be moved together or apart by means of a very finely threaded screw, with a dial to indicate down to one hundredth of a turn. (Thus, if the distance between two threads of the screw were, say, one tenth of an inch, and if the screw were moved one hundredth of a turn, you knew that the pointers had been moved one thousandth of an inch together, or apart.) By placing the micrometer at the point of focus of the telescope, once it had been focused on the object to be measured, and by then moving the pointers until they just touched either side of it, Gascoigne was able to make fairly accurate measurements of the diameters of the sun, the moon, and the planets.

Later, the idea was adapted for the microscope, and indeed for measuring any very small 'real', as opposed to optical, distance. Sadly, Gascoigne didn't live to see it. He joined the forces of Charles I in the English Civil War, and was one of the four thousand royalists killed in the defeat at Marston Moor in 1644.

That was just two years after the death of Galileo, who for the last four years of his life had been blind, due doubtless to years of looking at the sun with the naked eye. But Galileo had been associated with three other important inventions, all of which we use today.

One was a very basic idea, the pendulum, as a mechanism for regulating clocks. The story goes that when, at the age of seventeen, Galileo was at university in Pisa, he happened to be in Pisa Cathedral at the time of an earthquake. One of the great lamps, suspended on a long chain from the ceiling, started to swing back and forth. Galileo used his own pulse-beat to time the swings, and found that even as they grew larger, each oscillation took the same time. The fundamental principle he had discovered was that, within certain limits, the time taken for a pendulum to oscillate depends neither on the weight of the bob at the bottom, nor on the width of the arc through which it swings, but on the length of the pendulum.

Isaac Newton's reflecting telescope.

RIGHT *Galileo's escapement.* OVERLEAF *The great man is visited by another, John Milton.*

EUSTACHIO PORCELLOTTI
COSTRUITO A FIRENZE
L'ANNO 1883
M.R.CH.LAB.
337

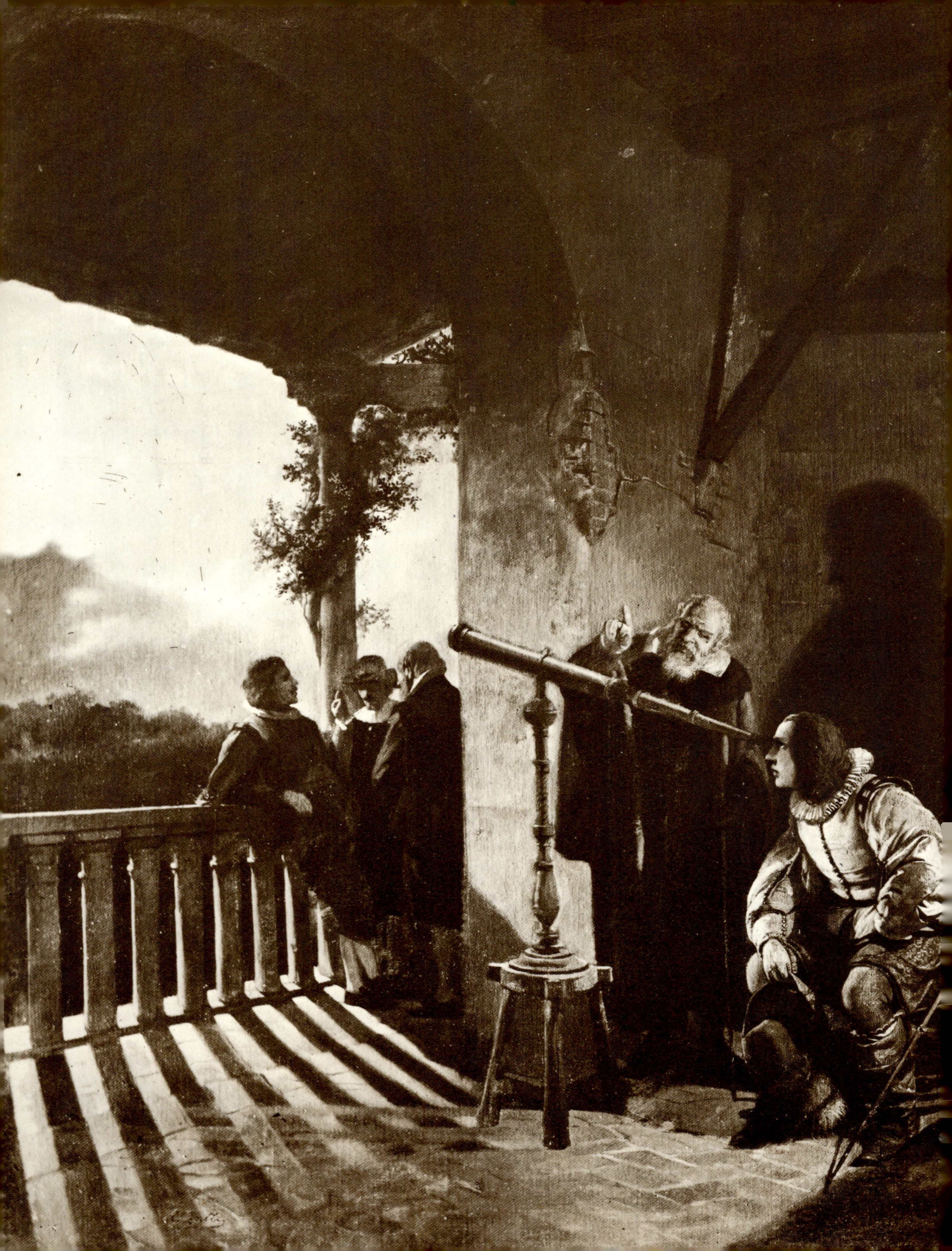

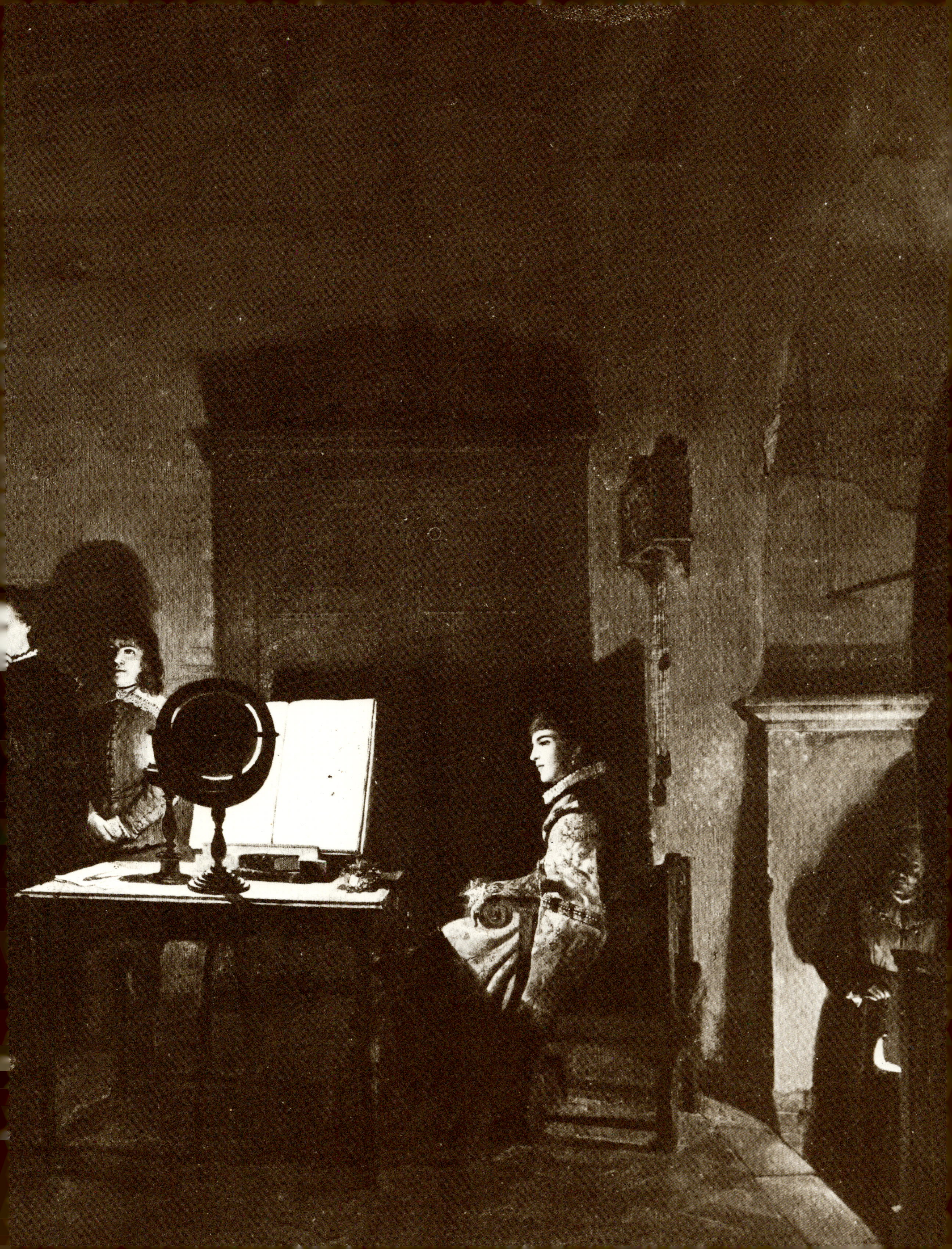

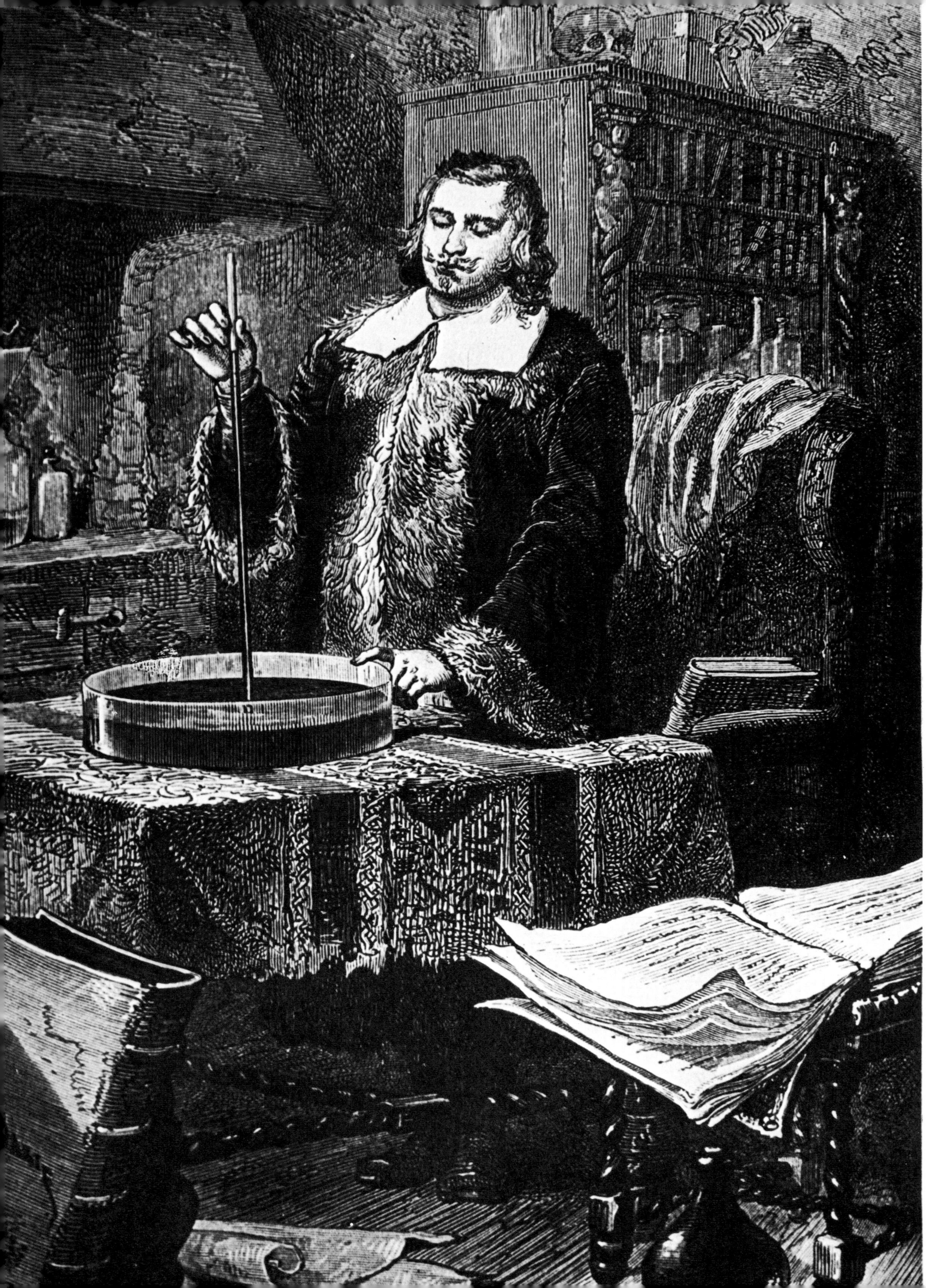

AN AGE OF GENIUS

Some have said that the story is apocryphal, but it doesn't really matter, any more than it matters whether Newton watched apples falling off trees or not. What is significant is the reminder that so many great inventors have succeeded by merely observing more closely what had been staring people in the face. There was no intrinsic reason why the secret of the pendulum should not have been realized thousands of years before.

At any rate, Galileo did little with the idea until the last years of his life, when, by now blind, he evolved the principles by which the pendulum could be used to regulate clockwork. It was left to the Dutch astronomer–physicist Christiaan Huygens actually to design and make such a clock, in 1656.

During the last three months of his life Galileo was joined in Florence by a brilliant thirty-three-year-old physicist from Faenza named Evangelista Torricelli. It was a fruitful meeting of minds. Up till that time, it had been thought, rather romantically, that the reason why pumps could raise water was that 'Nature abhorred a vacuum'. On the other hand, it had been known for a very long time that a vacuum would only raise water to a height of about thirty feet. Galileo pointed out, somewhat wryly, that it followed that if Nature did abhor a vacuum, its abhorrence only extended to thirty feet.

In 1643, the year after Galileo's death, Torricelli decided to see what would happen if instead of water he used mercury, which is 13.6 times denser than water. He part-filled a vessel with mercury, and then took a glass tube, with one end closed, and filled that too with mercury. Holding his finger over the open end to seal it, he tipped the tube upside down, put the open end under the surface of the mercury in the vessel, and took his finger away. The column of mercury in the tube dropped several inches, and then stopped. Torricelli correctly supposed that it had stopped at the point where the downward pressure of the mercury in the tube was being exactly equalled by the air pressure on the surface of the rest of the mercury in the vessel. The barometer was born.

In 1647, just after his thirty-ninth birthday, Torricelli died, but already in that year his ideas were being taken up and put to the test by the French scientist Blaise Pascal. From the glassworks in his native Rouen he got some huge glass tubes, about forty-six feet long. He believed that if Torricelli had been right, then a comparison between similar amounts of water and mercury in the tubes would prove it: since mercury is 13.6 times heavier than water, the column of water in one tube should, when it was equalized by the air pressure, remain at a height of 13.6 times that of the mercury in the other tube. It did.

Torricelli had also predicted that, since air pressure gets less the higher one goes, the mercury-level in his tube would drop if it were taken to the top of a mountain. In 1648, Pascal organized just that, when he sent his brother-in-law up the five-thousand-foot Puy de Dôme near Clermont-Ferrand. As a check, he kept a similar barometer at the bottom of the mountain. The mercury in that stayed at the same height all day, while his brother-in-law returned with the news that the mercury-level in *his* barometer had dropped lower and lower the higher he climbed.

LEFT *Evangelista Torricelli and* RIGHT *Galileo's thermoscope.*

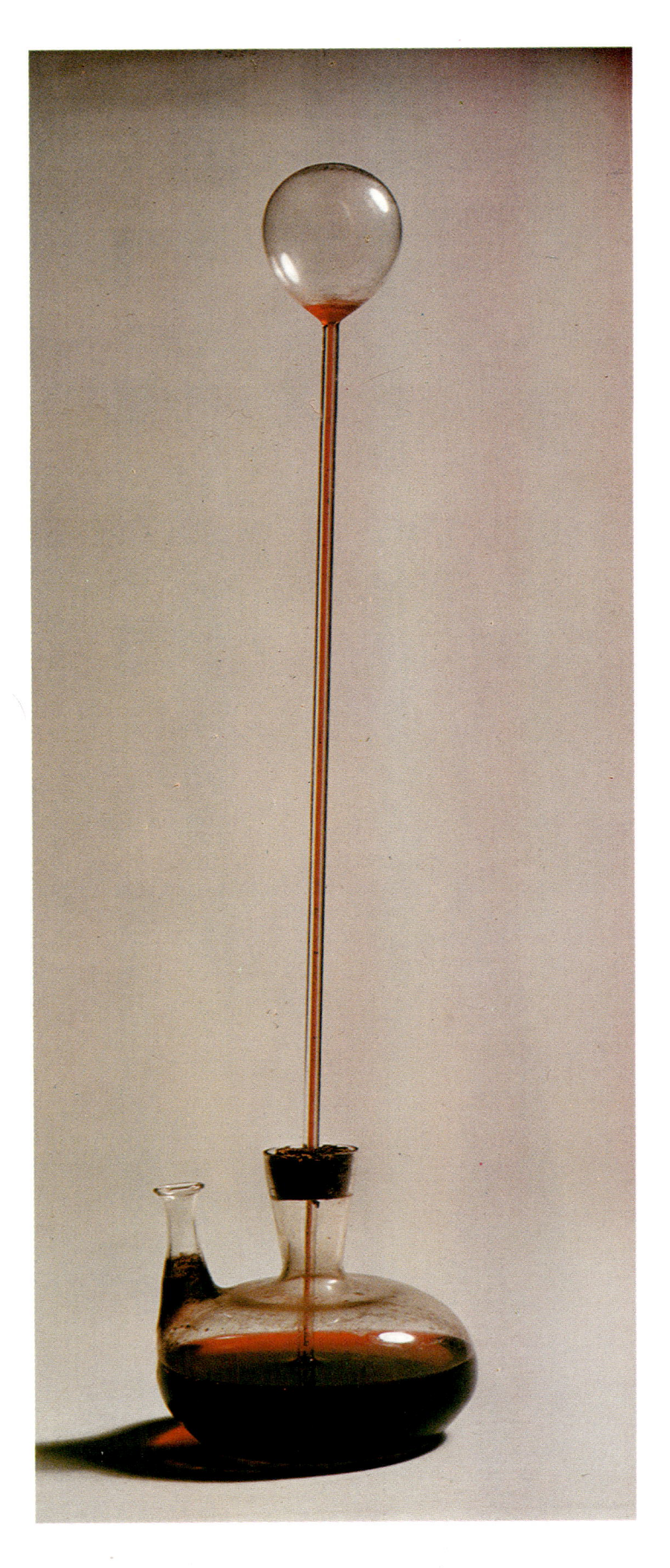

The final invention which we associate with Galileo is the thermometer. In its first form, it was an adaptation of an idea credited to the Greek inventor Philo of Byzantium, in the second century BC.

The Greeks, of course, had known all about the expansion of air when heated, and the 'thermoscope' that was built by Galileo's friend Santorio depended on the fact that if the end of a glass tube were placed in a man's mouth, the air would expand and drive some coloured water down the tube. Galileo's contribution was the idea of putting a graduated scale on the tube to indicate the temperature that had been reached.

It wasn't a particularly accurate or satisfactory instrument, and the true credit for the thermometer proper must go to a German instrument-maker named Gabriel Fahrenheit, who in 1714, while working in Holland, invented the thermometer based on a column of mercury sealed in a glass tube, as we know it today. He also devised the temperature scale by which we know his name, in which the freezing-point of water is 32 degrees, and the boiling-point 212 degrees.

A post-mill. The winch was used to pull the tail-pole round.

But if the forces of nature were being used for scientific inquiry, they were also being harnessed for more immediately practical ends. If there is any one axis around which progress in technology revolves, and upon which it utterly depends, it is the search for 'prime movers' or sources of power. This has been true from the day that man first controlled fire to the day that he first controlled the atom, and it will always be true, even though we cannot *conceive* the power-sources that will be used two thousand years from now.

This period saw the huge growth in importance of the windmill. The water-wheel continued to be a major power-source, but it was most useful in hilly or mountainous regions where descending water could be found. On the flat plains of northern Europe, however, the winds sweeping in from the Atlantic could be used to drive the windmill.

The first European mills were 'post-mills'. The whole mill was fixed to a massive post, which in turn rotated within a socket in a great horizontal beam. To make the sails face into the wind, the whole mill was turned by pulling on a long lever called a 'tailpole', which was fixed to the body of the mill.

The next improvement, in the mid-fifteenth century, was the tower mill. Instead of the grinding stones, the gears, and all the other parts moving around when the mill was turned, everything except the sails was housed in a fixed tower. Only the top of the tower, or 'cap', to which the sails were attached, moved around on top of the fixed tower. To turn the 'cap' around, winches were later installed which could be operated from within the tower.

Finally, in 1745, an Englishman named Edmund Lee made the wind itself do the job of turning the mill to face the wind. He attached a 'fantail' at right angles to the main sails. When the wind hit the fantail it turned the vanes on it, which were geared to wheels which ran on a track round the mill. As long as the wind was hitting the fantail, the mill turned. When it stopped, the sails were facing the wind.

The windmill was by no means confined to grinding corn. In Holland, for instance, it was put to work for land-drainage, in the constant battle against the sea. Elsewhere, windmills were used for draining water for the ever-increasing, ever-deeper shafts of the new mining industry.

This continual problem, and the demand for its solution, were to lead to a further series of important inventions. Torricelli's barometer had inspired great interest in the idea of producing a vacuum, in no one more than Otto von Guericke, the mayor of Magdeburg in Germany. In 1650 he built an air-pump which had a cylinder, a close-fitting piston, and two valves, one for intake, one for discharge. He used it to produce a vacuum in a vessel, and proved that it was indeed a vacuum by the fact that a candle burning inside the vessel was extinguished.

In 1654 he proved the power of a vacuum in a famous experiment with two twelve-foot hemispheres. He fitted them together to form a complete sphere, which he then evacuated with his air-pump. Then two teams, of eight horses each, were attached to the outside of each hemisphere and they attempted to pull them apart. They couldn't.

But if the power of the vacuum were to be used on a large

AN AGE OF GENIUS

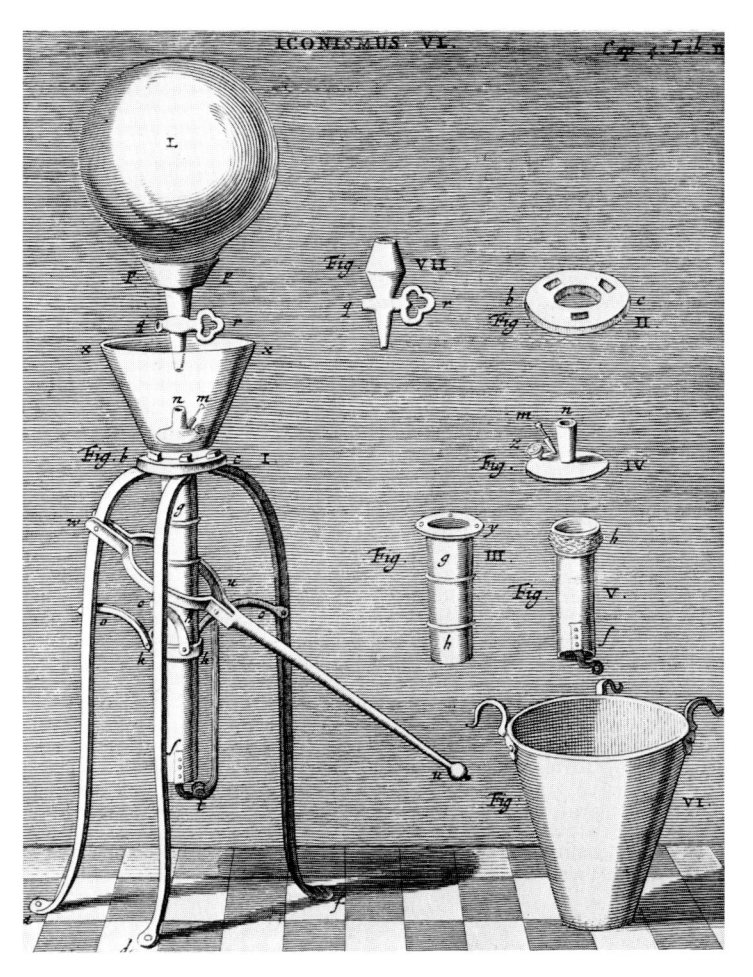

Von Guericke's air-pump. A candle proved the vacuum.

scale, the air-pump was clearly going to be too laborious a process. But how else? In 1698 the answer was provided by an Englishman, Captain Thomas Savery. The means? A new power-source which was to give its name to the succeeding age – steam.

Savery's engine, the first practical steam-engine, worked like this. A vessel was filled with water. Steam from a boiler was introduced into the top of the vessel, forcing the water out through a one-way valve. Then the outside of the vessel was cooled, condensing the steam inside, and thus forming a vacuum. The vacuum then sucked in a fresh supply of water through another valve, and the whole process started again. The 'fresh supply of water' was from the bottom of the mine shaft, which was why Savery's machine came to be called 'the miner's friend'. And Savery is said to have been the man who gave the world the word 'horsepower' to describe the performance of a machine.

Savery's engine worked all right, but it had a number of disadvantages, such as the lack of safety-valves – extremely dangerous when such high pressures were needed to drag water up from deep mines.

These problems were answered by a French physicist, Denis Papin, who had come to work in London. In 1679 he

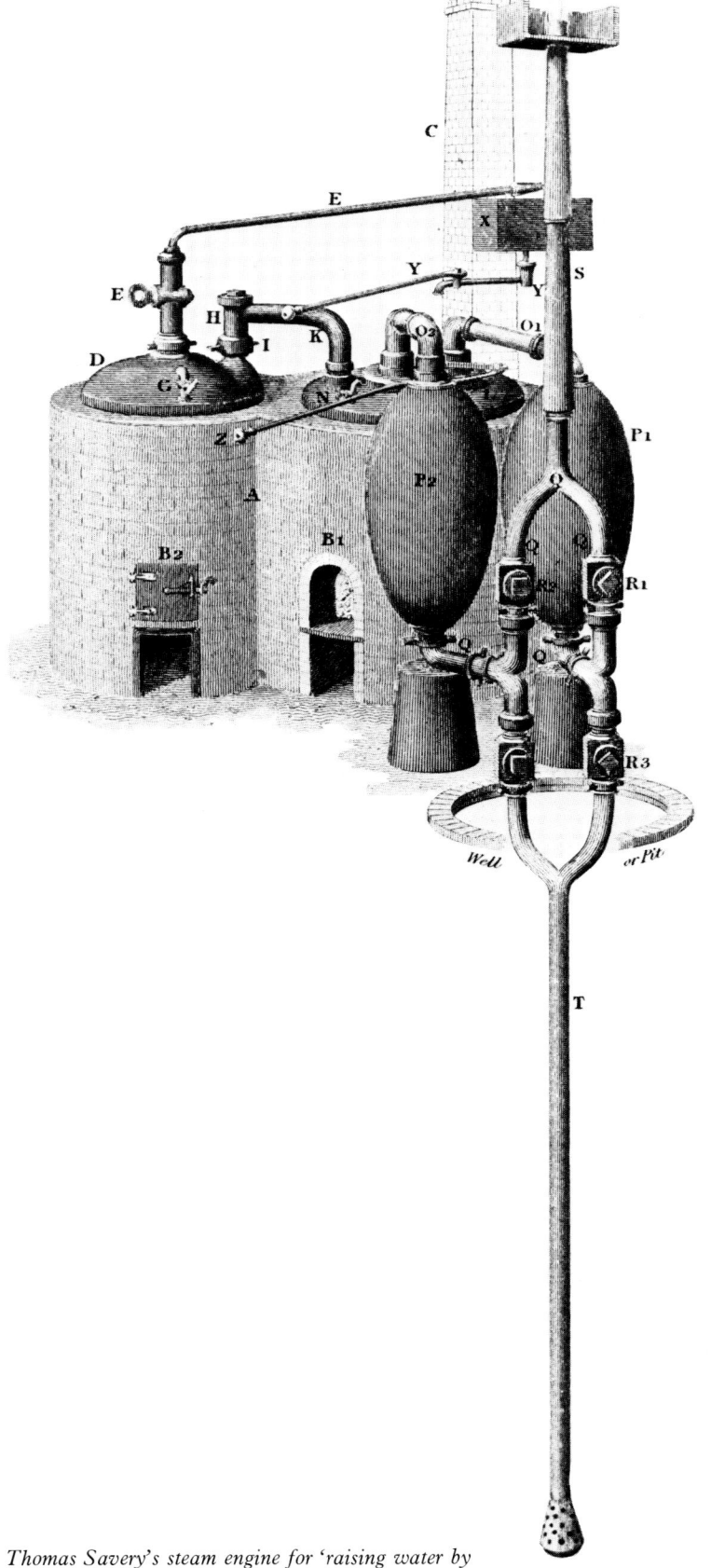

Thomas Savery's steam engine for 'raising water by fire'. To the man at the coal-face it was truly the Miner's Friend.

75

demonstrated to the Royal Society his new invention, the 'steam digester', which we have come to know as the pressure cooker. The important point Papin wanted to make was that the boiling-point of water depends on atmospheric pressure: the greater the pressure, the higher the boiling-point. To do this, he had to solve two problems. One was how to construct a vessel with a lid tight enough to withstand large pressures. The other, just in case the proposed solution to the first didn't work, was how to design a safety-valve, which would allow air to escape once a certain pressure had been reached.

And Papin had another idea. This was that if steam were used to drive a piston up a cylinder, then once the piston had reached its limit the steam could be condensed (as in Savery's engine), and the vacuum so caused would pull the piston down again. The trouble was that Papin wanted the boiler for the steam also to act as the cylinder.

It was left to a Devonshire ironmonger, Thomas Newcomen, to put all these ideas together, when in 1712 he installed the first steam-driven piston engine, for pumping water from a mine in Staffordshire. He made the boiler separate from the cylinder. Steam drove the piston up, cold water injected into the cylinder made the steam condense, and atmospheric pressure drove the piston down again – which gave it its name of 'atmospheric engine'.

Obviously, all these developments would have been impossible if there had not been a corresponding advance in tool-making. This was the period which saw enormous improvements in tools like the brace, for drilling, the spanner for use with nuts and bolts, the continuous-motion lathe, the vice, and the screwdriver, which was originally an 'unscrewer' for removing hammered nails which had been given a twist to make them more secure. (Curiously, it wasn't until the mid-nineteenth century that screws, as such, finally arrived as a regular means of fastening things. Curiously, because the notion of the screw *shape* had of course been known, and much used, since Archimedes.)

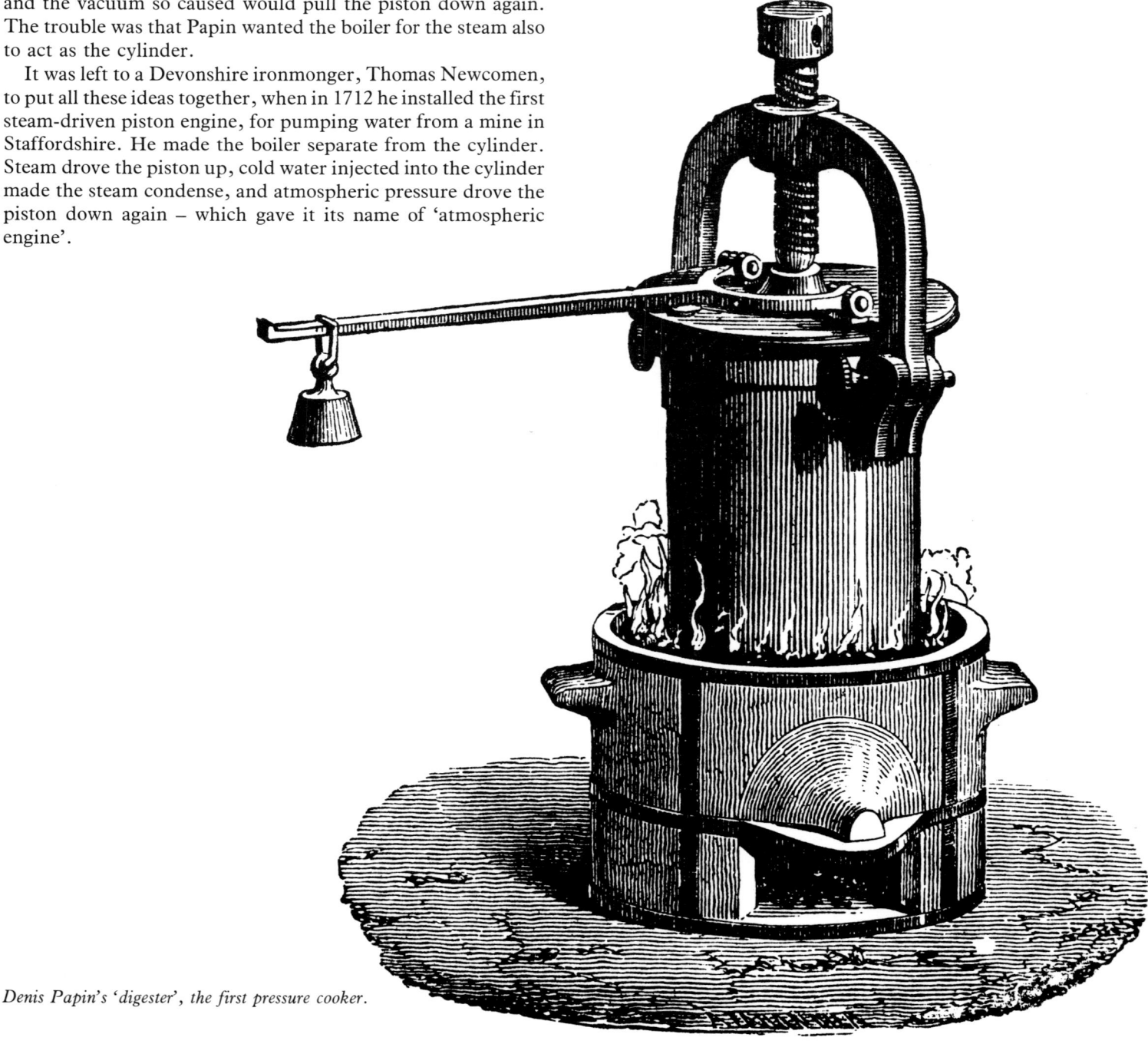

Denis Papin's 'digester', the first pressure cooker.

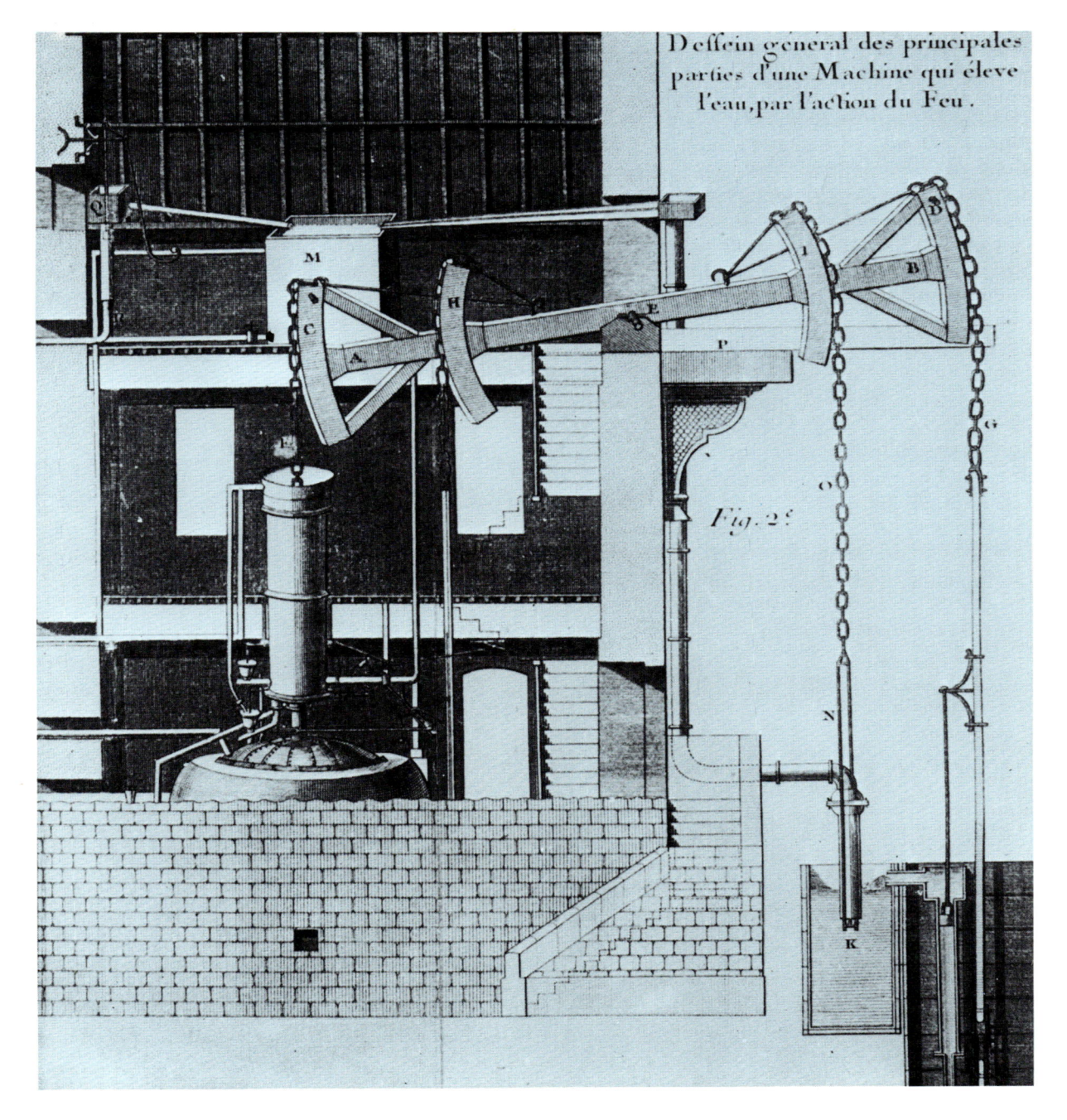

Newcomen's 'atmospheric' steam engine.

In metallurgy, great progress was being made in the search for efficient ways of making steel, together with methods of welding metals together.

And at sea, the navigators who had ushered in the age were provided with two important new instruments. One was the sextant, invented by John Hadley in 1731. Basically, the sextant is an instrument for measuring angles – a descendant of the astrolabe. But the use to which it was put was, and is, the measurement of the angle between the horizon and any given star, or the sun. Then, if you know what day of the year it is, and what time of day it is, you can calculate your latitude; that is, how far north or south of the Equator you are. The sextant incorporates a series of mirrors which allows the user to see both the horizon and the image of the sun (or star) at the same time. He moves the image, by turning one of the mirrors, until it appears just to touch the horizon – and can then read off the angle on a scale.

If you don't know the exact time of day, you can either aim at the sun at its highest point (noon), or you can, if it is night, choose one of the fixed stars. But what if you want to know what your longitude is? Only by knowing how many degrees east or west you are of some fixed point, and by crossing that line with

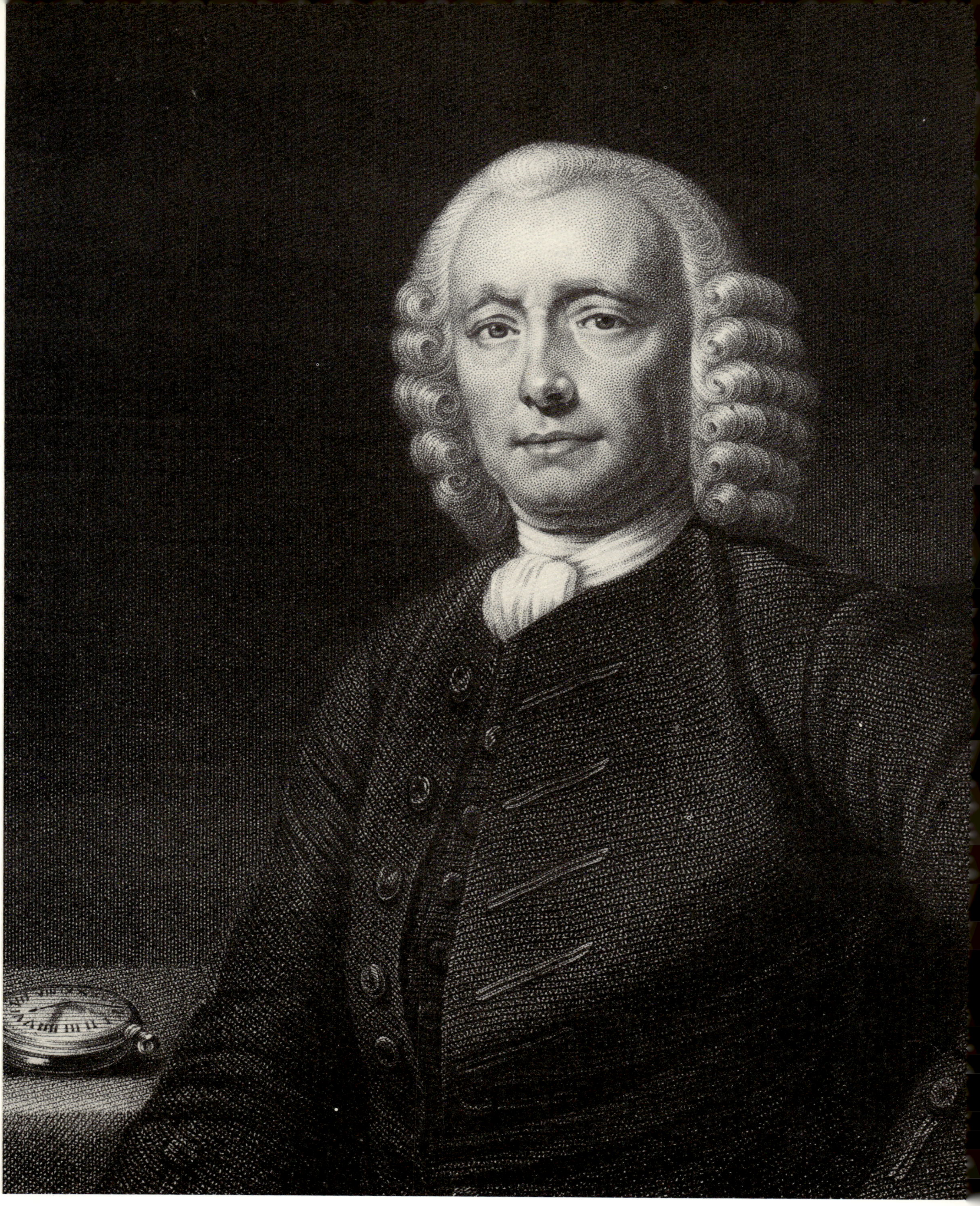

your line of latitude, can you find out exactly where you are on the surface of the globe. Merely knowing how far you have travelled will not tell you, because currents and winds can take you off a straight course. The only way of establishing your longitude is by knowing the exact time difference between where you are and the fixed point mentioned above – and *that*, since you know that the earth rotates once every twenty-four hours, enables you to calculate the number of degrees east or west that you are. And what that demands, obviously, is a very exact timekeeper, which will tell you what the time is at the fixed point – say, Greenwich.

During the late Middle Ages and the Renaissance, clocks had improved enormously. From the earlier sundials, sand-clocks, candle-clocks and water-clocks, they had progressed in the fourteenth century to ones using weights falling under the pull of gravity to drive the mechanism. By the late fifteenth century the idea of driving them with springs had been introduced. The escapements – the mechanisms which controlled the descent of the weight, or the rate of unwinding of the spring, and therefore the speed at which the clock's hand turned – had been vastly improved by Galileo's idea of using pendulums to regulate them.

LEFT *John Harrison. At his elbow is his No. 4 prize-winning chronometer, 'the most famous timekeeper ever made'.*

RIGHT *John Harrison's No. 2 chronometer.*

THE STORY OF INVENTIONS

By the beginning of the eighteenth century, however, there were still no clocks that would stay accurate at sea. The rolling of the ships was one problem. Another was that of changing temperature: since a pendulum's period of oscillation depends (as Galileo had shown) entirely on its length, even a slight expansion or contraction would make a very significant difference over a period of days or weeks.

Among the many countries to offer a prize for the solution, Great Britain in 1714 passed an Act of Parliament offering a scale of prizes. The size of the award depended on the degree of accuracy obtained, and the top prize of £20,000 was for a 'generally practicable and useful' method of finding longitude at sea, that at the end of a six weeks' voyage would produce readings accurate to within thirty miles. It was a lot of money for those

Hadley's sextant of 1785. With that and the chronometer, the ship's captain could now know his whereabouts!

days, but the world's navies were becoming desperate because of the number of disastrous wrecks that arose solely through not knowing the longitude.

For nearly fifty years the prize stayed intact, though there were countless attempts on it by inventors from many countries. The winner was to be the son of a Yorkshire carpenter from Barrow-on-Humber, who had managed to make some money from land-surveying and had taught himself the art of clock-making. His name was John Harrison.

In 1735 he made his first attempt on the prize, with a chronometer that he had taken six years to build. In essence he had substituted for the pendulum a pair of balances whose oscillation was unaffected by the ship's motion. The springs which controlled these balances were prevented from being affected by temperature by an arrangement of brass and steel rods, a 'gridiron', which varied the tension in the springs according to the heat or the cold.

Though Harrison's first chronometer didn't win, the Board of Longitude who controlled the prize thought he was close enough to get some support, and they started to advance him small sums of money. It took him two years to build his second large marine chronometer, and *seventeen* years to build his third, which was the one on which he lavished every possible effort of ingenuity.

It was ready for testing in 1757, but in order to have a double-check he decided to build a fourth chronometer, his No. 4 chronometer, which was more like a very large silver watch, and has been called 'the most famous timekeeper which ever has been or ever will be made'. Ironically, the No. 4, which had taken only three years to make, compared with the seventeen for No. 3, proved in trials that it was just as accurate. And it had the advantage of being much more portable.

On 18 November 1761, Harrison's son William took the No. 4 on board HMS *Deptford* at Portsmouth, and sailed for Jamaica. When the ship reached Jamaica, on 21 January, the incredible No. 4 was found to be just five seconds slow. Put another way, the longitude, as calculated by the chronometer, was accurate to within one mile.

Sadly, the Board acted with great dishonesty towards John Harrison. He had to fight even to get half the prize, and gave the other half up for lost. But in 1772 the Harrisons, father and son, were granted an audience with King George III at Windsor. He was fond of scientific men, and listened patiently to their troubles. He was heard to say beneath his breath: 'These people have been cruelly wronged'; and to John he exclaimed: 'By God, Harrison, I'll see you righted!'

In the end, under the royal and parliamentary pressure, the Board grudgingly gave in – though they still had the nerve to deduct £1250 in return for a similar sum they had much earlier paid Harrison for building his second and third chronometers!

Quite apart from his place in the history of clocks, John Harrison in a sense was the prototype of a new kind of inventor: one who did not rely on the flash of inspiration so much as on knowing precisely what the problem was, and what would be involved in solving it – and one who was prepared to devote more than thirty years to its solution.

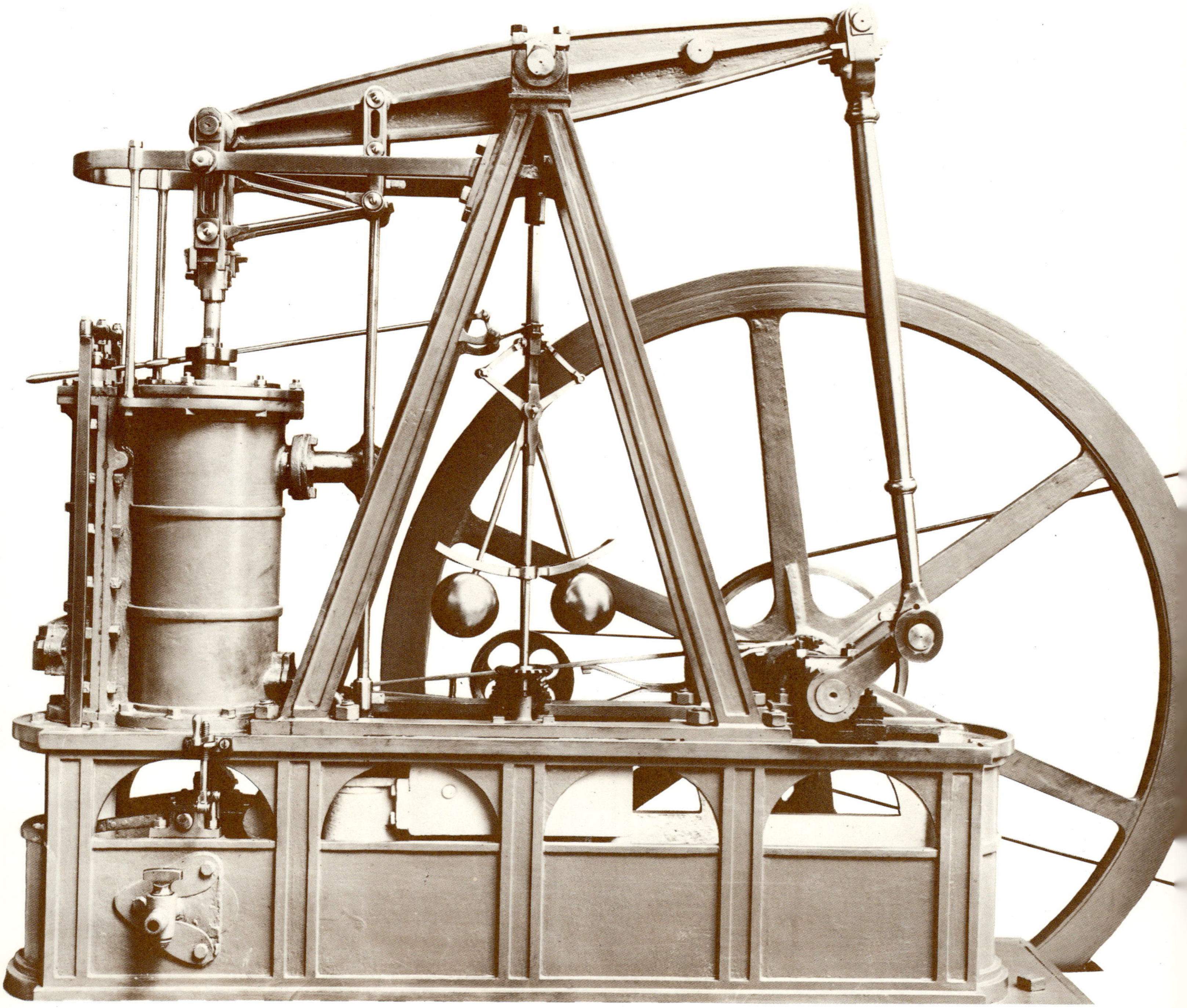

Industrial Evolution

The business of splitting history of any kind into compartments or 'ages' is at best inaccurate and at worst totally misleading. To give some sense to the older civilizations we are sometimes forced to do it, if only for lack of information – all we can say is that such-and-such was happening that was not happening a thousand years earlier.

Anyone alive today has no excuse for not realizing that history is continuous, and is being made 'before our very eyes'. Of course it always was so, and that is why the name 'Industrial Revolution' gives a false picture. The processes described in the previous chapter continued, and in time gave way to new processes. Nothing suddenly happened on 1 January 1750. Perhaps we should call it the 'Industrial Evolution'.

On the other hand, we *can* make some observations that are generally true of the period, and which give a general idea of how and why that evolution occurred.

At the start the centre of technological gravity, which had moved west from Italy, to Germany, France, Holland and Belgium, was now firmly rooted in Britain. Britain commanded the seas, and was creating a huge overseas empire which not only provided cheap sources of raw materials, but also a huge market for manufactured goods. Coal was becoming the prime source of fuel, and Britain was fortunate not only in having vast reserves of it, but also in having those reserves never far from the ports to which ores were brought from abroad for smelting.

Britain lost some of her empire when the American colonies declared independence in 1776, and over the following century the sheer abundance of natural wealth of the American continent attracted more and more migrants and meant an increasing importance for the technologies they had to evolve to cope with the New World.

Because of what one might call the 'technological imperative' – that is, the continual insistence on new ideas from any quarter and at any cost – there was a vast increase in mobility between classes. This is not by *any* means to say that the class system was breaking down. It was simply that the upper echelons of society,

James Watt's 'cabinet' steam-engine. At last the new power-source was being made effective.

the 'aristocracy by birth', were willing, indeed were forced by economic pressure, to accept into their ranks the aristocrats of invention, the men of ideas.

Those ideas, among other things, allowed man far greater control over the way his world was run. No longer did he have to go where the wind blew or the water ran. He could take steam anywhere.

The surge of invention that had just occurred in the field of scientific instruments now led to a whole new industry for producing them. This in turn gave a huge impetus to science, and perhaps one of the key happenings of this period was that science and technology, after a flirtation and courtship that had lasted some three thousand years, finally came to the altar and were wedded and bedded. The thousands of years of trial and error which had led, for instance, to the smelting of the earliest metals, now had to be compressed into a few years, or even months. Time was too short for trial and error. Only the scientist could allow the inventor to progress, and only the inventor could give the scientist new tools for his investigations. On top of all that, the different technologies were becoming inextricably interwoven.

To take just one example, but one whose ingredients sum up the whole period: to make the new textile industries more efficient demanded better steam-engines. That demanded more accurately machined parts, capable of withstanding greater pressures, which could only be answered by a vast increase in steel production. That was dependent upon efficient ways of turning coal into coke. And when *that* was achieved, the 'waste' products suddenly became the basic materials of two vast new industries: gas and chemicals. If we then add that gas provided better artificial lighting for shift work in the textile factories, and that the chemical industry provided the textile-makers with a vast new range of dyes – well, the circle is complete. Except that it didn't work as a circle, but as a continuous process of interaction.

Finally, it is almost certainly true that this period will prove to have been the heyday of invention. First, the inventor was in universal demand; and just as the pianist plays better if his audiences are full, and the farmer will grow more sheep if people

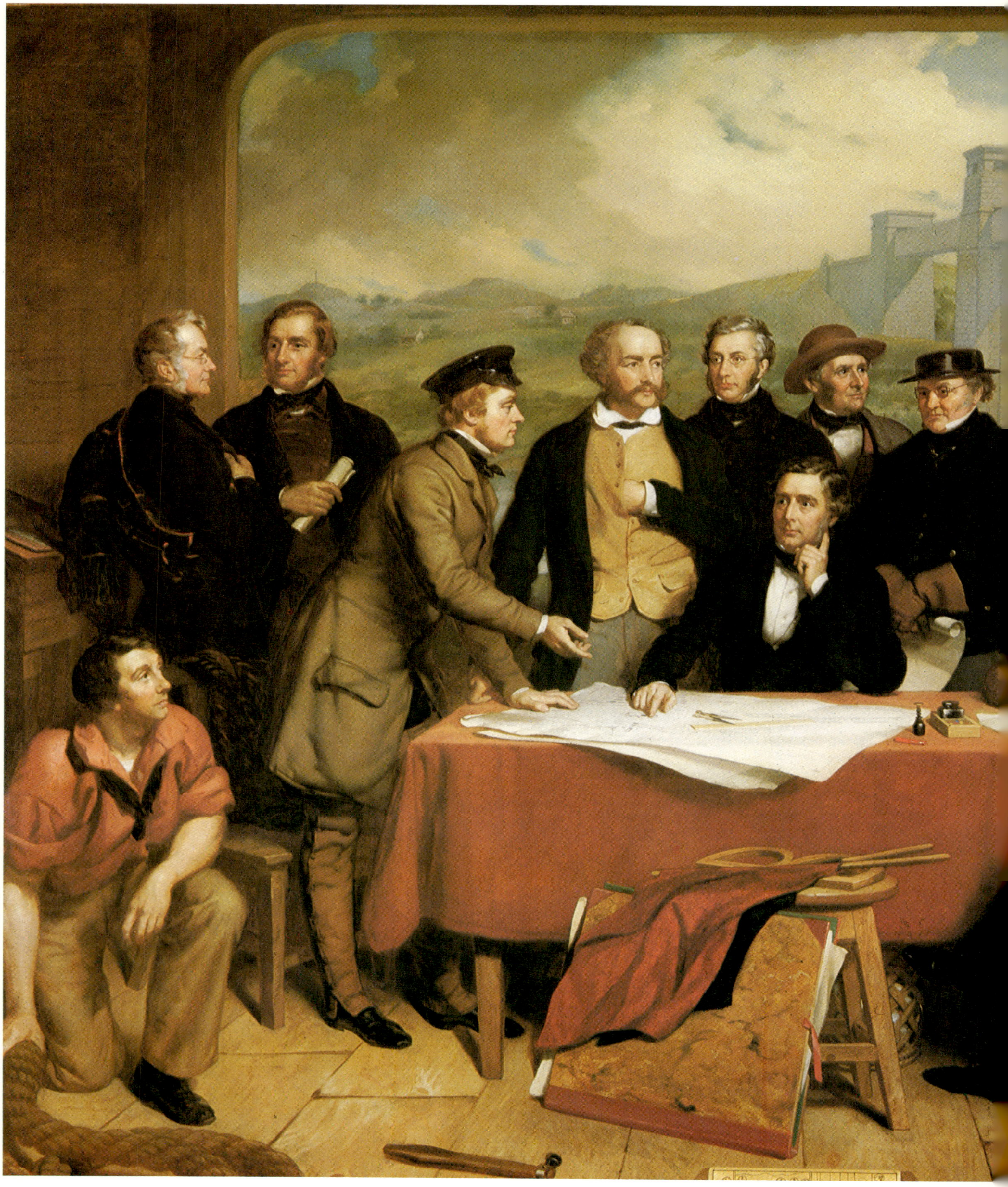

INDUSTRIAL EVOLUTION

want more wool and mutton, so, as in any field of activity, the inventor will tend to respond to what is required of him.

Secondly, the explosion of new materials (especially new metals), new tools, and new sources of power, was probably greater than at any time before or since.

Thirdly, and perhaps most important of all, the process of intercommunication of ideas, which had started with printing, had now reached a point where there was what one might call a 'total world information flow'. It was available to a man to know pretty well everything that was going on in his field, and what is more, he could *just about* take it all in. It was the last time that that was to be possible. Today, the second Flood, the Information Flood, is so great that, even in a very restricted field of science or technology, it is quite *impossible* for any one man to read and digest all that is going on within his speciality.

The basic search was, as it had always been and always will be, the search for the prime movers – the engines that provide the brute power to turn the wheels and gears of industry – and for the fuels with which to feed them. It doesn't always happen in that order, of course. Gas was discovered as a fuel before the machines were developed which could use it. On the other hand, the internal-combustion engine was thought of long before petrol arrived to fuel it.

The first breakthrough came with the Scottish engineer James Watt. The trouble with the steam-engines of Savery and Newcomen had been that they were clumsy, could only be used for pumping, and were extremely wasteful of steam (and therefore fuel). In his early twenties Watt became 'mathematical-instrument-maker' to the University of Glasgow, where, in 1764, he was given a model of Newcomen's engine to repair. As a result of that, and a study he made of the properties of steam, he came to two fundamental conclusions, which he built into his own engine, which he patented in 1769. One was that, since in order to get the best possible vacuum the steam should be condensed at as low a temperature as possible, the condensation should take place not in the cylinder itself, but in a separate condenser. The second was that, to avoid the inefficiency of the incessant heating and cooling which happened with previous engines, the cylinder should always be kept as hot as the steam which entered it – to achieve which he developed a number of ways of insulating the cylinder.

A Conference of Engineers by John Lucas. Robert Stephenson is sitting in the centre, Isambard Kingdom Brunel on the right.

85

THE STORY OF INVENTIONS

INDUSTRIAL EVOLUTION

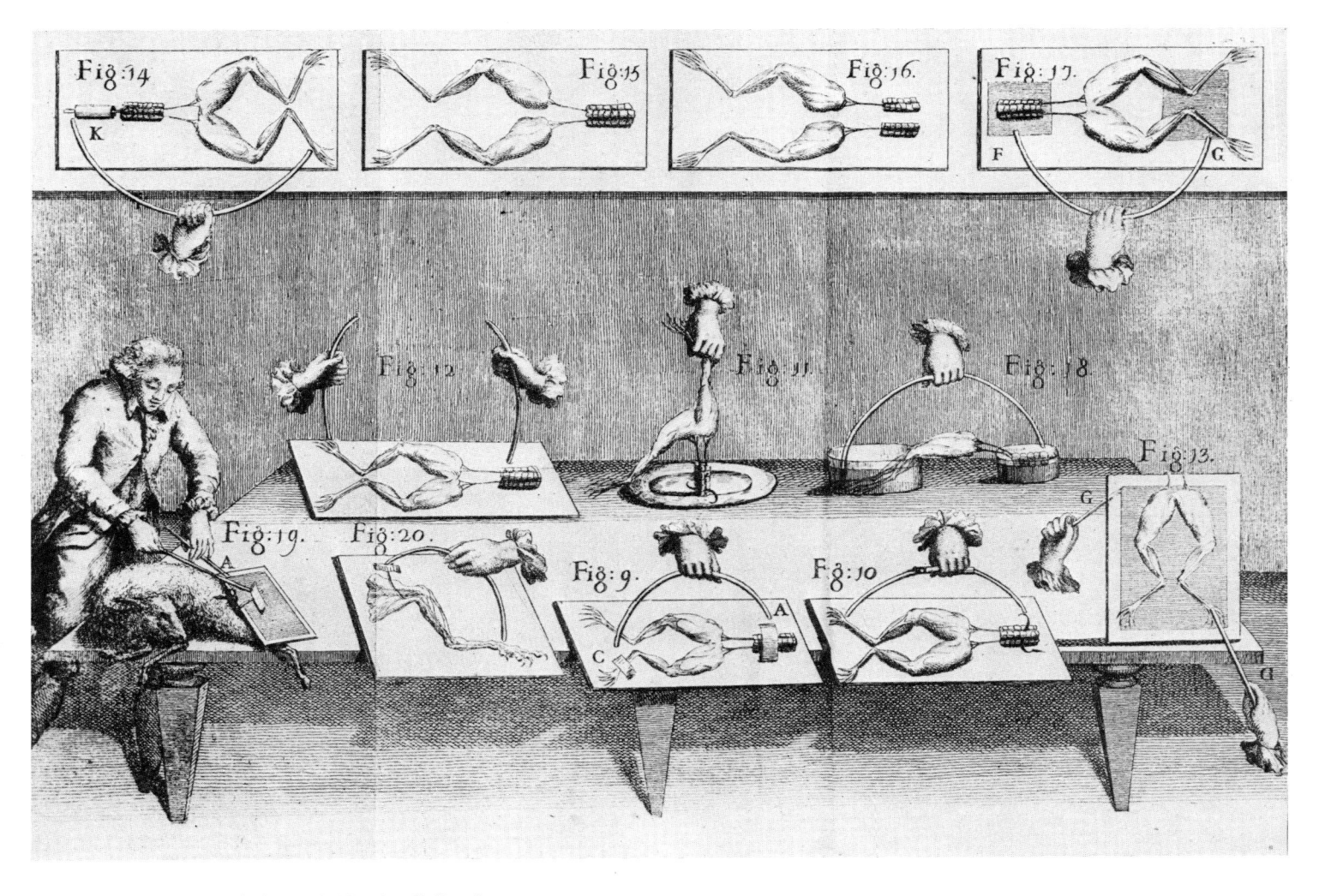

Luigi Galvani, with frog's legs twitching in all directions.

But the engine was still only to be used as a pump. However, over the next twenty years, he developed methods of adapting the engine so that its 'up-and-down' or 'reciprocating' motion was converted into a rotary motion – and from that moment, the steam-engine could be used to drive *any* sort of machinery.

At the very moment that steam was entering its period of unchallenged supremacy as the power-source of prime movers, an infant was being born which would ultimately overtake it: electrical power.

It was the culmination of a long search. Even the Greeks had known and wondered at the magnetic qualities of a piece of amber when it was rubbed. And since the thirteenth century the magnetic compass had been in general use. But it wasn't until the early seventeenth century that a serious attempt was made to understand these phenomena. From then on, the story is littered with famous names, many of whom have given those names to units of electricity. In 1748, the great American statesman–scientist Benjamin Franklin first suggested that electric charges exist in two states, positive and negative. Four

LEFT *James Watt, with designs for one of his engines.*

years later, by the extremely risky experiment of flying a kite in a thunderstorm, he proved that lightning was an electrical phenomenon (by the fact that a key attached to the kite-string became electrified). To him we owe the lightning-conductor.

Then, at some time in the late 1780s, an Italian lecturer in anatomy at Bologna University decided to dissect a frog. His name (the lecturer's, not the frog's) was Luigi Galvani, and he gave us the word 'galvanize'. He cut the frog in half, hung the bottom half from a copper hook, and then proceeded with his dissection, using an iron scalpel.

One of the frog's legs twitched. Fascinated, Galvani conducted a number of similar experiments, which ended with his belief that what he had discovered was 'animal electricity'. In 1791 he published a paper about his 'discovery' and sent a copy of it to his friend, another Italian, a physicist named Alessandro Volta.

Volta at first went along with Galvani's ideas, but became sceptical, and started a series of experiments which ended with his deduction that it was not 'animal electricity' but 'metallic electricity'. In a famous paper read to the Royal Society in London in 1800, Volta announced not only his findings, which

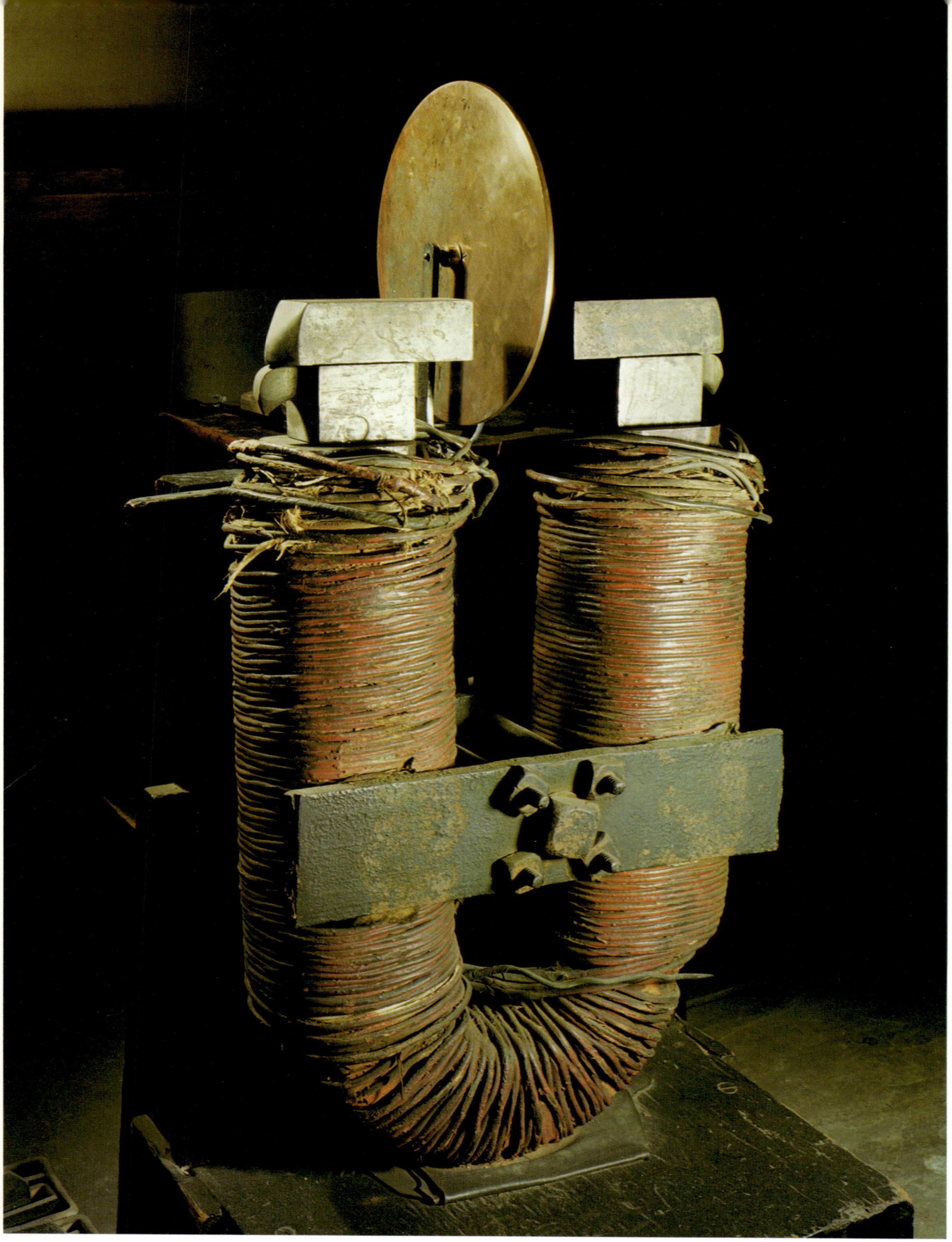

were that the twitch had been induced because the hook and the scalpel had been of different metals, but also his invention of the 'electrochemical pile' – or battery.

It was composed of a stack of discs. First there was a silver disc, which we now know as the cathode, then a disc of paper or cloth soaked in a salt solution, which we would call the electrolyte, then a disc of zinc, which we call the anode, then another silver disc, and so on.

Twenty years later, in Copenhagen, a professor of physics named Hans Christian Oersted made a vital discovery while he was in the middle of a lecture on Volta's 'battery'. On his table was a pivoted magnetic needle, like a compass. He suddenly realized that when he placed a wire carrying electrical current parallel to the needle, the needle swung away at right angles to the wire. The connection had been made between electricity and magnetism.

What followed was one of the most dramatic demonstrations in the history of technology of how quickly one discovery can beget others. Oersted announced his discovery in July 1820. That September, a French physicist named André-Marie Ampère (after whom amps are named) saw a demonstration of the new discovery in Paris, and within a week had shown that not only did an electric current affect a magnet, but it could also *produce* magnetism.

The following year the scene moved to the Royal Institution in London, and a young blacksmith's son who had become the laboratory assistant there. His name was Michael Faraday, and it was he who turned the new discovery to practical use. He placed a vertical magnet in a vessel nearly filled with mercury. Next to it he suspended a stiff wire from a swivelling hook, with the bottom end of the wire in the mercury. As soon as he passed an electrical current from a battery through the wire, it started to spin rapidly. It was in essence the first electric motor, in that it converted electromagnetic energy into mechanical energy. Ten years later he made the equally important demonstration of the dynamo, which would do exactly the reverse – convert mechanical energy into electrical energy. The world had a new source of power.

At exactly the same time, a whole new lease of life was being given to one of the oldest forms of power, the water-wheel. The trouble with the traditional water-wheels (whether 'undershot', i.e. with the bottom of the wheel placed in the stream, or 'overshot', i.e. with water directed from above the wheel into buckets round its circumference) was that there was no movement of the water relative to the buckets. In other words, once full, they continued on their own way without contact with the running water. This meant that they were enormously inefficient, and used only a fraction of the potential water-power available. But way back in the first century AD, Hero's aeolipile, based on the principle of action and reaction, had given the clue as to how this might be improved.

Since the beginning of the seventeenth century men had been experimenting with ways of adapting this principle to the wheel.

LEFT *Faraday's disc dynamo. With it, the electrical industry was born.*

Ampère, the man who 'made' magnetism.

The problem was finally solved in 1827, when a young Frenchman named Benoît Fourneyron built the first effective water turbine.

In essence, it was a tube with a wheel built into it, with its axis in the same direction as the tube. The wheel was unusual in that it was actually composed of a number of curved blades. As the water was passed through the tube, it was directed by a number of guide vanes through the middle of the wheel. Then, as it passed through to the far side of the wheel, the curved blades of the wheel directed it outwards against the walls of the tube, causing the wheel to spin, giving it its name of 'reaction turbine'.

Fourneyron's first model gave six horsepower. By 1833, he had developed a turbine delivering fifty horsepower, and in that year won the 6000-franc prize offered by the French Society for the Encouragement of National Industry, for 'the best application, on a great scale, of hydraulic turbines . . . to mills and manufactories'. (Given the encouragement, inventors will invent!)

Within twenty years a number of important variations on the theme had been developed, and hundreds of machines were built as prime movers for factories. But towards the end of the century, as electricity became more and more developed and practical, the main use of the water turbine came to be the

THE STORY OF INVENTIONS

Parsons' steam-turbines fitted in the packet boat Queen.

generation of electricity – which thus became, in effect, a means for transporting 'water-power' to wherever it was wanted.

The water itself, of course, had to stay where it was, which limited the use of the water turbine as a direct source of power to factories to those places where there was a sufficient flow or drop of water. But now that the new family of turbines had been born, it wasn't long before men began to work to intermarry it with the older family of steam.

The steam-engine, of course, *could* be moved wherever it was wanted. But there was still a loss of efficiency due to the fact that the up-and-down motion of the piston had to be converted by cranks or gearing systems into a rotary motion. The obvious idea was to make the steam turn a turbine, an application which was even closer to Hero's original idea. The problem was that where the piston engine got its power from 'brute force', the steam-turbine would have to get *its* power from turning incredibly fast.

In 1884, this was solved by Charles Parsons, a son of the Earl of Rosse. Unlike that of the water-turbine, the wheel of the steam-turbine was given vanes, like those of a windmill, which would be turned by the pressure of the steam acting directly on to their faces. However, as the wheel was turned, a lot of the steam's energy would escape past it and be lost. So Parsons built a *series* of wheels along the shaft, getting larger as they went, so that as the steam pressure dropped, when it passed each wheel, so there was a larger wheel to make use of lower pressure.

In this way, Parsons' first steam-turbine achieved the then unbelievable speed of eighteen thousand revolutions per minute. Twelve years later he installed a steam-turbine into the first turbine-propelled ship, a launch named the *Turbinia*, which in 1897, at the Spithead Naval Review to celebrate Queen Victoria's Jubilee, caused a sensation with its unheard-of speed of thirty-four and a half knots.

INDUSTRIAL EVOLUTION

These advances in machine-construction had only been possible because running parallel to them had been a series of enormous advances in the metal industry. In the previous chapter we saw how the use of wood to make charcoal for smelting had made people turn to coal to heat their homes. Now the process moved a stage further. Since wood was becoming both scarce and too expensive for the owners of the iron-foundries, they, too, turned to coal.

Iron-smelting works on the principle that the iron-ore is heated together with a fuel (charcoal up to this time) which has been pre-heated so that it doesn't have enough oxygen to burn on its own. In order to burn properly, the fuel combines with the oxygen in the iron-ore (iron-ores are basically iron and oxygen in different combinations). What you are left with then is iron, on its own.

Pure coal, then, is no good for smelting, because it contains oxygen, as well as a number of impurities like sulphur and phosphorus. But if it is pre-heated in the same sort of smothered conditions that turn wood to charcoal, the result will be coke, which, like charcoal, is a form of carbon. The trouble is that with certain types of coal some of the impurities remain in the coke, and iron as a material is very susceptible to these. Even small amounts will ruin it.

It was the three generations of a family named Darby, all of them christened Abraham, who made coke-smelting possible. They had an iron-foundry at Coalbrookdale, on the River Severn in Shropshire, and the three generations spanned the eighteenth century. The essence of their achievement was the realization that the best sort of coke for smelting came from the deeper parts of the mines, where the coal had fewer impurities – and that the coke used had to be in the form of large, hard lumps, which would allow a free circulation of air in the furnace.

Using these discoveries, they succeeded in making purer and purer cast-iron in increasingly large quantities. The climax of their efforts, which finally convinced people of the usefulness of cast-iron for major building works and of its reliability, came in 1779, when Abraham Darby III built the world's first cast-iron bridge, across the Severn at Coalbrookdale, where it still stands. It had a span of a hundred feet, and it came just in time to serve the great generation of British civil engineers who built Britain's system of canals, roads, railways and bridges – men like Isambard Kingdom Brunel, Thomas Telford, John Rennie and John McAdam.

The next great improvement came with the development of the hot-air blast for the furnaces. It had always been thought that the air had to be as cold as possible. But in 1828, a Scotsman named J. B. Neilson realized that the reverse was true – the hotter the blast of air, the less fuel would be needed to get the furnaces up to their huge running temperatures. And he devised a method of pre-heating the air before it was used for the blast.

Cast-iron, though a marvellous material, has one great disadvantage. It is very brittle – it will hardly bend at all without cracking, and this clearly limited the number of uses to which it could be put. Since very early days men had been aware of the comparative advantages of wrought-iron and steel, but the making of steel in particular had always been a lengthy business. The answer came in 1855.

Henry Bessemer was the son of a Hertfordshire type-founder,

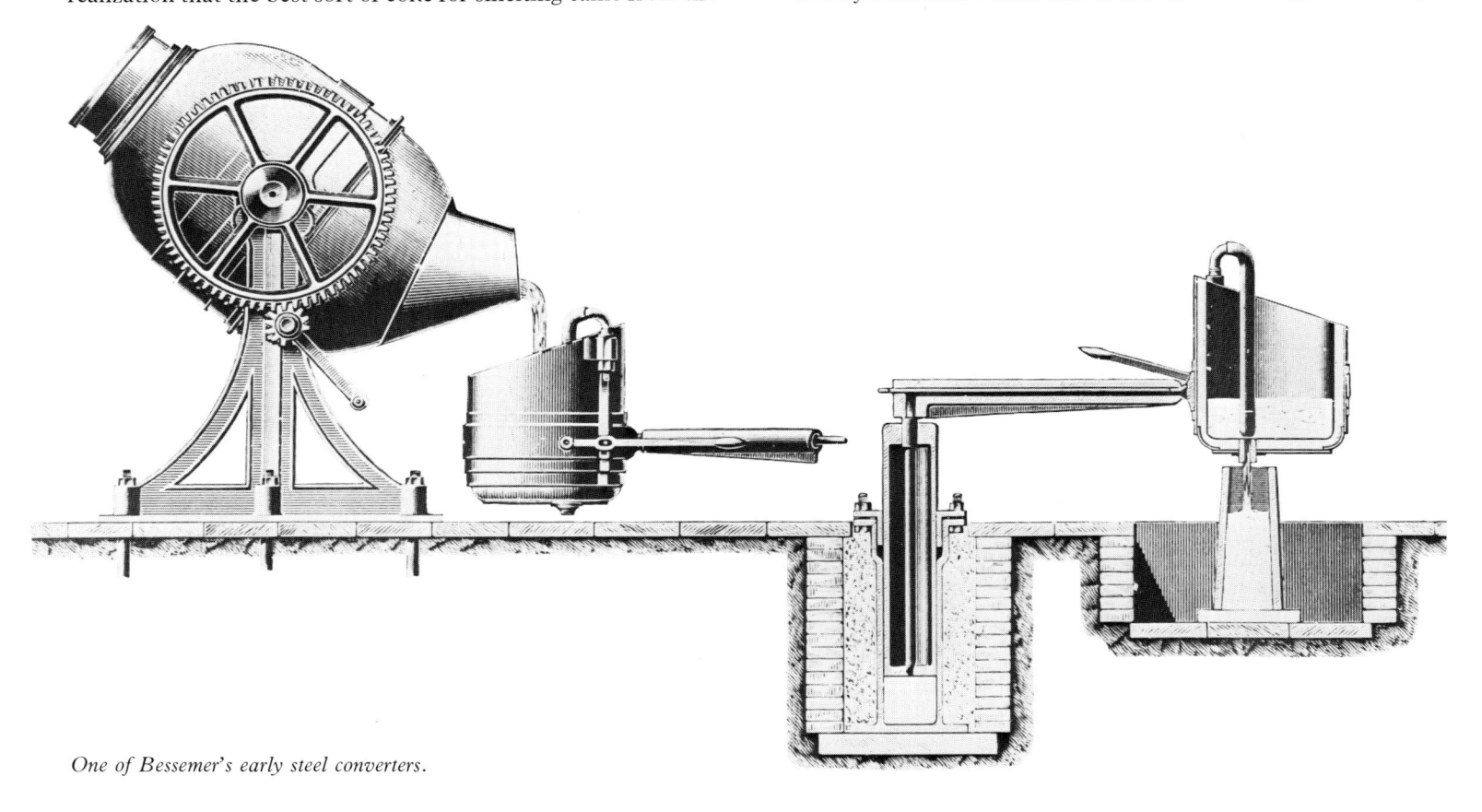

One of Bessemer's early steel converters.

THE STORY OF INVENTIONS

Mining will always be dangerous, but the Davy lamp helped.

and grew up to be an inventor by profession. During the Crimean War he had come to realize the drawbacks of cast-iron for making artillery, and so he set out to find a way of making good-quality steel in large quantities. His solution was the 'Converter'. The basic idea of it was that crude pig-iron (cast-iron that had been poured into rough moulds) was heated until it was molten. Then a blast of air was blown through the molten metal which would burn off the impurities in it, including any carbon. That left a 'pure' iron, to which the correct proportion of carbon could then be added, mixed up, and poured out as liquid steel. Within a few years the process had spread worldwide, and the Age of Iron gave way to the Age of Steel – and Henry got a knighthood.

At this point, we should remember the men who were providing the basic fuel for this technology, the miners. Although the various new engines meant better drainage and better ventilation, mining remained what it probably always will remain, a dirty, hard and dangerous occupation. And the greatest danger of all was that of explosion, which could happen at any time if a significant amount of methane, known as 'firedamp', a gas held in natural 'reservoirs' in coal seams, was ignited by the open flames of the miners' lamps. In 1815, the year when men were dying of rather different causes at Waterloo, the Society for Preventing Accidents in Coal Mines approached the brilliant young professor of chemistry at the Royal Institution in London, Humphry Davy.

Within a year he had the answer, the miner's safety lamp. It was based on his discovery that if a flame is applied to a metal gauze, the strands of the gauze conduct the heat away so quickly that the flame will not go through it. Accordingly, he surrounded the flame of the lamp with a cylinder of metal gauze, and enclosed the whole thing in a lantern.

To his great credit, at a time when everyone seemed to be patenting everything they could think of, he refused to patent

RIGHT *Davy lamps, showing the gauze which contained the flame.*

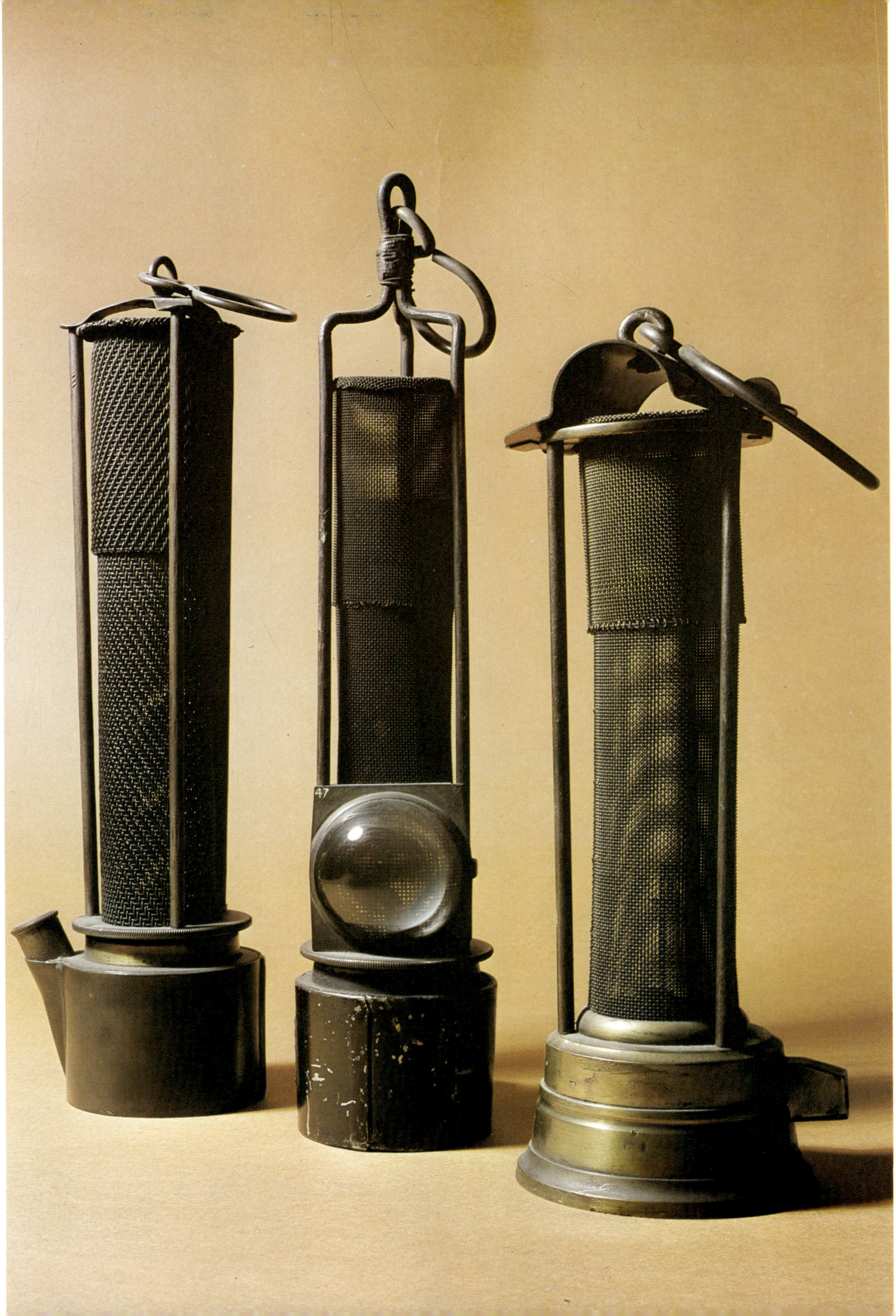
47

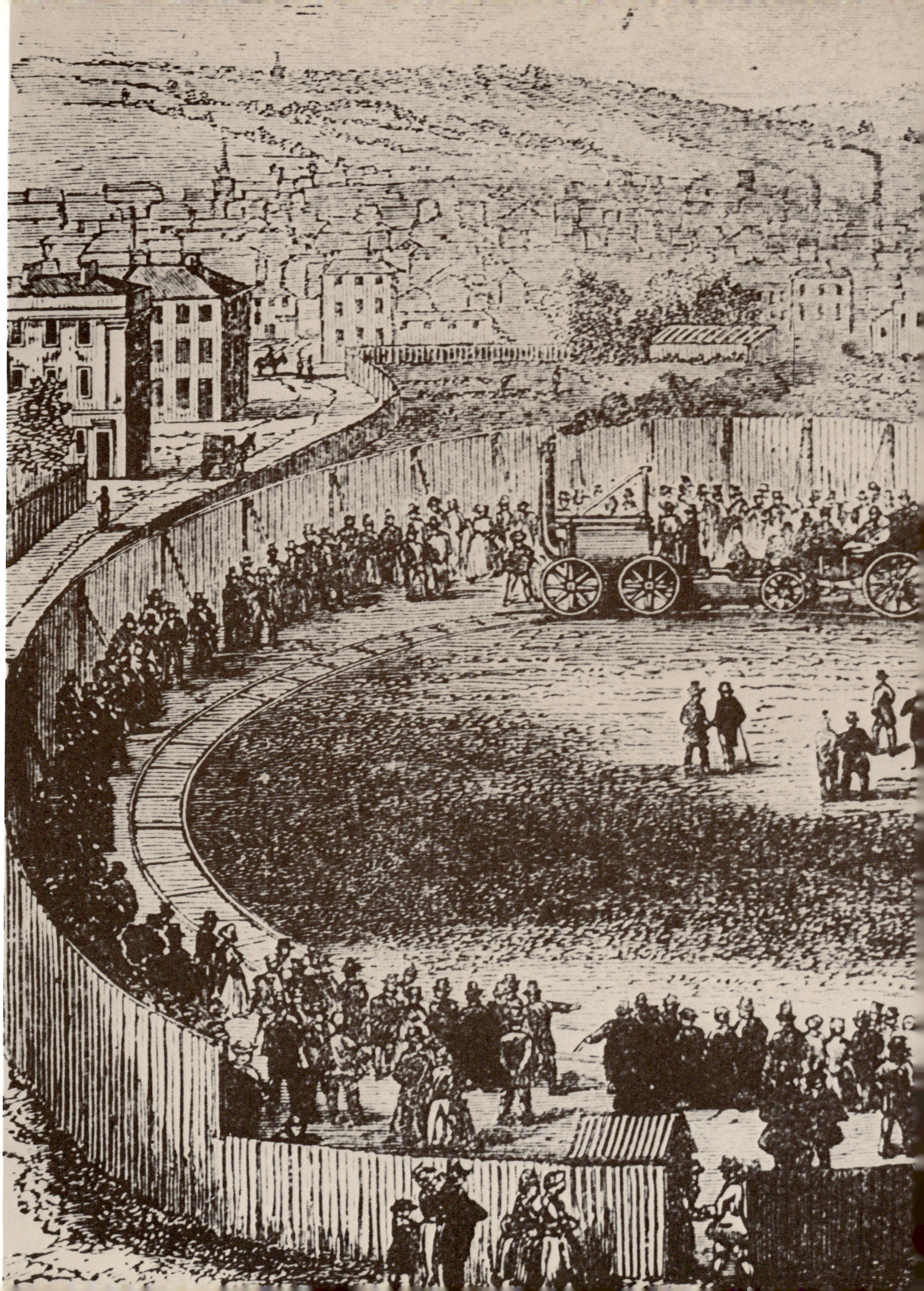

INDUSTRIAL EVOLUTION

his invention, which must have saved more lives than it is possible to estimate. But the 'Davy lamp', as the miners called it, and his brilliant chemical discoveries, did earn him a knighthood.

Meanwhile, the mines themselves were providing the key to an invention that would revolutionize transport – the railway. Since the early sixteenth century the ores and the coal had been transported from the mine face to the bottom of the shaft on wagons which ran on rails. And in the late eighteenth century, now that the steam-engine could produce rotary motion, it wasn't surprising that men should be thinking of adapting it to transport. On Christmas Eve of 1801, a young Cornishman named Richard Trevithick drove his new steam-carriage, carrying passengers, at speeds of up to nine miles an hour, along a road at Camborne. Unfortunately, he then tried to drive it up a hill, where it ran out of steam.

Part of Trevithick's achievement was to develop an engine that could use a much higher steam pressure than previously, but he was still only thinking of road transport. Then in 1804, at Merthyr Tydfil, in Wales, he built his first locomotive, which he had decided to run on iron rails, since it was clear that the roads were in no condition to support the heavy machine. The locomotive was called *Catch-me-who-can*, and with it he hauled five wagons, ten tons of iron, and seventy wary passengers at the devastating speed of five miles an hour. He had proved the vital point that there was sufficient friction between wheels and rails to make it possible to run a steam railway.

But that wasn't what the rest of the world thought. They liked the notion of railways for public transport, but the idea persisted that the carriages should be pulled by horses. Many railway companies were formed, and one of these was the Stockton and Darlington Railway in north-east England. In 1822, a young Northumbrian named George Stephenson was called in as consulting engineer on the building of the line.

Stephenson persuaded the owners to use a steam-engine instead of horses, and on 27 September 1825 the world's first public passenger service opened, the train being pulled by Stephenson's locomotive with the suitable name of *Active*. Four years later, in 1829, George and his son Robert built what was probably the most famous steam-engine of all, *Rocket*, which they entered for the trials, organized by the directors of the new Liverpool and Manchester Railway, 'to discover and test the most improved locomotive engine'. *Rocket* won, of course. In front of thousands of spectators, at Rainhill near Liverpool, it pulled a twenty-ton load over the sixty-mile course at an average of some fifteen miles an hour, reaching a top speed of nearly thirty.

Needless to say, the idea of using steam had also occurred to the boat-builders. In 1707 Denis Papin, the inventor of the pressure cooker, had built a steamboat driven by a paddle-wheel. He intended to sail it from Cassel, in Germany, to London, but sadly the local boatmen thought such an invention would put them out of business, and they destroyed it before it could set off.

Trevithick's Catch-me-who-can *being demonstrated in London in 1808.*

ABOVE *The most famous steam-engine of all, George Stephenson's* Rocket.

RIGHT *'The New Steam Carriage' by G. Morton, 1827.*

Astonishingly, there was then a gap of nearly eighty years, until 1783, when the French Marquis de Jouffroy d'Abbans took his paddle-steamer *Pyroscaphe* for its first run on the River Saône at Lyons. She was 138 feet long, and weighed 182 tons, and was built of wood.

But this was, after all, the age of iron, and in 1821 Aaron Manby laid down the keel of the first iron-hulled ship at Tipton in Staffordshire. The following year she made her maiden voyage to Paris, carrying a cargo of linseed and iron, and the rather self-centred name of *Aaron Manby*.

Just as the water-wheel had been superseded by the turbine, so the paddle-wheel, for similar reasons, was to be superseded by the propeller, though curiously, in view of the prevailing knowledge, the paddle-wheel, made famous by the river boats of the Mississippi, lasted much longer than it ought to have done. As early as 1804, the American Colonel John Stevens had demonstrated his five-ton *Little Juliana*, driven by twin propellers, with which he achieved a speed of eight miles an hour.

But the advances on land and at sea were now to be challenged in that third medium of transport of which man had dreamed ever since Daedalus and Icarus escaped from the Minotaur's labyrinth on wings of wax – flight through the air.

In 1783, a month before the first steamboat sailed, a crowd assembled in the town square of Annonay, near Lyons. In the centre of the square sat a huge cloth-and-paper bag, beneath which the brothers Jacques and Joseph Montgolfier lit a fire.

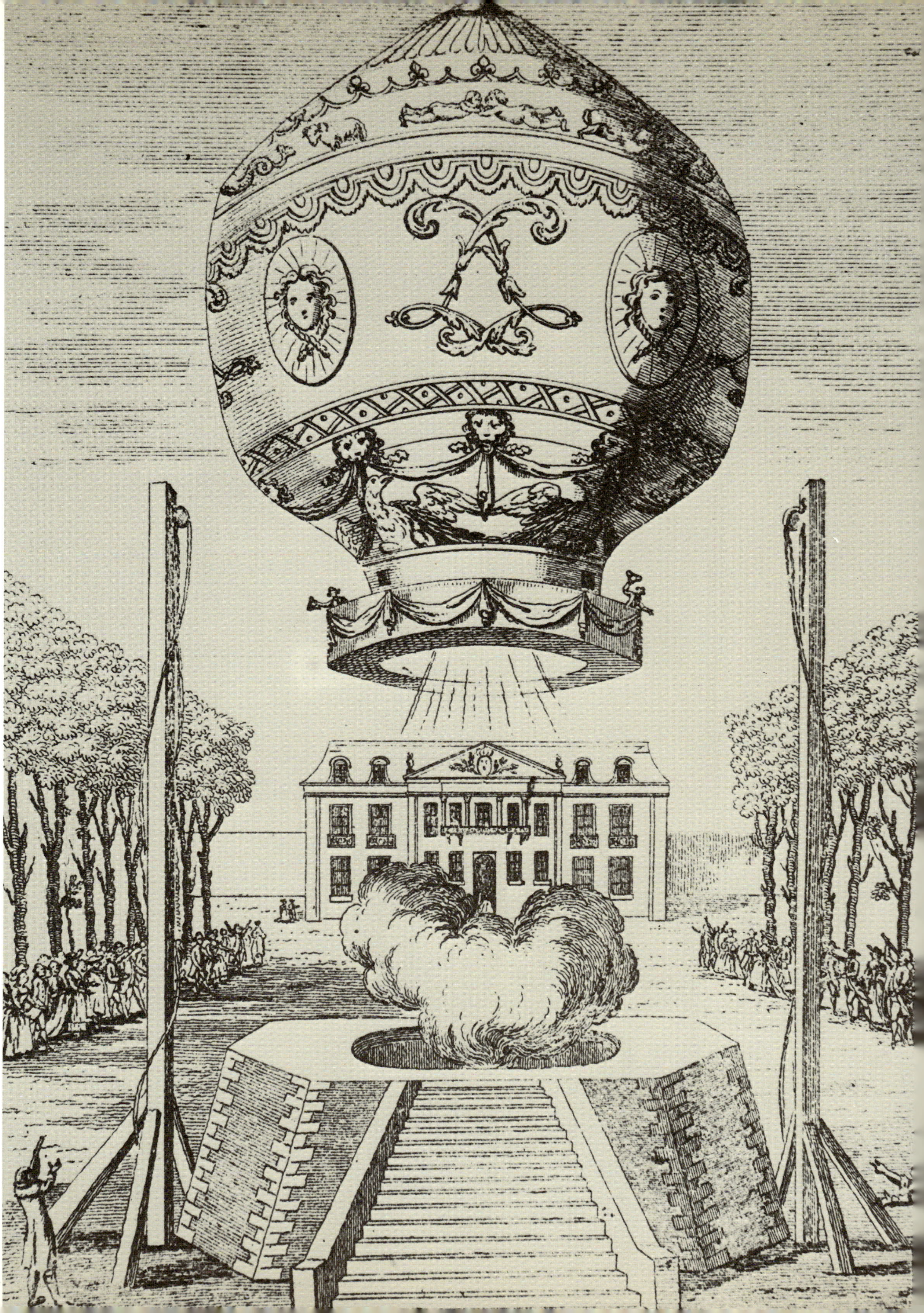

INDUSTRIAL EVOLUTION

The hot air filled the bag, the bag was released, and it ascended to a height of fifteen hundred feet. Astonishment among the crowd.

More was to follow. A few months later, at Versailles, in front of the ill-fated Louis XVI and the 'cake-eating' Marie Antoinette, the brothers sent up an even larger, highly ornate balloon, this time with three passengers in a basket suspended from it – a duck, a sheep and a cock.

It is not known how the 'passengers' felt about it, but it is interesting to note how closely the pattern of experiment was later paralleled by the steps towards space-flight.

Finally, on 21 November of that year, a balloon ascent was made from the Bois de Boulogne in Paris. The balloon was made by the brothers Montgolfier, but the ascent, made standing in a gallery surrounding the neck of the balloon, was by a doctor and a nobleman, Jean Pilâtre de Rozier and the Marquis d'Arlandes. Within twenty-five minutes the intrepid pair had covered five and a half miles across Paris – and at last, man had flown.

Within a fortnight, a French professor of physics named J. A. C. Charles made a successful manned flight of twenty-seven miles. But his balloon was filled with hydrogen rather than hot air, and so set the pattern for most of the later balloons. Just over a year later, Jean Pierre Blanchard and an American doctor named Jeffries (early balloonists seem to have realized the usefulness of keeping a doctor handy!) crossed the English Channel from Dover to a wood inland from Calais, and international flight had begun.

Immediately, the scientists and engineers started to look for ways of making the balloon truly practical by giving it a means of steering, and of course of propulsion, since the wind was not dictated by airline schedules. But it wasn't until 1852 that Henri Giffard, a French engineer, succeeded in flying the first airship, which took off from the Hippodrome in Paris. It was powered by a three-horse-power steam-engine, which turned a propeller, and Henri covered seventeen miles at an estimated six miles an hour.

On the ground, lesser mortals had to content themselves with getting from A to B on a newfangled contraption, the bicycle. The idea of man propelling himself along on wheels went back to the sixteenth century, but unfortunately that is exactly what he had to do – sitting astride the machine and running along with his feet on the ground, unless of course he chose to go downhill, which would have been hazardous since brakeless.

But in 1839, Kirkpatrick Macmillan, from Dumfriesshire in Scotland, devised a bicycle that could be pedalled, thus enabling a man to travel faster under his own 'steam' than he could run. It had two rods suspended from pivots below the handlebars, one rod on either side of the front wheel. At the bottom of the rods were pedals, from which a second pair of rods ran back to either side of the rear wheel. Here they were attached to a pair of arms joined to the rear axle, and fixed at a hundred and eighty degrees from each other, so that as the pedals were alternately pushed forward the back wheel was turned – rather like the principle now used on children's pedal cars.

LEFT *The Montgolfier balloon ascends from the Bois de Boulogne.*

An early gas-filled balloon. Hot air is now back in fashion.

It has been suggested that the bicycle had an unforeseen social effect, especially in the countryside, where marriage (and therefore breeding) had tended to be restricted, for lack of transport, to the immediate locality. Now it was possible for suitors to find out if the grass beyond the hill really was greener!

They would have been uncomfortable courtships, however, since the early bicycles had wooden wheels with 'tyres' made of iron. That problem was solved in 1888, by John Boyd Dunlop, a Scottish vet who lived in Belfast. His son complained to him about the hazards of riding his tricycle over the cobbled streets of Belfast, and Dunlop responded with an invention which was to be of enormous importance to the motor-car – the pneumatic tyre, which had a rubberized casing and which was inflated through a valve. We have had a softer ride ever since, and the

THE STORY OF INVENTIONS

The Cripper tandem tricycle of 1877. Jolly for outings.

company started by Dunlop has grown into one of the world's great corporations.

But it wasn't all fun, and balloons and bicycles. It was, after all, an *industrial* evolution, and no industry stood more clearly for the changes that took place than the textile industry.

There are two basic elements to the making of cloth: spinning the raw material, be it wool, silk or cotton (or today's artificial fibres), into yarn or thread, and then taking that yarn and weaving it into the cloth. Processes like bleaching, fulling and dyeing, though important, are incidental to the two main processes, which had traditionally been run as family-operated, home-based industries. From the mid-eighteenth century to the mid-nineteenth, a whole series of inventions truly 'revolutionized' the making of textiles, turning it into a factory industry, and speeding the process of manufacture beyond belief. It is an indication of the degree of change that at the end of that one-hundred-year period, Britain's imports of raw cotton were almost exactly a hundred times what they had been at the start.

Never has the idea of one invention 'begetting' another been more clearly demonstrated. Competition between the manufacturers, and demand for textiles, meant that a machine had hardly been invented before it was being improved upon, or required the invention of further machines. Of many brilliant ideas, there is only room to mention a few. The first of these was the Flying Shuttle, invented in 1733 by John Kay, son of a Lancashire farmer. The shuttle was the container which held the thread which made the 'weft' (or crosspieces) of the cloth as it was woven between the 'warp' (or longitudinal threads which form the 'skeleton' of the cloth). The only way to pass the shuttle across the divided yarns of the warp, to form a new line of weft, had been by hand, a tedious and lengthy process, which in the case of broad cloths needed two workers to do it.

John Kay not only made it far quicker, but also removed the need for a second worker. He gave the shuttle a track, called a shuttle race, on which it ran from side to side of the loom. After it had crossed over, the shuttle was collected in an open box, the shuttle box, which was tapered, so that the shuttle wouldn't bounce back. Inside each box there was a horizontal spindle, along which ran an attachment known as the 'picker'. As the shuttle entered the box, it knocked the picker back to the end of it. But each of the pickers was attached to a cord, and these two cords were suspended from the middle of the loom. At the point where they joined, there was attached a wooden handle called a 'picking peg'. The weaver jerked the peg away from the side where the shuttle was sitting, forcing the picker to run along its spindle, in doing which it flicked the shuttle along its 'race' and across to the other side of the loom. As soon as the next set of warp threads were raised, the weaver flicked it back again.

The immediate effect of this invention, apart from provoking the wrath of the old-style weavers, was that cloth was being woven at a far greater rate than the spinners could produce the yarn: it had previously been reckoned at four spinners to one weaver. Now, spinning too had to be mechanized.

The spinning-wheel had seen many improvements since it was first introduced in the thirteenth century, but there was still a large amount of hand-operation in the process, and it was slow. That was all changed in 1764 by one of the most famous machines ever invented, the Spinning Jenny. The man who invented it, James Hargreaves, was a spinner and weaver in his early forties who lived near Blackburn in England. He was poor and uneducated, a reminder that inventive genius is not the prerogative of the leisured or the learned.

It was a complicated machine, which imitated the action of the hand-spinners but was able to spin eight threads at a time with only one operator. With the aid of a moving horizontal carriage, or draw-bar, through which the roving, or textile fibre, passed on its way to the spindles, the operator drew out a given length of yarn by moving the bar away from the spindles and from the bobbins which held the roving. The roving was then clamped tight, and the eight spindles were set to spinning by the operator turning a wheel, which at the same time pulled the draw-bar even further back. Since the yarns were attached to the tops of the spindles, this gave a twist to the yarn. At a point at which the yarn was fine enough, the wheel was stopped, and the draw-bar pushed back sufficiently to make the thread between itself and the spindles slack. Then a wire dropped down on to the threads where they joined the spindles, pushing them down to the point where they were now located at the main body of the spindle. Then the wheel was again turned, but now the spindles, instead of twisting the yarn, simply wound it on to themselves. Hargreaves patented his machine in 1770.

A year before that, Richard Arkwright had patented his machine, the 'water-frame'. The importance of this was that it was water-powered, and used a technique by which the thread was drawn out through a series of rollers.

Then, in about 1779, the best features of both Hargreaves'

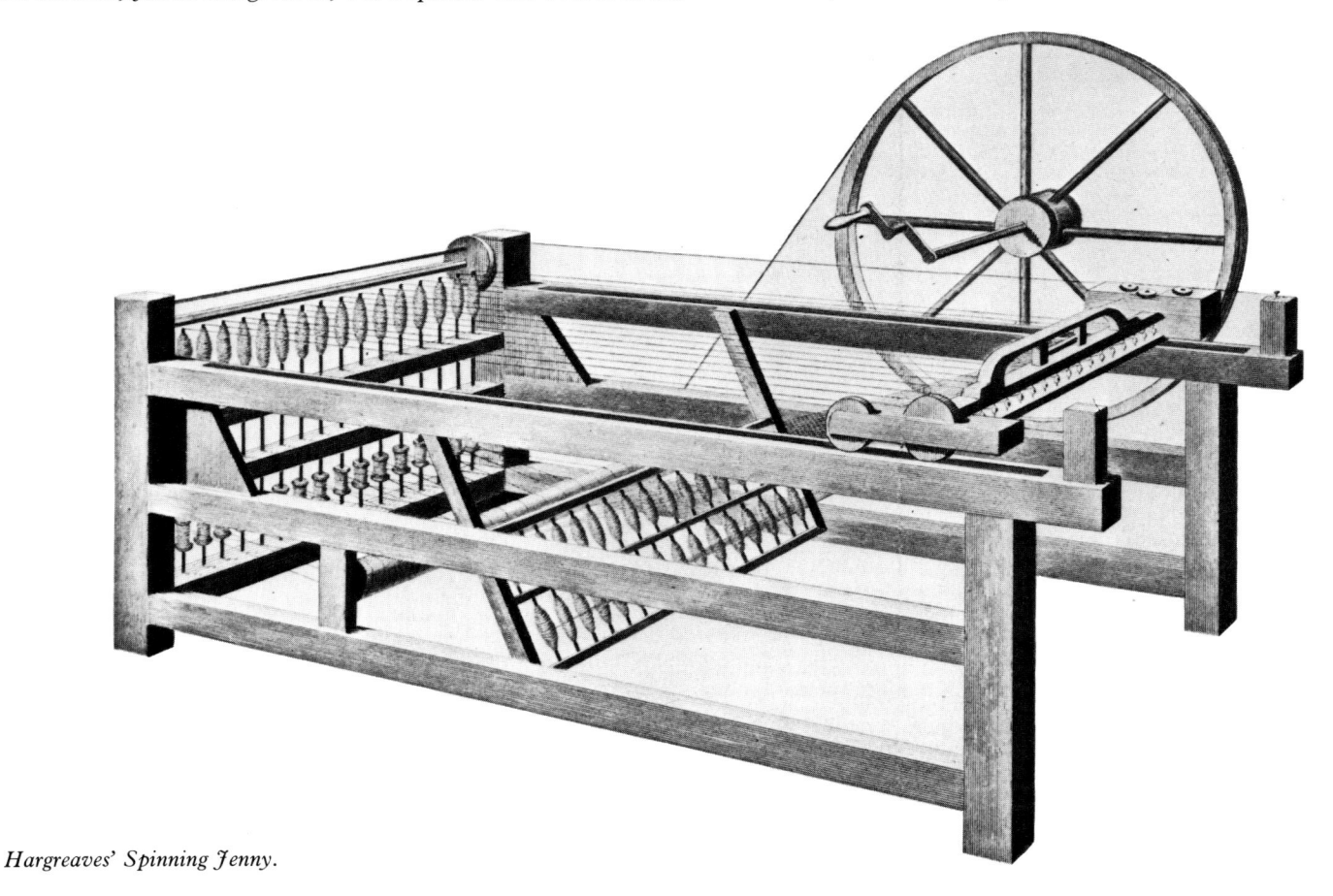

Hargreaves' Spinning Jenny.

THE STORY OF INVENTIONS

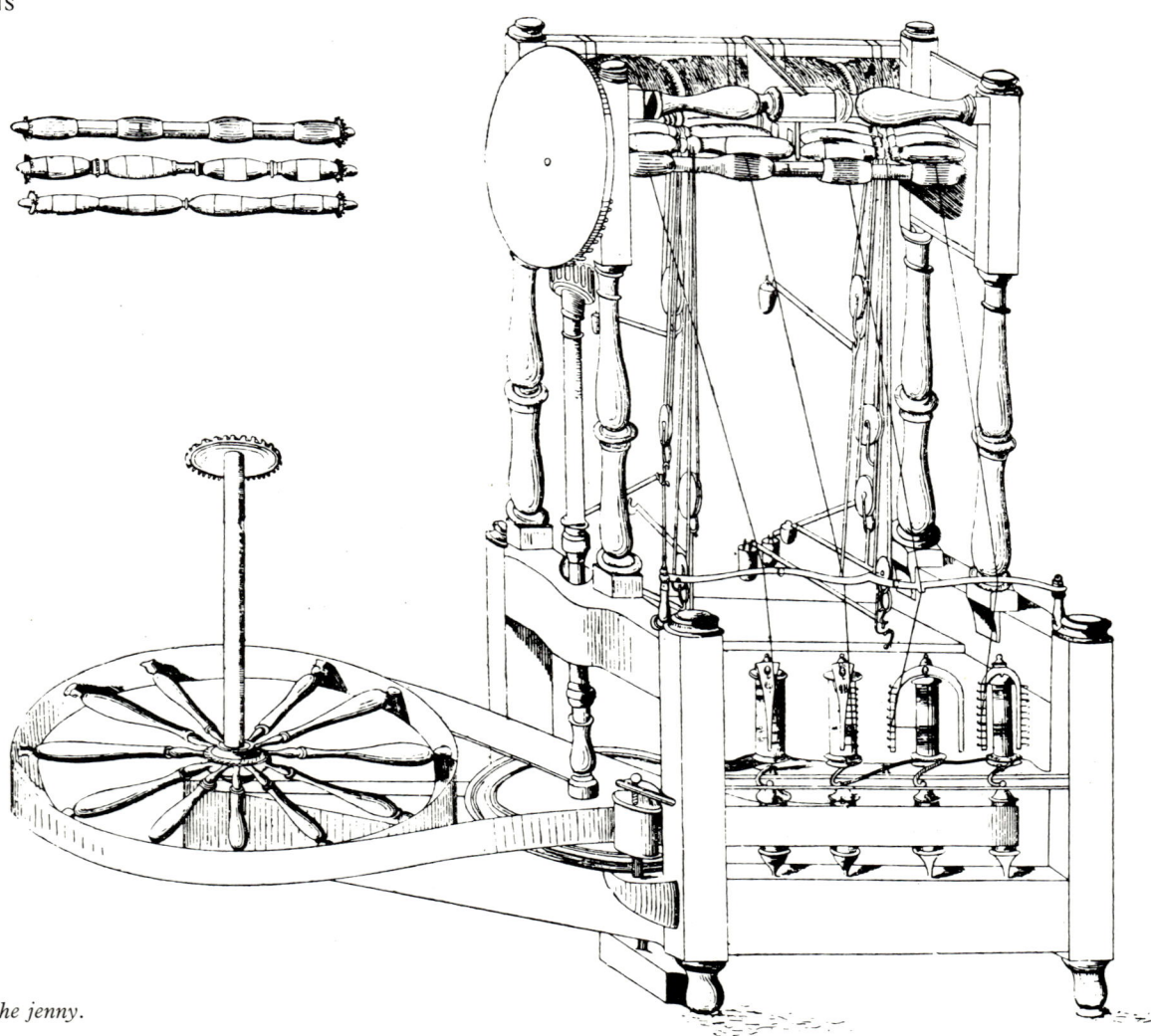

ABOVE *Arkwright's version of the jenny.*

and Arkwright's machines were combined by a twenty-six-year-old Lancastrian named Samuel Crompton. For years he had spun cotton, but was dissatisfied with the jenny and decided to improve on it, helping to finance his efforts by playing the violin at the theatre in Bolton, where he lived.

Crompton's machine incorporated the idea of using rollers to draw out the thread, and combined it with a rolling carriage. Unlike those of the jenny, the spindles were mounted on the carriage, and therefore moved back and forth, while the drawing mechanism of the rollers stayed in a fixed position. The machine produced a finer yarn than had been thought possible, and it was given the name 'Crompton's Mule' because, like that much-maligned creature, it was the child of mixed parentage.

One other invention in the field of weaving must be mentioned, because of its application, a century later, in a multitude of fields other than that of textiles. It arose from the desire of the weavers to produce intricate designs. The more intricate the design, of course, the greater the number of combinations of warp threads that have to be lifted for each throw of the shuttle. In order to make this possible, the draw-loom was evolved, in which the warp threads were controlled by individual cords, which were operated in the required combinations by a 'drawboy'.

At first, this drawboy had to sit on top of the loom – presumably a fairly uncomfortable experience – though later a mechanism was devised to allow him to operate the cords from the side. But it still meant an extra worker (to be paid) for the process, and of course he could make mistakes in the combination of threads he selected.

The question was how to select the threads automatically. The answer came from Joseph Marie Jacquard, who was born in the French silk-making city of Lyons. After an adventurous life fighting on both sides in the French Revolution (which in its own way had consequences as far-reaching as its industrial counterpart) he settled down in Lyons and studied the problem. And in 1805 (the year his country's navy did badly at Trafalgar) he demonstrated his invention.

The cords controlling the warp threads hung from S-shaped hooks rather like butchers' hooks. They were raised by a bar which engaged the top end of the hook. But the top end of the hook was attached to a horizontal needle, which could either allow the hook to engage on the rising bar or prevent it from engaging by pushing it out of the way.

RIGHT *An operator sitting at a Jacquard loom.*

OVERLEAF *Power-loom weaving in the mid-nineteenth century. The dresses may look pretty, but conditions rarely were.*

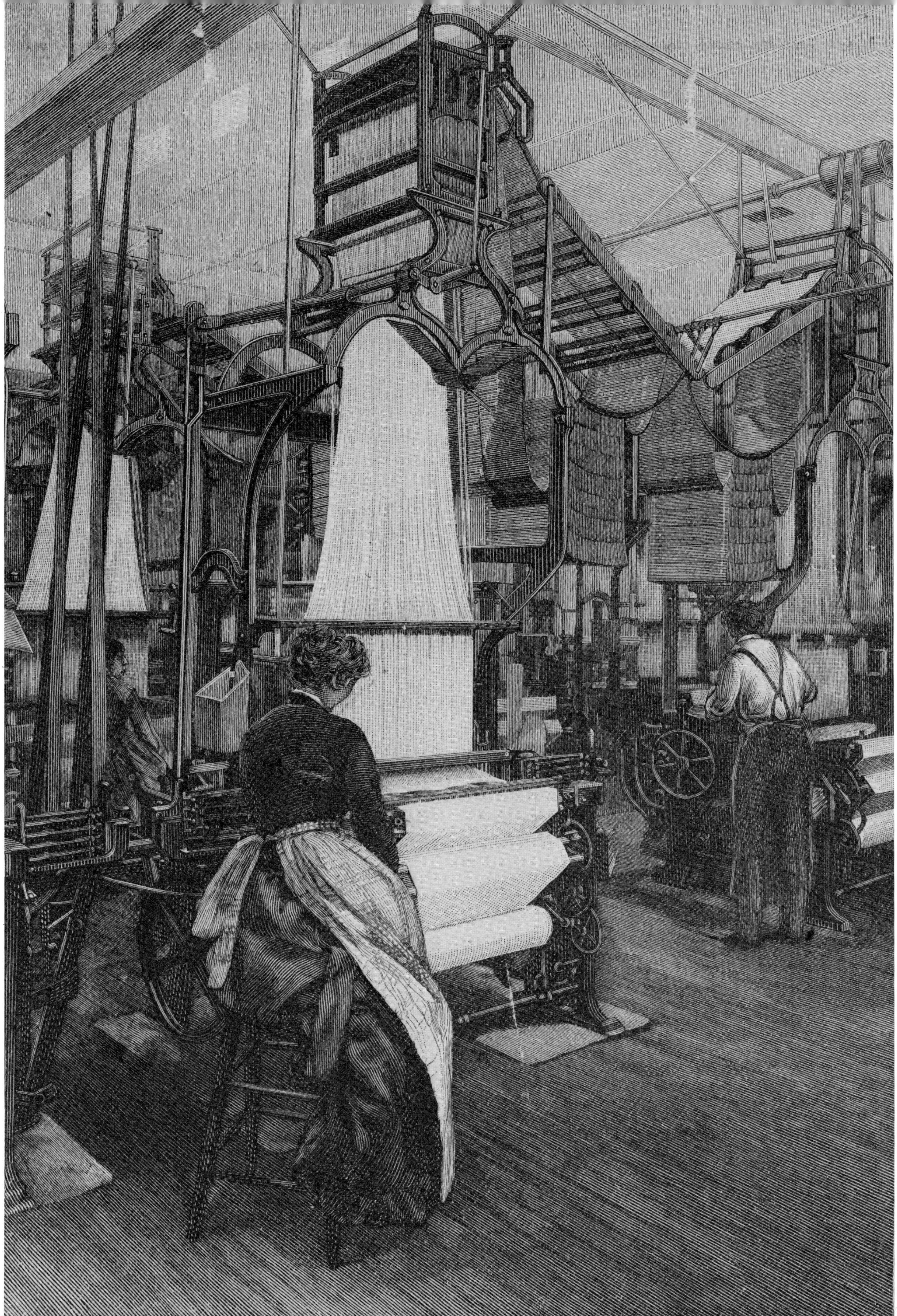

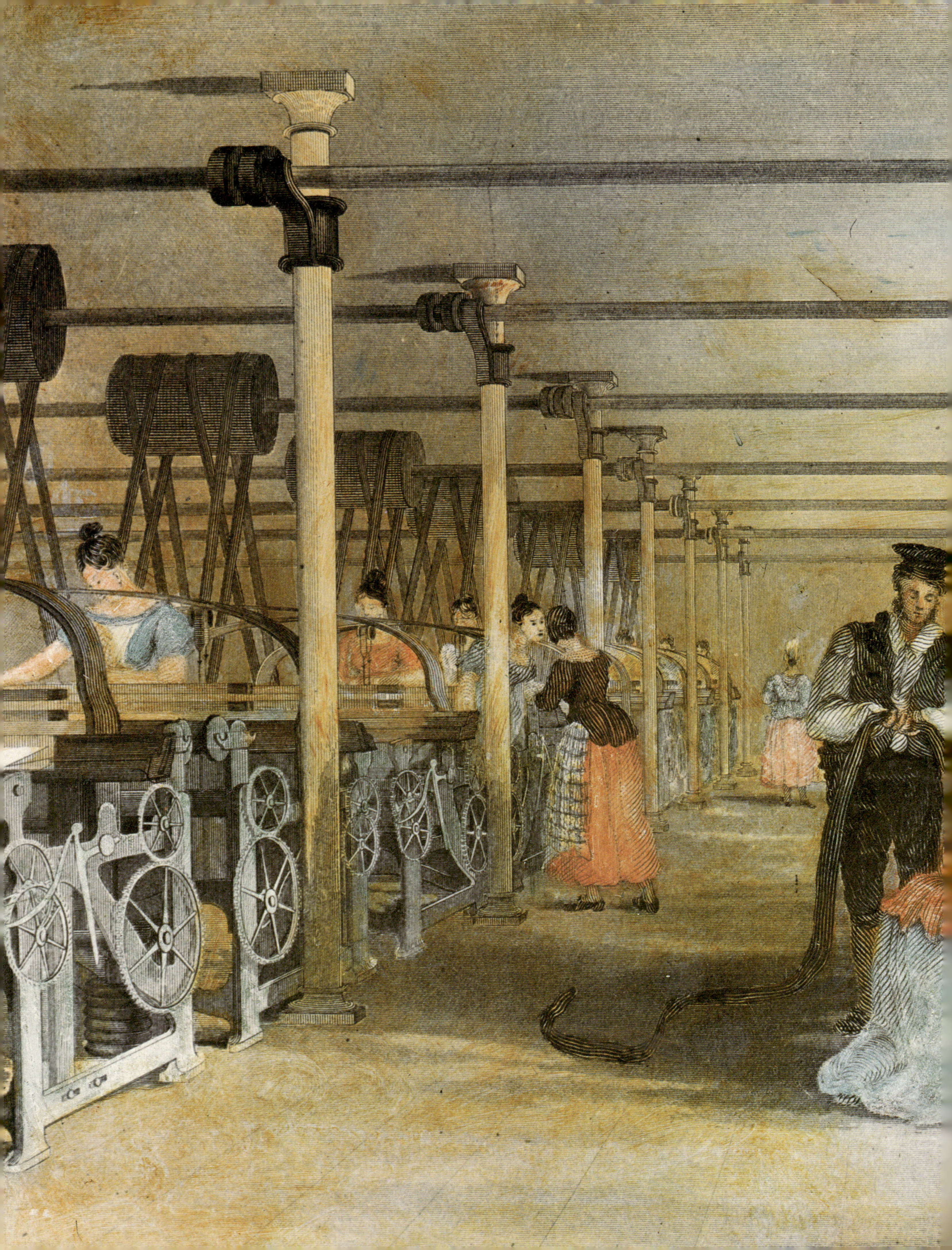

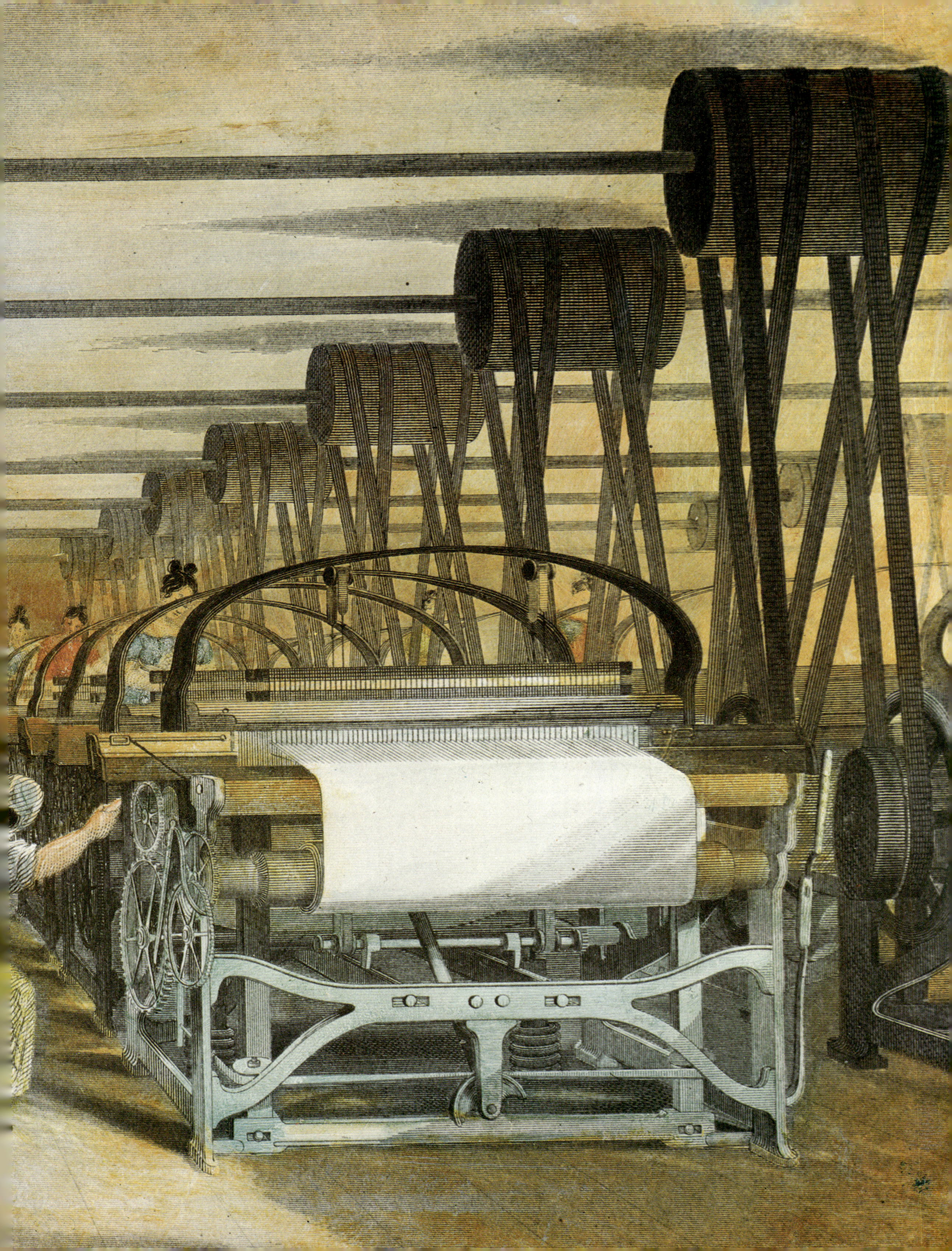

THE STORY OF INVENTIONS

The way that Jacquard decided, for each throw of the shuttle, which needles would push the hooks away, and which wouldn't, was a series of cards with holes punched in them. Each pattern of holes controlled a different pattern of needles, and thus a different pattern of warp threads.

It was one of the truly brilliant inventions, which owed nothing to what had gone before, and today punch-cards have a thousand different applications.

This technological race between the spinners and the weavers, improving efficiency in both, could leave only one problem, that of a sufficient supply of raw materials, and in particular cotton, of which the main suppliers were the Southern plantation owners of the United States, served by that power-source of classical times, the slave. But even slaves could only work so fast. And the trouble was that the only cotton which would grow successfully there was a type known as short-staple upland cotton. It had green seeds which were tightly attached to its fibres, and it could take a slave a whole day to clean a pound of cotton by hand – 'pick a bale of cotton'.

This uneconomic proposition was changed almost overnight by a young farmer's son from Massachusetts, Eli Whitney. In the winter of 1792, after graduating in law at Yale, he went to Savannah, Georgia, where he was friendly with the widow of Nathanael Greene, a general in the War of Independence. Through Mrs Greene's planter friends he heard about the problem, and by the following April, 1793, he had the answer – the cotton-gin.

Like all the best ideas, it was a very simple one. The cotton was fed into one side of a grid, which had very fine slits in it, so fine that the cottonseeds would not go through. On the other side of the grid was a cylinder covered with very thin spikes, which were arranged so that when the cylinder was turned they

Eli Whitney's cotton gin. Like the American Civil War, it transformed the South.

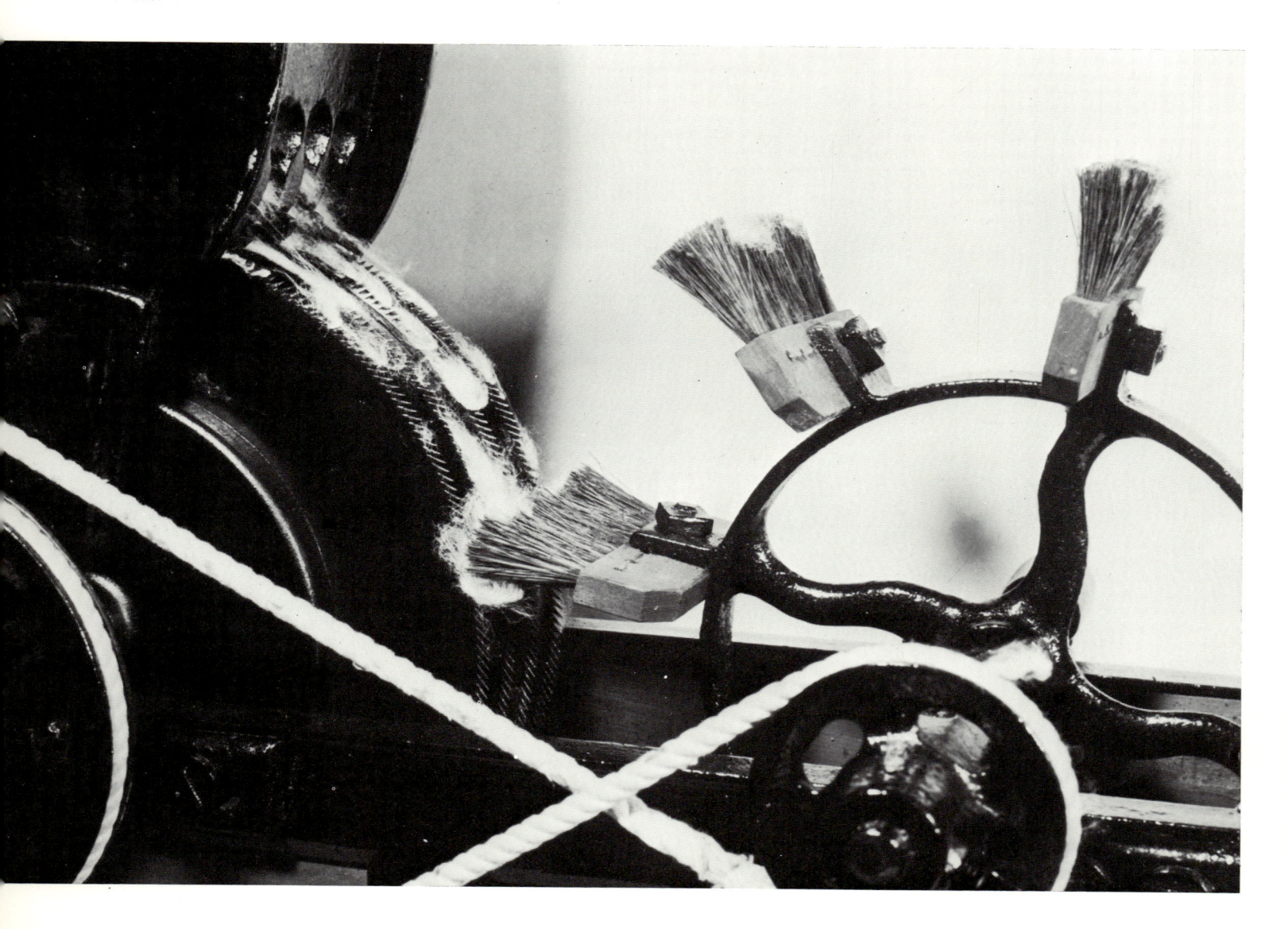

passed through the grid. Revolving in this way, they dragged the cotton fibre back through the slits with them, forcing the seeds to drop off. Then a second revolving cylinder, a brush, cleaned the cotton off the spikes, before they returned through the slits to pick up more cotton. The machine could clean fifty pounds of cotton a day (equivalent to what fifty slaves could do), and completely transformed the South, more and more of whose farmers could now afford to turn to growing the profitable cotton.

Seventy years later, the South was again to be transformed, as a result of the American Civil War, which saw the first mass use of those new weapons, the repeating rifle and the revolver. By one of history's huge ironies, Eli Whitney, the man who had brought prosperity to the South, contributed posthumously to its downfall. Disgusted with frequent infringements of his patent on the cotton-gin, and the mass of consequent lawsuits, he went to New Haven, Connecticut, where in 1798 he set up a fire-arms factory at which he pioneered the idea of interchangeable parts, a principle we see today in everything from a motor-car to a vacuum-cleaner, and one that lies at the very heart of mass-production.

Although Whitney died in 1825, it was to his factory, because of its experience in accurate machining, that a young man of seventeen came in 1831 with his new invention, the revolver. His name was Samuel Colt, and the previous year he had run away to sea and sailed to India. It was during the voyage that he dreamed up the idea, carving the prototype model out of wood.

As every lover of westerns ought to know, the key to the success of the Colt revolver was its mechanism by which, each time the hammer was cocked, the cylinder containing the cartridges rotated until the next chamber was in the position to be fired. In the first models the cocking had to be done by hand, but later the trigger performed all the functions: cocking the hammer, rotating the cylinder by means of a ratchet, and then, when the trigger was fully pulled, firing the gun.

Colt, who went on to make a fortune at his own factory in Hartford, where he developed and perfected Whitney's ideas on interchangeable parts, applying them to the first true production line, also fitted his revolving cylinder into rifles, turning them into repeaters.

The small-arm had come a long way. In the fourteenth century it had been a 'hand-cannon', a cumbersome and dangerous affair that was fired, like a cannon, by putting a red-hot wire to the touch-hole. By about 1450 that had been superseded by the 'matchlock', in which a trigger was used to apply a slow-burning 'match' (a length of rope soaked in saltpetre) to the charge. At the start of the sixteenth century the wheel-lock appeared, in which the spark was obtained by turning a rough-edged wheel against a piece of iron pyrite (the same principle as used in most modern cigarette-lighters). A century later, that gave way to the 'flintlock', in which the cocking mechanism rammed down against a piece of steel to produce the spark.

But the modern system of firing was born in 1805, with an invention by a Scotsman, Alexander Forsyth, who was a clergyman (of the Church militant, presumably!). He discovered that there were certain chemical compounds, in his case potassium chlorate, which would make a flash if they were struck sharply – percussion firing.

At that time, most weapons were still smooth-bore. The idea of rifling the barrel to make the bullet spin, and therefore give greater accuracy, had been understood since the mid-fifteenth century. But there were many drawbacks. One was that powder tended to clog up in the grooves. Another was that the process of rifling the barrel was very difficult and expensive. Most important of all, if the rifling were to have any effect it had to fit the bullet (or ball as it then was) very tightly; so the ball was made to a size which meant that it had to be hammered repeatedly to force it down the barrel. That took a long time, which is why, well into the nineteenth century, armies preferred the smooth-bore muskets which, though only accurate up to about a hundred yards (against the three hundred yards of the rifles of the time), could be reloaded and fired in about fifteen seconds. The generals preferred quantity (of fire) to quality.

Two inventions changed all that. In 1849, a French army captain, Claude Minié, perfected an idea first put forward twenty years previously by a captain in the English army, Captain Norton. Instead of being a ball, the bullet had become the cylindrical shape, with a conical nose, which we know today. At the base of the bullet was a hollow cavity, which expanded under the force of the explosion so that it gripped the rifling tightly.

Three years earlier, a Paris gunsmith named Houiller had made the first completely self-contained ammunition, in which the bullet was held at the end of a metal case which contained both the charge and a percussion-cap filled with fulminate of mercury. He also used the fulminate of mercury as a charge, but it was too weak, and it was not until ten years later, just in time for the American Civil War, that two young American gunsmiths, Horace Smith and Daniel B. Wesson, perfected the cartridge. They used a proper charge of black powder instead of the fulminate, which they retained only for the percussion.

The American Civil War happened just too soon for the machine-gun, or at least one that was effective. In fact the device had been invented by an English lawyer, James Puckle, who came from Sussex. In his patent of 1718 he called it 'a portable gun or machine called a defence'. It stood on a tripod, and had a cylinder, with nine chambers, which was turned by a crank. It fired square bullets, but it was made and tried, and it did work, though one major drawback was that it was produced in the days of flintlock firing.

Exactly one hundred years later, in North Carolina, a boy was born named Richard Jordan Gatling. In his early thirties he became a doctor, but when the Civil War broke out he set himself to inventing fire-arms, on the dubious grounds that more men killed more quickly would end the war sooner – which, taken to the extreme, it obviously would!

The machine-gun he invented was much like Puckle's idea, except that where Puckle had used only one barrel, and rotated the cylinders, Gatling used a number of barrels rotating, hand-cranked, around a central shaft. It was gravity-fed, from a drum sitting on top of the cylinder containing the barrels, and after each barrel was fired the bullet was ejected. By 1862, the second

THE STORY OF INVENTIONS

The Gatling gun. A contemporary print shows delight in the versatility of the new means of death.

year of the war, he had a gun that could fire 350 rounds a minute, which was not bad even by modern standards; but the Union authorities didn't accept it until 1866, when the war was over. Its complicated mechanism had been made possible by the fact that the recently perfected cartridges, mentioned earlier, were now made of lightweight brass.

Gatling died in 1903, leaving a bequest to American gangsterdom in the form of its slang name for a gun – a 'gat'. The story of guns, with key roles played by a priest, a lawyer and a doctor, proves that efficient means of effecting death are not solely the interest of soldiers.

The Civil War also saw the first successful use of a device that today has become one of the main arms of the deterrent strategy, the submarine. It had an even longer history than the gun, with its foundations in ancient Greece. I mention this as a reminder

that so many 'firsts' are by no means original, but are notions which have had to wait until their technological time arrived. (A good example is the Vernier instrument, a brilliant device for highly accurate measurement invented by the Frenchman Pierre Vernier shortly after 1600. It wasn't until 1775 that the technology existed to make it satisfactorily.)

There were many ingenious, and at times ludicrous, attempts to make submarines, including that of one gentleman in 1615 who delighted the court of King James I by *rowing* his submarine beneath the Thames from Westminster to Greenwich.

In 1863, the Confederate States of the South launched the first submarine attack to do real damage. The craft was called *David*; it was some 50 feet long, shaped like a cigar, and had a crew of four. It was driven by steam, and had to keep its funnel above water, which rather spoiled the effect, but it attacked the Federal ironclad *New Ironsides* and succeeded in damaging her badly.

The following year the Confederates used a true submersible, the *H. L. Hunley* – named after the man who put up the money for it. It succeeded in sinking the Federal sloop *Housatonic* in a night attack, though the submarine was actually on the surface at the time, a disappointment which was enhanced by the fact that the submarine also sank.

The weapons these submarines used were 'spar-torpedoes', which were explosive charges attached to long spars (whence the name) sticking out from the front of the submarines like very long bowsprits.

The weapon which finally made the submarine effective was, of course, the torpedo proper. It was invented by a British engineer from Lancashire named Robert Whitehead. He started with the idea, given him by an Austrian Navy officer in 1864, of a boat, loaded with explosives and self-propelled, which would be steered by long ropes towards its target – a sort of elaboration of the fireship technique that Sir Francis Drake had used so successfully against the Spanish.

Whitehead tried it, decided it wouldn't work properly, and in 1866 built the first torpedo proper, which he improved over the next few years. It was about fourteen feet long and carried eighteen pounds of dynamite in its nose. It was driven by a single propeller powered by a compressed-air engine, giving it a speed of about six knots and a range of up to seven hundred yards.

The dynamite it carried was the brand-new invention of one of the most ironic figures in this story, the Swede Alfred Nobel, who went on to make a fortune out of explosives and then used the fortune to found the Nobel Prizes for Literature, Science, and . . . Peace.

In 1846, an Italian chemist had discovered the extremely powerful explosive nitro-glycerine. The trouble with it was that it was so unstable that it was likely to go off at the slightest excuse. The solution clearly lay in soaking the nitro-glycerine up in something else, and in 1866, Nobel, after years of trying

OPPOSITE TOP *Colt's Patent Fire Arms Manufactory, where interchangeable parts became the standard practice.*

OPPOSITE BOTTOM *The US submarine* Turtle *approaches Admiral Howe's flagship,* HMS Eagle. *The attack, however, failed.*

108

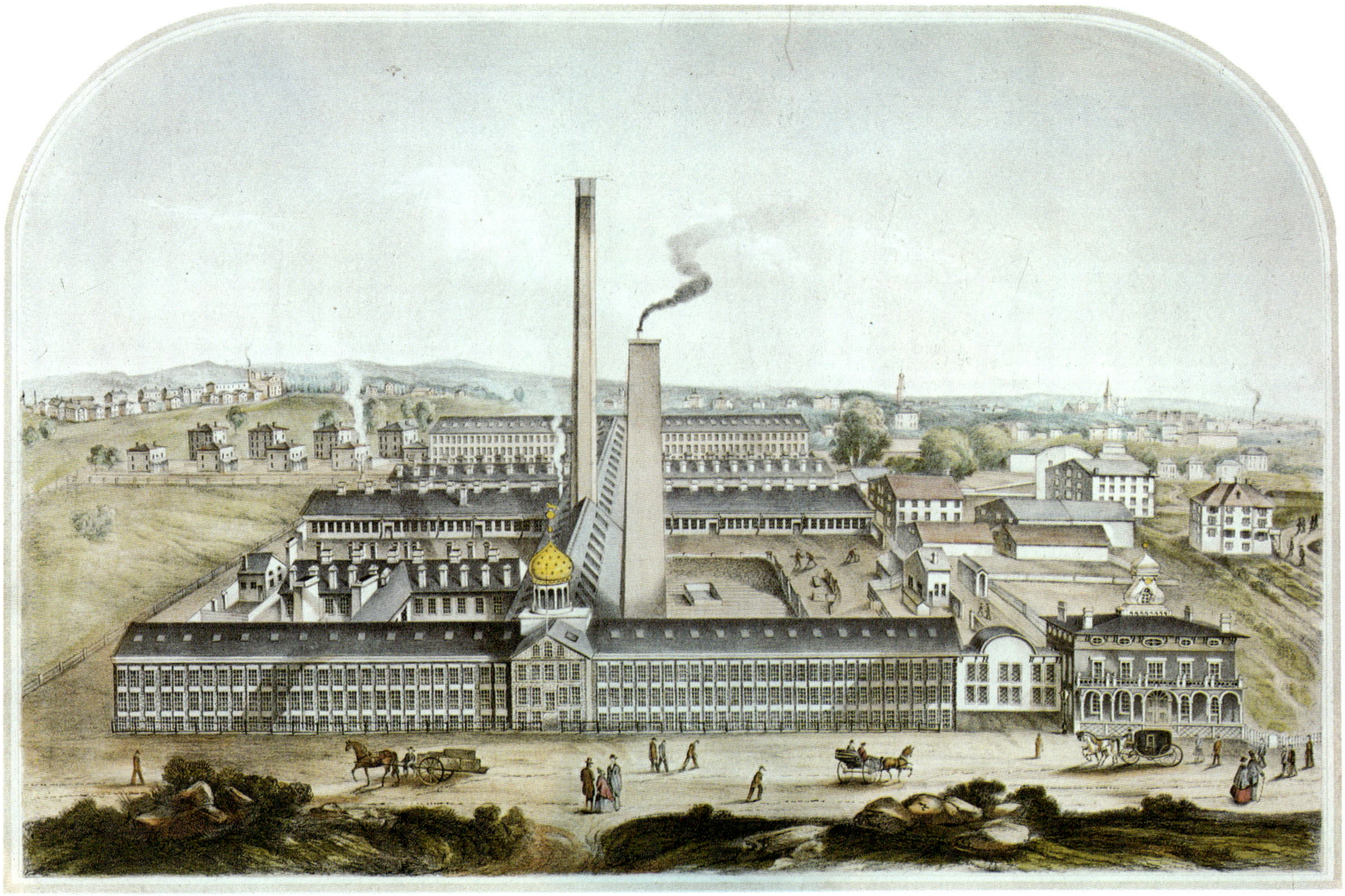

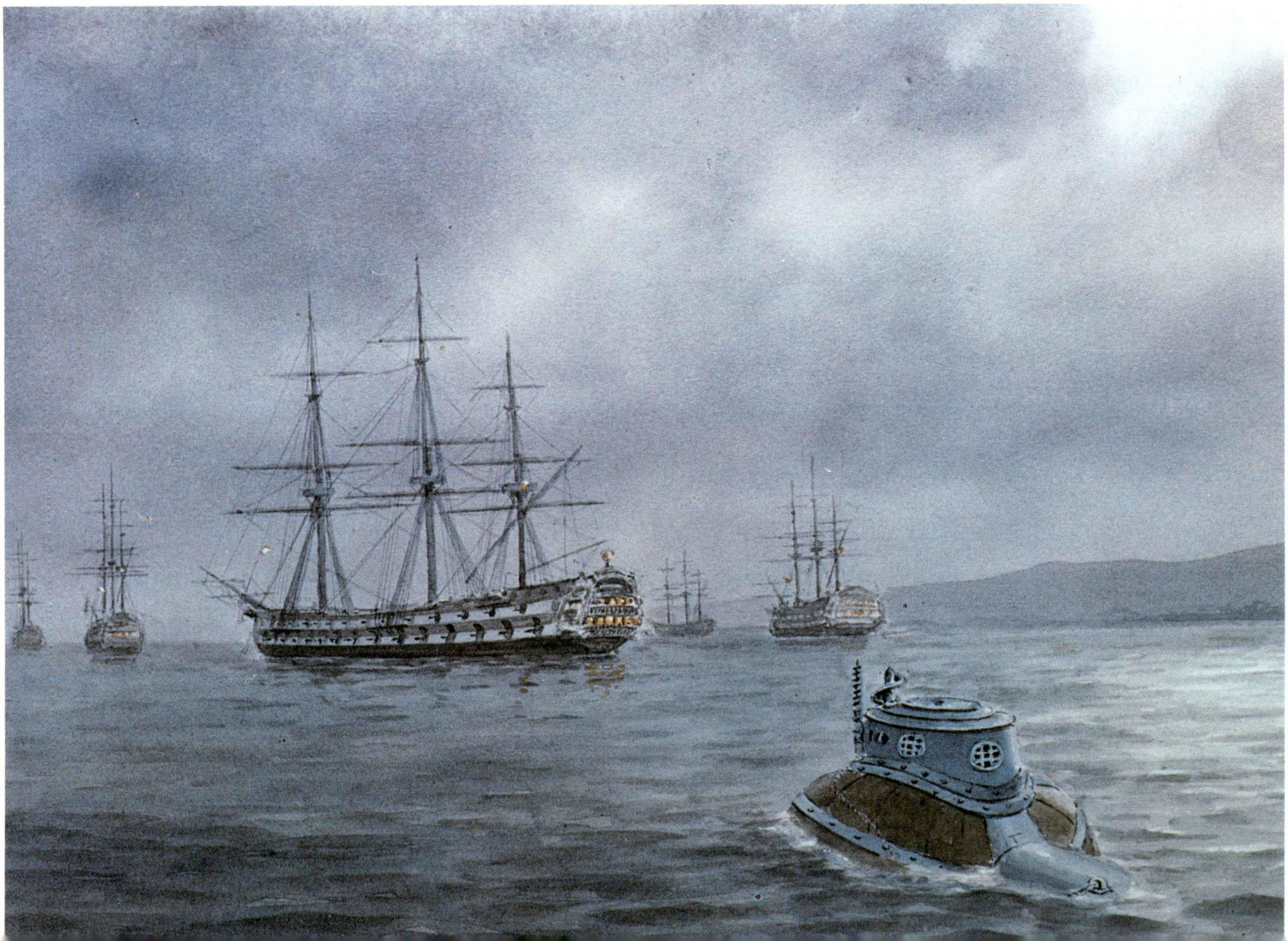

THE STORY OF INVENTIONS

An early canning factory. The tops were soldered on by hand.

everything from paper to clay, hit on the perfect soaker-up – an absorbent, inert mineral called kieselguhr. The combination was, in every sense of the word, dynamite.

It did also have its uses in peacetime, going some way towards showing that good can come of war, and undoubtedly the most dramatic example of this was in the field of food-preservation.

In 1795 the French were at war with Britain. At sea, the scourge of all navies was scurvy, which killed the sailors because of their lack of fresh fruit and vegetables. On land, armies had to take food from the local people where they were fighting, which was not only unreliable from the soldiers' point of view, but disastrous for the civilians. The French Government therefore offered a prize of 12,000 francs for the invention of a method of preserving food, so that the sailors and soldiers could take their supplies with them. A French chef, Nicolas Appert, set to work at his confectionary business at Massy. His experiments were given continual impetus by the great marches of Napoleon's armies.

In 1810, Appert finally had the answer, on which today's canning industry still depends. It was that if the food were cooked in a jar, or bottle, from which the air was excluded, and which, after the cooking, was sealed so that the air couldn't get in, then the food would keep. He tried it with about seventy different foods, from soups to syrups, fruit and vegetables, and it worked.

What he couldn't have known was that it worked because, by excluding the air, he also excluded bacteria carried in the air, and because bacteria in the food itself had been killed by heating. But he won the prize, and in 1822 was rightly given the title 'Benefactor of Humanity'. Rightly, because from that moment on, man was no longer dependent on the vagaries of harvest and weather in order to have enough to eat.

Appert's invention soon gained an ally, when in 1834 Jacob Perkins, an American living in England, took out the first patent for a refrigerator, which worked on the vapour-compression system. Basically, a volatile liquid like ether is allowed to evaporate. Evaporation has the effect of cooling (which is why we sweat when we are hot). The gases given off during evaporation

110

are then collected in a condenser, where they are returned to their liquid form, when they can be used all over again. In 1850, commercial refrigeration plants were opened both in America and Australia, and both for the same reason, the need to keep fresh the vast quantities of beef that each was producing and exporting.

In America the great wheatlands of the Midwest were also benefiting from technology, when in the Shenandoah Valley of Virginia, in the year 1831, Cyrus Hall McCormick invented the mechanical reaper. He was just twenty-two at the time.

Before that, farmers had been limited in the amount of grain they could sow by the amount they knew they would be able to gather, with the manpower available, at harvest time. The reaper changed all that. It was pulled by a horse, and ran on a wide master wheel, like a roller. As this turned, it supplied the power to its two essential moving parts – a knife that moved backwards and forwards as it cut, making sure no stalks were left uncut, and the revolving reel, whose horizontal arms scooped up the cut grain as they rotated and passed it on to a platform at the back of the reaper. It also had a 'divider', that pulled in each new row of wheat towards the knife.

The cut wheat still had to be tied into bundles by hand, but by 1850 a device had been invented that tied them mechanically. The final development, of course, was the combine harvester, which not only cut the wheat but threshed it as well. Although it was invented in 1836, and saw some use in California, it didn't come into general use until the twentieth century.

If war sometimes gave to peace, so peace made what was to become one of the most horrible contributions to war, with the invention of barbed-wire. Several people had thought of it, but the 'credit' must go to the man who developed a practical way of manufacturing it, Joseph Glidden, a rancher from Illinois. He had first seen it at a county fair, and in 1874 took out a patent for a machine that was able to thread the barbs into the twisted wire.

The railroad companies used it for keeping cattle off the tracks. The wheat farmers used it for keeping the cattle off their wheat. And Hollywood later used it as the basis for a thousand western plots, re-enacting the range wars which it brought in its train. It spelled the end for the open range, and for the already legendary cowboy who for a century had made his home on it.

But by then, another kind of wire strode across the continent, the telegraph wire. Its inventor? So many names are associated with its development that it is unfair to credit it to any one man. Indeed, the first suggestion of using electrical currents to transmit messages came in an anonymous letter to a Scottish magazine in 1753.

The first working telegraph seems to date from 1816 and to have been the brainchild of Sir Francis Ronalds, who set it up in his garden in Hammersmith, in London. At each end there was a disc with letters round the edge. In front of each was a second, masking, disc, with a hole in it which would allow one letter at a time to be seen. The lettered discs were turned slowly by clockwork, and were synchronized, so that the letter appearing at one end was always the same as that appearing at the other. An electric impulse from the sender activated a pair of pith balls at the receiver, indicating that the letter then visible was the one being sent.

An operator transmitting a message by Morse telegraph.

Bell opening the telephone link between New York and Chicago.

A trial of the McCormick reaper in Virginia in 1831.

OPPOSITE LEFT *Cooke and Wheatstone's two-needle telegraph. The messages were indicated by deflections of the needles.*

OPPOSITE RIGHT *An early version of Bell's telegraph receiver.*

By 1838, William Cooke and Charles Wheatstone had developed a system by which the electrical impulses were used to deflect a magnetic needle (using the principle discovered by Professor Oersted) which was pivoted in the centre of a wire coil which received the charge. The deflections were made intelligible by means of a code. That year, one of their systems was set up on the Great Western Railway between London and West Drayton.

But the most famous code of all, still used, was that of an American clergyman's son, Samuel Morse. In the system he developed, the dots and dashes were recorded by a pencil on a clockwork-turned strip of paper. The pencil was attached to a lever, deflected by a current passing through an electromagnet. In 1843, he built America's first telegraph line, from Baltimore to Washington, and when it was opened the following year, the first message he sent was: 'What hath God wrought.'

But the world wasn't going to be content with dots and dashes – and already many inventors were in search of the 'speaking' telegraph, the telephone. It was patented, in the centenary year of American independence, 1876, by Alexander Graham Bell, who had emigrated from Scotland and now lived in Boston. He actually invented it in 1874.

The basic idea was a membrane, or diaphragm, into which the voice was spoken. At the back of this diaphragm, and attached to it, was a piece of iron, which, as the voice made the diaphragm vibrate, would itself vibrate, in front of an electromagnet. This would make the electromagnet produce an undulating electric current, which would be sent down the line to the receiver, which was the same as the sending instrument, but would operate in reverse.

Bell, who was then twenty-seven, doubted, however, whether it would actually work, and didn't bother to make the instrument. But the following year he was experimenting with some multiple telegraph equipment, whose instruments had thin metal strips as part of the operation, when his assistant, Thomas Watson, who was in another room, happened to twang one of these strips, and sure enough, the sound was reproduced at the instrument Bell was using. So it *would* work.

Bell and his assistant immediately set about making the telephone as he had devised it the year before, and on 10 March 1876, Bell transmitted the first complete telephonic sentence: 'Mr Watson, come here; I want you.' Peremptory, but at least a useful and necessary message. Since then, telephone companies have made fortunes out of the billions of words of unnecessary chatter that the instrument has induced.

To match these leaps forward in communication, the media of 'record' also moved on. There are three basic ways of 'recording' something: the written word, the picture, and sound.

For four centuries, the first of these had enjoyed the enormous benefit of printing. And since the beginning of the eighteenth century inventors had been trying to perfect the 'individual printing machine', the typewriter.

It wasn't until 1868 that the first practical machine, which could type far faster than the hand could write, was patented. Its inventor was an American printer, Christopher Latham Sholes, and within five years he had perfected it to a point where it was in its essentials very like today's machines – including the arrangement of the letters on the keyboard, which Sholes designed so that the most used letters were spread apart, eliminating the risk of jamming the keys.

Late in life Sholes wrote: 'Whatever I may have felt, in the early days, of the value of the typewriter, it is obviously a blessing to mankind, and especially to womankind.'

It certainly had a profound social effect, in that it led to the almost entirely female profession of shorthand-typing, thus admitting women to the world of business, albeit in a junior capacity which many later came to think of as degrading. And like the telephone, it has itself undoubtedly given rise to a great deal of work – the number of letters dictated expanding to fit the time available for dictating them. A similar observation might equally be made about the invention that overtook the painter as the pictorial recorder, the camera.

The photograph, the picture which is produced by light, must be one of the most easily observed of natural phenomena. If you remove an object that has lain on a lawn for a couple of sunny days, or a picture that has hung on a painted wall, you will see a photograph, or at least the basic chemistry of a photograph. Optically, any cave-dweller with a chink in the covering over the entrance to the cave, or a tented nomad with a hole in his goatskin wall, could observe the principle of 'camera obscura' at work.

The first person truly to understand the principle was the Arabian scholar Alhazen of Basra, who lived from 965 to 1038. He first noticed it in prison, where he had been committed after feigning madness to escape a sultan's wrath. He went on to write about the fundamental principles of optics, recognizing the relationship between the size of the aperture and the sharpness of the image, and the way in which the image was inverted.

The idea of the 'camera obscura' was taken up again during the Renaissance, and therefore many inventors looked for ways of 'fixing' the picture. By the beginning of the nineteenth century it seemed that everyone was after it, but the honour of producing the first permanent, chemically fixed, camera photograph went to an amateur scientist, Joseph Nicéphore Niepce.

The year was 1826, and the picture he took was of the courtyard of his house near Chalon-sur-Saône in France. It shows a pigeon-house, a bakehouse, a barn and a pear tree, all pleasantly rural and the only one of his pictures to survive.

Niepce's photographic plate was made of pewter, and rendered sensitive to light by a covering of a kind of asphalt known as bitumen of Judea. But it had been a close race. In 1835, the English inventor William Henry Fox Talbot succeeded, using different chemicals and in 1837 another Frenchman, Louis Daguerre, who had collaborated with Niepce, produced his 'daguerreotype', which was produced by exposing an iodized silver plate in a camera and then 'fuming' the plate with mercury vapour. The picture was 'fixed' in a solution of common salt.

Since those days, techniques have improved, but the principles involved, both in the optics of the camera lens and in methods of fixing, have remained basically the same.

The third 'medium of record' was, of course, the record, or gramophone recording. In a sense it was the greatest breakthrough of the three, since, although writing and painting had existed, there had never been any way of recording sound. And unlike so many inventions, which were either the result of many people working at around the same time (thus leading to the endless 'patent battles' of the nineteenth century) or had evolved over centuries, it was indisputably one man's idea and his alone.

An early typewriter. Design had not yet surrendered entirely to function!

Thomas Edison experimenting in his laboratory.

Ernemann Kinox

Der ideale Familien-Kinematograph

INDUSTRIAL EVOLUTION

At the age of twelve Thomas Edison had been a newsboy, after having had only three months' education, and when he was fifteen he became a telegraph operator. But he had an enormously inventive mind (by the end of his life he had 1033 patents to his credit), and when the telephone was invented he immediately thought of ways of improving it.

One idea was to replace the vibrating piece of iron in Bell's instrument with a short needle. Then, in his own words: 'I was singing to the mouthpiece of a telephone when the vibrations of the voice sent the fine steel point into my finger. That set me thinking. If I could record the actions of the point, and send the point over some surface afterward, I saw no reason why the thing would not talk.'

There was no reason. He tried it out with a strip of waxed paper, shouting 'Hallo' as the paper moved beneath a steel needle. When he ran the paper back, he got his answer: 'Hallo.' That year, 1877, he produced and patented his 'phonograph', in which a stylus followed a path in some tinfoil wrapped round a cylinder in which spiral grooves had been cut. Another stylus had previously been used to 'record' the message, the first of which once again fell somewhat short of the heroic. It was 'Mary had a little lamb'. Just that, no more – not even the whole verse. But it was the very first number one in the hit-parade, and many performers, a high proportion of them of indifferent talent, have made fortunes from it.

The following year, Edison went to work on the electric light bulb, and in 1879, within a year, had turned it into a practical reality, starting another whole industry, which was to supersede the gas lighting that had reigned for most of the century.

Edison was just thirty-two, and went on inventing till 1928, three years before his death.

Edison invented the phonograph and a whole new industry called 'pop'.

BELOW *A portrait photographer's studio, a world away from family 'snaps'.*

OPPOSITE *A German poster c. 1913. Even then, home movies were the rage.*

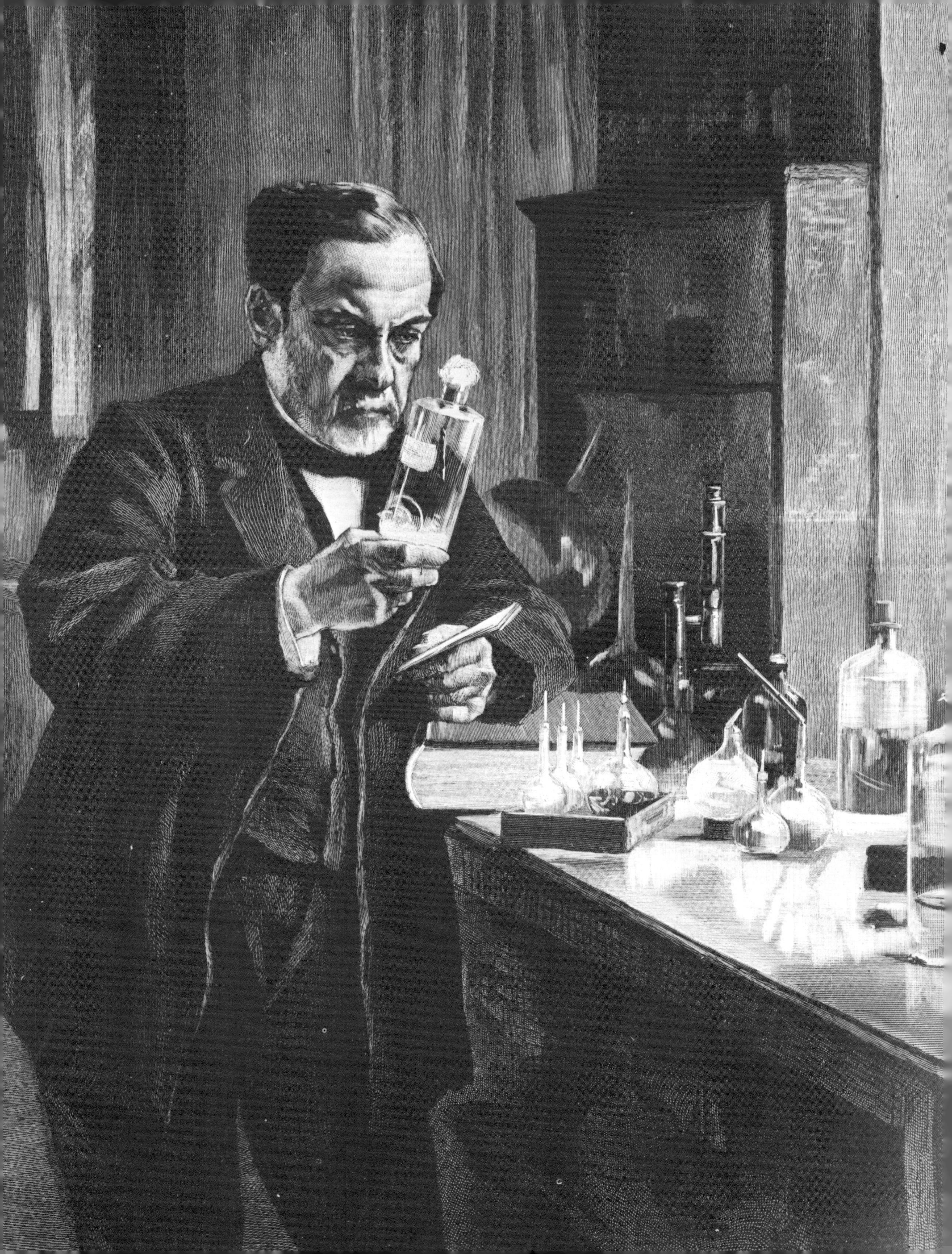

Here Today, Where Tomorrow?

If only we could project ourselves five thousand years forward in time, we might be able to make some adequate judgement about this, the twentieth century. As it is, we can have no idea. The temptation for most of us, apart from the few visionaries who have graced all ages, is to believe that we are basically 'where it's at'. We can see that a few problems remain to be solved, but most people find it hard to believe that technology could advance very far beyond its present state.

In fact, the reverse is true, and must be true, for the simple reason that there is no end to the question 'Why?' Every scientific problem that we solve, and every discovery we make, and every invention that is created, inspires *at least* one question, and usually many, many more. So, like a tree that just keeps on growing, dividing at the end of each twig into two more twigs, the number of questions *always* exceeds the number of answers. Since man is by nature curious, and having posed a question, tends to be unhappy until he has the answer, the assumption must be that the number of questions will continue to grow. The sum of our ignorance grows faster than the sum of our knowledge. So this last chapter can be at best only a guess as to what will prove to have been the key inventions of our time and the decisive influences that were their background.

Perhaps the single most important of these influences has been the growth of the world's population. At the time of writing it stands at nearly four thousand million, which is four times what it was in 1850. Estimates are that by the year 2000 it will have doubled to eight thousand million, despite the invention in the mid-'fifties, by American doctor Gregory Pincus, of the birth-control pill.

The main cause of this explosion of the living has been that fewer people are dying young, and that is due to the huge advances in medicine over the last century or so.

At the beginning of the nineteenth century Dr Edward Jenner introduced vaccination, giving protection against the decimations of smallpox. In the 1840s, anaesthetics came into general use. In the 1880s, Louis Pasteur vastly widened the scope of the immunology that Jenner had begun. Medical diagnosis was given its greatest single weapon in 1895, when Wilhelm Röntgen discovered the X-ray. The discovery was an accident, as was that which in 1928 led Alexander Fleming to penicillin, which by 1939, together with Howard Florey and Ernst Chain, he had turned into the life-saving drug which won the three of them a Nobel prize in 1945.

It had come, of course, just in time for the Second World War. The *Second*. Perhaps history will nominate the notion and practice of global warfare as the century's greatest influence. Perhaps the verdict will be astonishment that the technological explosion was not accompanied by better ideas for settling arguments.

The two world wars alone, without counting the almost continuous lesser struggles, cost the world some hundred million dead. It seems a lot. It *is* a lot. But that is the rate by which the world's population is now rising roughly every two years. We come back to population.

More people means less to go round, and faster exploitation of the world's natural resources. In many areas the scientists provided the answers: what nature couldn't provide in sufficient quantity, man would provide artificially. Perhaps this will be known as the Synthetic Age: synthetic foods, fibres, drugs, fertilizers – even synthetic minerals. (After all, diamonds are among the best friends of industry, as well as of girls – though they *did* get false eyelashes!)

The increase of production, and the new materials, and the new techniques led to vast problems of pollution – though, to be fair, it is doubtful whether this century has changed the face of the earth to the extent that it was changed by that devastating trio, the axe, fire, and the plough.

Much of the pollution was due to the search for more energy. All progress in technology (and that includes every aspect, from agriculture to zoological gardens) depends ultimately on adequate and efficient sources of power. The reason India has remained so poor so long has been her massive dependence on an extremely inefficient power-source – the bullock.

The demands for more power, combined with the running-

LEFT *Louis Pasteur, the man who made milk safe to drink.*

A new Age begins, with a roar that makes the earth shudder.

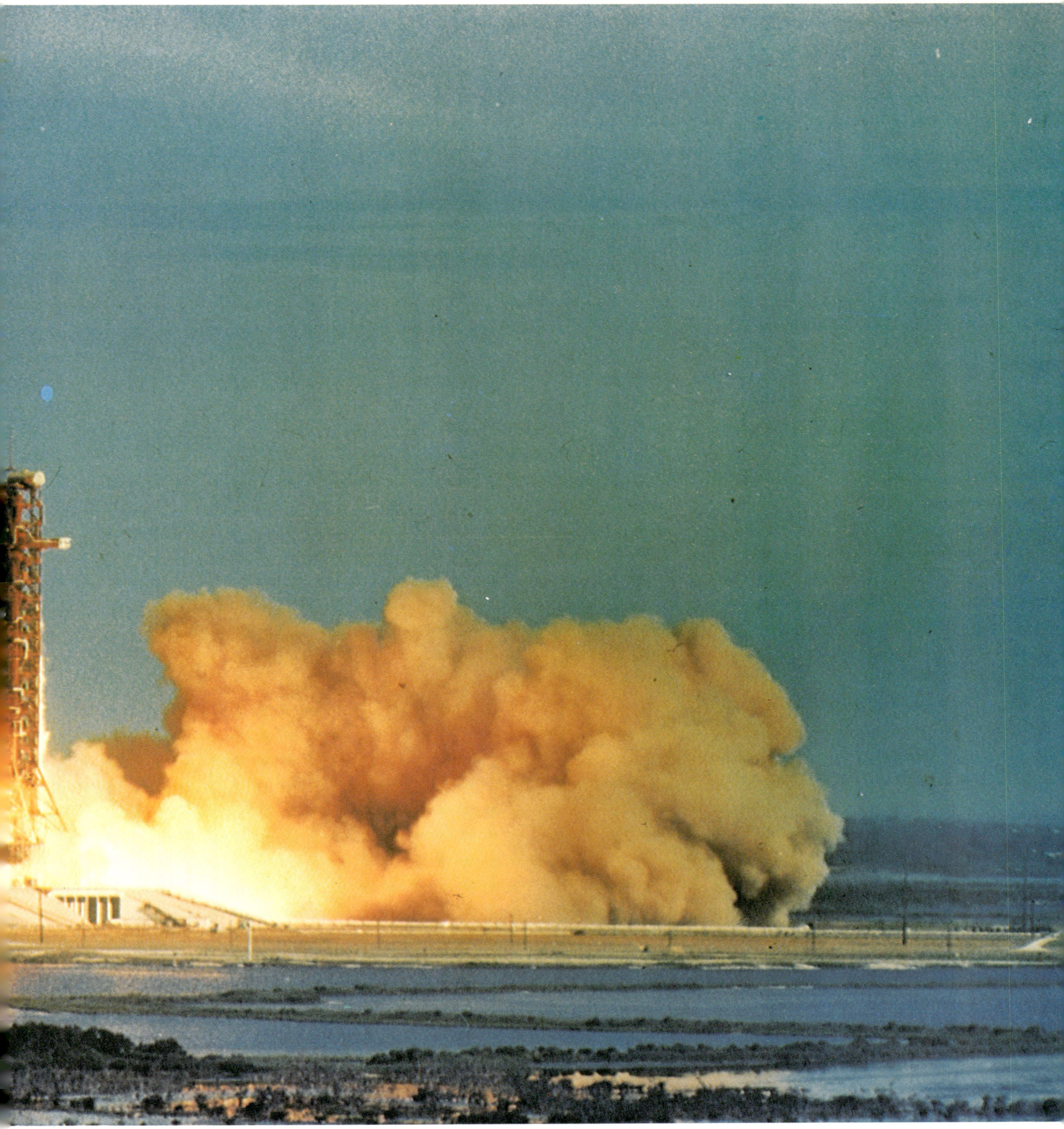

THE STORY OF INVENTIONS

down of supplies of the traditional fossil fuels, seemed to be answered by the harnessing of atomic energy. But the waste from nuclear plants threatens a far deadlier pollution than any other. Will this be known as the Atomic Age? If those problems are solved, perhaps it will. On the other hand, within a few decades we may discover new power-sources which will give atom-splitting a shorter life than the water-wheel.

Another possibility is that our century will be known as the Age of the Masses – the time when the great proportion of the world's workers, lower classes, proletariat, whatever you want to call them, realized their own political power and began to have a real say in the running of affairs. As far as the theme of this book is concerned, the importance of that was that it led to an enormous spreading of wealth and spending power, and so to the creation of vast 'consumer societies' – with the consequent need of machines that could deliver the goods. The Consumer Age, perhaps?

There are other candidates. What about the Computer Age? Up till now, machines could only be a substitute for men's physical labours. Now, it could do their calculations, and a great deal of their thinking – not genuinely 'creative' thinking as yet, but already there are computers that can be programmed to suggest the sort of programmes with which they should be fed.

The Communications Age is another possibility. For the first time it was in theory possible that every being on earth could see and hear a single event as it happened. Not so much theory, either: already, audiences for events like association football's World Cup are measured in hundreds of millions. Radio and television have been absolutely crucial, both in informing the great mass of people as to what is happening in their world, thereby creating a genuine 'public opinion', but also in manipulating that opinion.

The world-wide television network depended, of course, on satellites, on the final candidate for supremacy in our time, space. Are we the beginning of the Space Age? It is possible. The moon could be colonized, in artificial atmospheres, but it's really quite small. Venus, we now know, is too hot for comfort; Mars, fairly inhospitable. But it's not *inconceivable* that we might colonize other planets. If that proves to be the answer to overpopulation of earth, then our first faltering steps into space will truly have been the most significant events of our time.

Five thousand years in the future? The only way to get an idea of how we will seem is to glance back at the second chapter of this book – man had not yet learned the alphabet, nor how to make iron, nor started to build the pyramids.

But I suppose that most people, if asked which single machine has been the greatest transformer of life in the twentieth century, would nominate the motor-car.

The idea of a self-propelled vehicle was, of course, a very old one; and the early decades of the nineteenth century had seen a number of steam-driven road vehicles. But steam, though very powerful, has a disadvantage other than that of weight. It is an inefficient user of the fuel it consumes, for the simple reason that it is an external-combustion engine – that is, the fuel is burned outside the engine itself.

Engineers realized well enough the advantages to be gained by burning the fuel *inside* the engine, the internal-combustion engine. But it wasn't until 1860 that Etienne Lenoir, a Frenchman who, like so many other inventors, was completely self-taught, built the first successful internal-combustion engine.

Like the early steam-engines, it was designed as a static engine. Its fuel was 'illuminating' gas (the coal-gas used for street lighting, which had developed as a 'spin-off' from the need for coke for steel-making) mixed with air. It had one cylinder, and was double-acting; that is, there was a combustion chamber each side of the piston. As the piston moved along the cylinder, the chamber on one side would have the combustion mixture sucked into it. As it reached the end of its run, a spark ignited the mixture, driving the piston back in the other direction, which at the same time sucked fresh mixture into the

Mr Benz had his motor car . . .

. . . and Mr Daimler had his.

Henry Ford started small, and grew and grew and grew.

chamber on the other side, and so on. It wasn't very efficient, giving less than two horsepower at 100 revolutions per minute, representing about four per cent of the potential energy in the gas. But it did work, and several hundred of them were sold.

That same year, 1860, a newspaper carrying an article on Lenoir's machine was read by a twenty-eight-year-old travelling salesman from the Rhineland named Nikolaus August Otto. Perhaps, knowing how valuable the motor-car has become to travelling salesmen, he should have been made patron saint of that profession – because he immediately started to experiment on his own account, and in 1876, after many mechanical detours, produced the first engine using the four-stroke cycle.

The vast majority of cars today use this system, whose success depends on the fact that the mixture is compressed before firing. On the first downstroke of the piston, the mixture is drawn into the cylinder through a valve. On the following upstroke, the mixture is compressed. At the top of that stroke it is ignited, so that the next downstroke is the power stroke, in which the piston is forced down by the expanding gases. And the final upstroke, the exhaust stroke, drives the used gases out through another valve. The system is called, after its inventor, the Otto Cycle.

Now the hunt was on for a practical way of making the internal-combustion engine drive a vehicle. It had to be a light engine. It had to be capable of a great number of revolutions a minute. It had to be run on some sort of liquid fuel, since gas would require huge containers if reasonable journeys were to be achieved.

The man generally credited with success was Karl Benz, who in the spring of 1885 drove his three-wheeler round a cinder-track at his factory in Mannheim, Germany. It ran on petrol, which fed a one-cylinder four-stroke engine, producing one and a half horsepower. It did ten miles an hour, and since history records that he was accompanied on the circuit by his workers, and his wife clapping enthusiastically as she ran, one can only assume that either they were all very fit, or that he slowed down out of kindness.

Sixty miles away, at Bad Cannstatt, two of Otto's old assistants had set up their own business. They were Gottlieb Daimler and Wilhelm Maybach, and in November of the same year they successfully drove the first motor-cycle, which had the advantage over Benz's engine, which could only do 250 rpm, that its air-cooled engine did 900 rpm, the first true high-speed internal-combustion engine.

By one of the strange freaks of history, it is worth recording

THE STORY OF INVENTIONS

A Zeppelin under construction.

that not only did Daimler and Benz never meet, but they had never even heard of each other – though in 1926, long after Daimler's death, their firms were finally to merge, to produce the car we know as the Mercedes-Benz.

To Maybach goes the credit of perfecting, in 1893, the first really efficient carburettor, and to Robert Bosch, in 1902, the key to a workable sparking-plug, the high-tension magneto. Daimler had produced *his* ignition by a tube heated by an open flame!

Four years later, in 1897, the compression-ignition engine, which needs no spark, was built at Augsburg by yet another German engineer, the thirty-nine-year-old Rudolf Diesel. The principle was, and is – for diesel engines have run parallel with petrol engines as their heavy-duty counterparts – that if air is compressed sufficiently (far more than in petrol engines) it will get so hot, from the mere fact of compression, that when the fuel is then sprayed into the cylinder the heat of the air will ignite it.

The diesel engine has the disadvantage that it will do far fewer revolutions a minute than the petrol engine. Of course, gearing will help make up for this, but acceleration is far slower (which is why lorry- and truck-drivers don't like slowing down!). On the other hand, it has two great advantages: it will burn very low-grade fuel (cheaper, because it hasn't had to go through the refining processes of petrol), and it is far more efficient in its use of the fuel's energy – 35 per cent against the 28 per cent of the best petrol engines.

At the start, the motor-car was the rich man's plaything. But not for long. In 1903, a farmer's son from Michigan set up a car factory. His name was Henry Ford. He soon saw that the car would become not a luxury, but a necessity, and in 1908, when he was forty-five, he launched his immortal car for every man, the Model T, known as the Tin Lizzie.

By the time the last of them was produced, nineteen years later, he had sold fifteen million of them, and the way he did it was in its own way a major contribution to the twentieth century, the conveyor-belt assembly line. The chassis starts at one end and, as it passes along the line, workers skilled and trained for one particular job add more and more pieces to it, until the completed car rolls off at the other end. It certainly proved the key to mass-production, though present thinking suggests that the tedium which accompanies it has had disastrous social effects.

Meanwhile, the internal-combustion engine had taken to the air. On 2 July 1900, an enormous airship, 420 feet long, rose from a floating hangar on Lake Constance, in Germany. She was the brainchild of a retired army officer, Count Ferdinand von Zeppelin, after whom she was named, and she was driven by two 16-horsepower Daimler engines.

The previous year, an American bishop's two young sons had become interested in flying. At the time they were working in the bicycle shop which they had opened, and had been reading about the experiments in gliding made by the German Otto Lilienthal (using a hang glider similar to those now so popular). The brothers were Wilbur and Orville Wright.

Over the next three years they built a series of biplane gliders, with which they experimented with the problems of controlling an aircraft in flight. In 1903 they installed a 12-horsepower engine in their latest glider design, which drove two 'pusher' propellers, and by the end of the year they were ready.

On 14 December they tried to take it off the ground, and failed. But on 17 December, at Kill Devil hill (it should have been renamed Dare Devil) near Kitty Hawk, in North Carolina, Orville lay once more at the controls. The plane, under its own power, ran forward along its wooden launching rail, and for twelve seconds was airborne – the first powered heavier-than-air flight.

They made three other flights that day, and on the last of them the plane stayed in the air for 59 seconds, covering a distance of 852 feet. Since there was a strong breeze against it, the machine was credited with distance through the air of half a mile. And for once an historic machine was given a suitable name. With proper optimism they had called it 'The Flyer'.

By 1905, they had perfected their third version, Flyer III, to such an extent that it could perform all the manœuvres now regarded as standard in flying – banking, turning, circling and making figures-of-eight. It could do 35 mph, and stay in the air for half an hour. The age of manned flight had truly begun – and

Wilbur Wright's first European flight in 1908.

Le Petit Journal

SUPPLÉMENT ILLUSTRÉ

5 centimes 5 centimes

ABONNEMENTS

Le Petit Journal
CHAQUE JOUR — 6 PAGES — 5 CENTIMES
Administration : 61, rue Lafayette
Les manuscrits ne sont pas rendus

Le Petit Journal agricole, 5 cent. — La Mode du Petit Journal, 10 cent.
Le Petit Journal illustré de la Jeunesse, 10 cent.
On s'abonne sans frais dans tous les bureaux de poste

	SIX MOIS	UN AN
SEINE et SEINE-ET-OISE	2 fr.	3 fr. 50
DÉPARTEMENTS	2 fr.	4 fr. »
ÉTRANGER	2.50	5 fr. »

Dix-neuvième Année — DIMANCHE 30 AOUT 1908 — Numéro 928

WILBUR WRIGHT

L'AÉROPLANE DE WILBUR WRIGHT EN PLEIN VOL

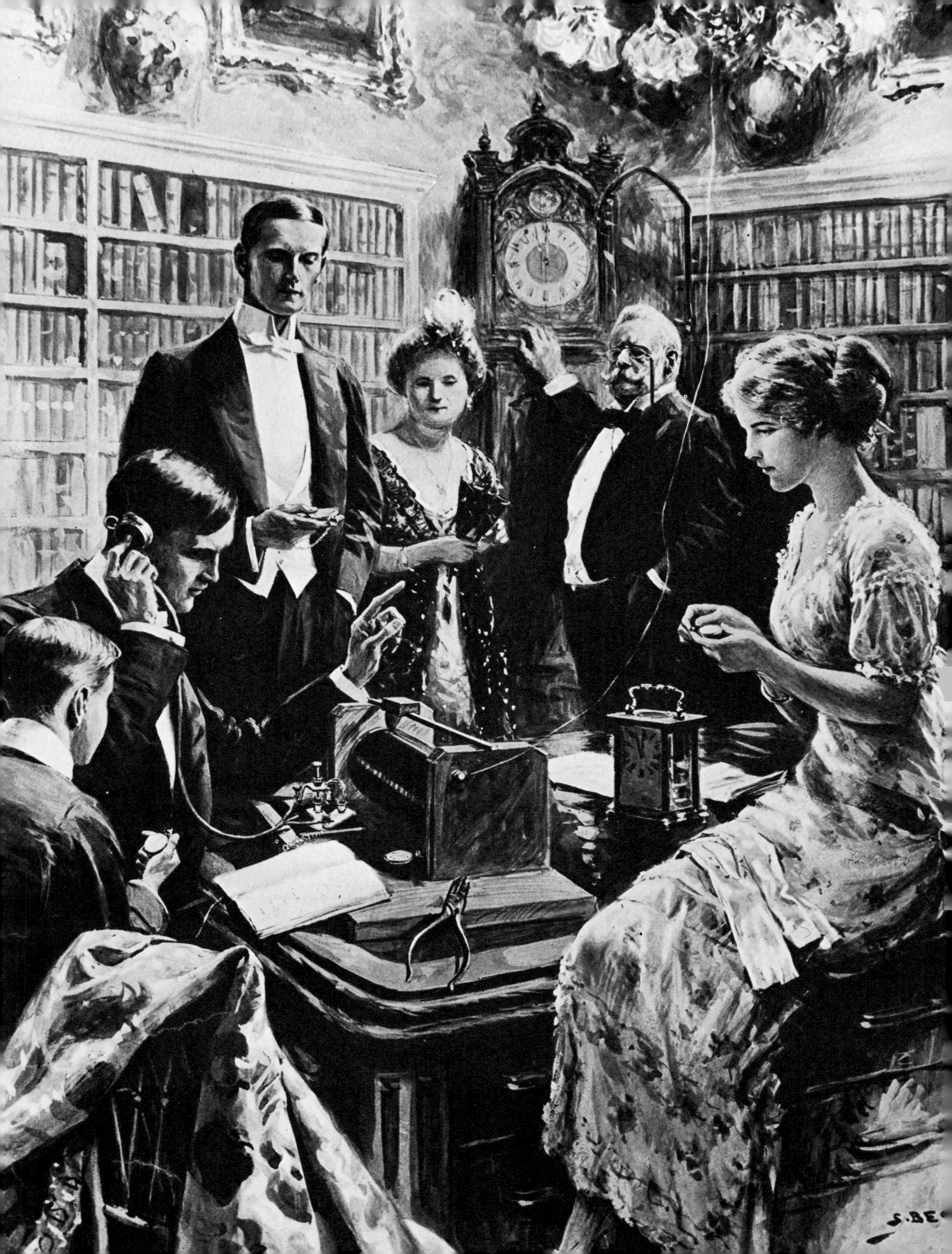

two years later, in 1907, Leonardo's dream came true when a Frenchman, Paul Cornu, took off at Lisieux in France in a helicopter.

Running parallel to this dramatic improvement in man's ability to get from one place to another was an equally exciting breakthrough in the possibility of sending messages instead: the wireless telegraph, which came to be the radio.

The story had begun with Faraday's discovery of electromagnetism. It was taken up by a brilliant Scottish physicist, James Clerk Maxwell, who, after years of experiment, demonstrated that electromagnetic forces travel in a similar wave-pattern to those of light. He also confirmed that the speed with which an electric current flows along a wire is the same as the speed of light – roughly 186,000 miles per second.

Maxwell came to an absolutely startling conclusion. As he put it: 'We can scarcely avoid the inference that light consists in the transverse undulations of the same medium which is the cause of electric and magnetic phenomena.' In plain language, light and electricity were variations of the same thing – as indeed they are.

Since light can travel through the air, why not electromagnetic waves? Maxwell died in 1879, aged only forty-eight, but within ten years his theory was proved experimentally by an equally brilliant young German, Heinrich Hertz. As his 'transmitter', he used a spark generated between two metal plates. A few feet away was his 'receiver', which was a loop of wire with two brass balls at each end of it. The loop was bent round until the two balls were only separated by the tiniest gap. In a darkened room it was possible to see that when the first spark was generated, another spark jumped the tiny gap between the balls. The first spark had generated an electromagnetic wave which had been picked up by the wire loop and re-converted into an electrical current.

Hertz, like Maxwell, died tragically young, at the age of thirty-seven. The year was 1894, and in the two top rooms of his father's country house near Bologna, a young Italian now wore the mantle of invention and discovery that had passed from Faraday to Maxwell and Hertz. He was then twenty, and his name was Guglielmo Marconi. By the following year, he had turned all that had gone before into practical reality. As his receiver he used a device called a 'coherer', which had been developed as a result of independent research by American, French, Italian and English physicists – a reminder that scientific advances were coming more and more to depend on the efforts of many individuals and groups.

The coherer was a glass tube filled with iron filings. In normal circumstances, an electric current would not pass through the filings, but it had been discovered that if they were exposed to electromagnetic waves they would 'cohere' – in plain language again, 'stick very lightly to each other' – allowing a current to pass through. So, if a battery were attached to the coherer, in such a way that it was always trying to pass a current through it, then the moments when it *succeeded* in passing a current would indicate the presence of electromagnetic waves. The coherer was fitted with a mechanical 'decoherer', which was simply a way of continually shaking the iron filings loose again, ready to indicate the presence of the next signal.

To help his 'transmitter' spark he put it at the top of an aerial, which increased the range to a mile and a half. The question was: would the waves be affected by high ground between transmitter and receiver? In the September of 1895, he sent his brother Alfonso to the far side of a hill near their home, the Villa Grifone. Guglielmo transmitted – and a shot from his brother's rifle told him that the message had been received.

Unbelievably, the Italian government showed scant interest in Marconi's work, and in 1896 he came to England, where he got immediate support from the Post Office. Improvements followed rapidly, until finally, on 12 December 1901, the letter 'S' was transmitted in Morse code from a station at Poldhu in Cornwall – and was received by Marconi in St John's, Newfoundland, seventeen hundred miles away.

Nine years later the use of radio became a public sensation when in 1910 a transatlantic call to the captain of the ship *Montrose*, near Quebec, led to the capture of the fugitive murderer Crippen, and his lover Ethel Le Neve. It was a curious case of history repeating itself, because sixty-five years earlier the first public telegraph service had been used to catch a murderer who had caught a train from Slough. When he arrived in London, the police were waiting for him, just as Inspector Dew was to wait for Crippen.

If electromagnetic waves could be used to transmit sounds, why not pictures? The idea had occurred to an awful lot of people. Since the early days of the telegraph there had been ideas, some of which worked, for sending crude images over telegraph-wires.

But these were not moving pictures, since they had to be built up, piece by piece. That was the crux of the problem: how to break down a picture into a great number of small component parts, and having done that, how to 'look at' or 'scan' across all those parts in such a way that when they were transmitted they could be reassembled as 'one picture'.

There were two basic lines of thought. The first was to look at the picture mechanically. In 1884 a German named Paul Nipkow devised a disc which had a series of holes in it, starting at the edge and moving towards the centre in a spiral. The spiral was designed in such a way that, when it was rotated, the first hole passed along the (imaginary) top line of the picture, the second hole the next line, and so on. According to what the picture was, the strength of the light passing through the holes would depend on the degree of light or darkness on each line of the picture. This was converted by a photoelectric cell into a series of different electric values, which were converted back again at the receiving end into the original values of light-intensity, and passed through another Nipkow disc (rotating at exactly the same speed as the first) to form the lines of the picture.

This was basically the system used by the Scotsman John Logie Baird, when he gave the first public demonstration of television on 27 January 1926, at the Royal Institution in London. Two years later he had transmitted pictures in colour, and had sent pictures across the Atlantic. In 1932 the BBC began a regular television service, using Baird's equipment.

Radio time-signals reach London from the Eiffel Tower, 1913.

THE STORY OF INVENTIONS

The trouble with his system was that it could only achieve a very low definition – that is to say, because of the limitations of the disc, there were only thirty lines to each picture, which meant that the image was crude.

It was the second line of thought that was to lead to today's television, as well as to a host of other devices which today we take for granted. It was based on the realization, right at the end of the nineteenth century, that atoms were not the smallest constituent parts of our universe. Atoms were composed of a number of smaller parts, some of which were negatively charged particles which came to be known as electrons.

In 1897, the German Karl Ferdinand Braun had built a cathode-ray tube. The cathode is the negative terminal of any electrical power-source, like a battery. It had been discovered that if a hot cathode were discharging into a vacuum, it gave off a stream of these negative particles, electrons. Braun built his cathode into the end of a glass tube, the other end of which was made fluorescent. He made the stream of electrons pass through two sets of plates, one set of which would move the stream up and down as it passed through the vacuum, the other from side to side. The results were visible on the screen at the other end. It was an oscilloscope, just as we use today in instruments like those in hospitals for monitoring heart-beats and other functions of the body.

The degree by which the two sets of plates deflected the beam from side to side and up and down depended on the electrical voltage passing across them, and it was a Russian professor, Boris Rosing, who first saw this as a way of producing an electronic picture. But he still used a mechanical device like Baird's for transmitting the picture.

But in his laboratory at St Petersburg, now Leningrad, was a young student named Vladimir Zworykin, who emigrated to the United States in 1919. By 1928 he had adapted the principle to produce his 'iconoscope' camera tube. Now, both the transmitter and the receiver did their scanning electronically, and the television age was born.

Zworykin's camera broke the picture down into 120 lines. Today there are two standard systems: the American, which uses 525 lines, and produces 30 complete pictures every second; and the European, which has 625 lines but only 25 pictures a second.

These researches into the properties of light, electromagnetism, radio waves and heat, all of which, it was now understood, were directly related to one another, spread into a hundred different branches of technology – and it is beyond the scope of this book to describe even a fraction of them. What is more, the high points of modern invention, which appeal to the layman because he can understand their usefulness or their dramatic qualities, are often only the last step in a chain of discovery whose previous steps are of prime interest only to the scientist (so that, for instance, the team under Robert Oppenheimer who built the first atomic bomb were the end of one particular chain that went back to Albert Einstein, with his Theory of Relativity, and before him).

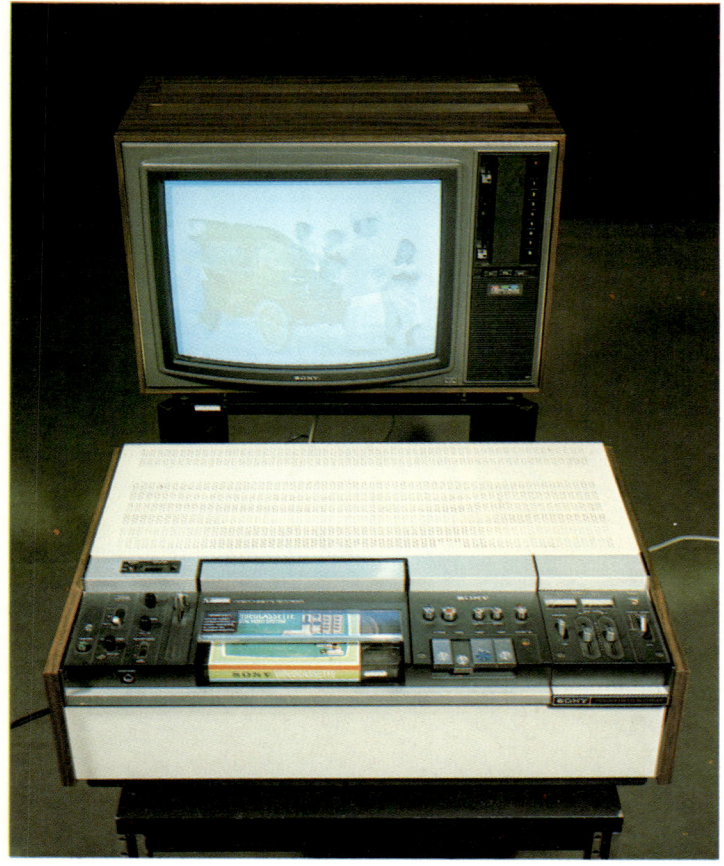

TOP *The arrest of Dr Crippen and his lover, Ethel Le Neve.*
ABOVE *A modern video-cassette.*

In addition, it becomes more difficult to single out great inventive individuals who are responsible for truly 'new' concepts. One such would be Sir Barnes Wallis, famous in the public eye for his invention of the bouncing bombs for the 'Dambusters', but the innovator also of far more important and radical ideas – like the 'swing-wing' or variable-geometry aeroplane. More often, the breakthroughs come through the work of large teams, in universities and in corporations.

Of course, these 'chains' do not *end* with a great invention. They continue on other paths. Zworykin's work in television, for instance, started a separate chain that led to the electron microscope, which was first built by others in the early 1930s. He himself joined in that new chain, and in 1939 built an instrument that could magnify a hundred thousand times. Two years later, we had our first photograph of the flu virus.

We explored inwards, and we explored outwards. By the early 1940s, after it was realized that radio 'interference' was due to faint radio waves reaching us from outer space, the giant dishes of radio telescopes began to be built, collecting and amplifying the signals and allowing us to build up pictures, not just of our own universe, but of other galaxies.

Nearer to home, the detection of moving objects at sea and in

The Parkes radio telescope, Australia.

THE STORY OF INVENTIONS

Whittle's first turbo-jet engine. The world of technology had come a long way since Hero's aeolipile.

the air was made possible by the development of radar. It had long been realized that the reason Marconi's radio waves could be heard by his brother on the other side of the hill was that radio waves bounce off the ionosphere, a layer in the earth's upper atmosphere. If they'd bounce off that, why not off anything else?

Much of the credit is usually given to Robert Watson Watt, who in the mid-'thirties was head of the radio department of Britain's National Physical Laboratory. This is partly because the radar he developed was to prove so crucial to Britain's defences in the Second World War. But in fact, parallel development was going on in the United States, France and Germany, and it was actually a German, Dr Rudolph Kuhnold, working for the German Navy, who built the first successful radar, which by 1934, a year before Watson Watt's first experiments, could detect both ships and aircraft.

The idea of radar is essentially very simple. Radio signals are sent out at a given frequency and strength. If they hit something, they return like an echo. Since you know the speed at which they are travelling, and you know when you sent them out, then the time at which they return allows you to calculate how far the object is away. If you then put that information as an electronic 'dot' on a screen, which represents a map of the area you are looking at, and continue to get a series of echoes from the object, you can determine how fast it is travelling, and in what direction. As in television, the instrument used for forming this 'picture' is the cathode-ray tube.

'Radar' stands for 'radio detecting and ranging'. We live in an age of acronyms, and few more important than 'laser', short for 'light amplification by stimulated emission of radiation'. It was a crucial invention, first made to work by scientists at Malibu, in California, in 1960, and it is a supreme example of the way in which scientists, for so long separated from the inventors, have today for the most part *become* the inventors. We owe the basic principle involved, as with so much else that we take for granted today, to the work of Albert Einstein, one of the supreme figures in the history of science.

Put as simply as possible, a laser works like this: atoms of a given kind (different atoms will produce different kinds of laser) are excited in such a way that they have a surplus amount of energy to give off. If they are then exposed to an electromagnetic or light wave of a given frequency, they will give off radiation at the same frequency.

But ordinary light spreads out from its source in all directions, which is why an electric bulb will illuminate a whole room. The final, key step, taken by the laser is to so organize the emission of the light waves from the excited atoms that they do not spread out. To all intents and purposes they travel as a single beam. The nature and strength of the beam will depend on the atoms that are involved in the first place. And the use varies accordingly. Already lasers are being used for high-speed metal-cutting, and for the delicate precision required by surgeons for 'welding' together damaged parts of the human eye. Another use, which like the laser itself is still in its infancy, is for producing three-dimensional photographs called 'holographs'.

But laser's greatest usefulness will probably be in the field of communications. To give an idea *how* useful: it has been calculated that the different frequencies which make up the visible light spectrum could in theory carry eight hundred million telephone calls at the same time.

The laser is a truly twentieth-century idea. In other areas the chains of invention went back far earlier. Hero of Alexandria's aeolipile, which had led to the water- and steam-turbines of the nineteenth century, had evolved during the 1930s into the gas-turbine – and that was used to power the jet engines pioneered by the German Dr Hans von Ohain and the Englishman Frank Whittle.

They came into operational use towards the end of the Second World War, at the same time that another old idea was finally made practical – the computer. In a sense that was one of the oldest ideas of all, the aid for doing mathematical calculations – for which, of course, nature provided man with the original foolproof decimal system, his ten fingers.

The first external mathematical aid, devised by the early Babylonians, was the abacus, such as small children still use today; and in the mid-seventeenth century the French scientist–philosopher Blaise Pascal, while still in his teens, devised an adding machine to help his father with tax-collecting in Rouen. Thirty years later, the great German philosopher–mathematician Gottfried Leibniz designed one that would multiply and divide. He also gave the world the definitive statement about the need for computers: 'It is unworthy of excellent men to lose hours like slaves in the labour of calculation which could safely be relegated to anyone else if machines were used.'

Babbage's 'difference engine', the first computer.

131

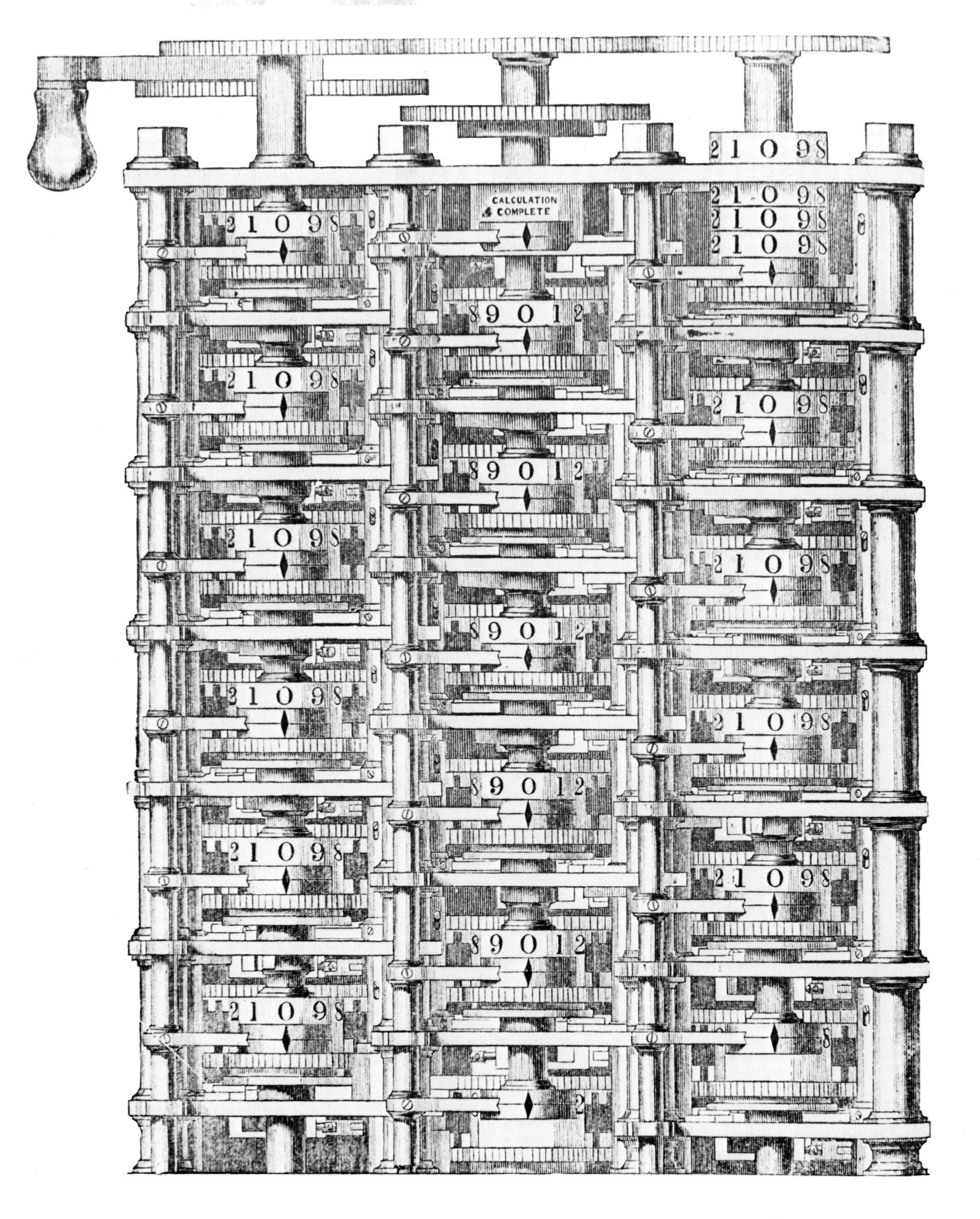

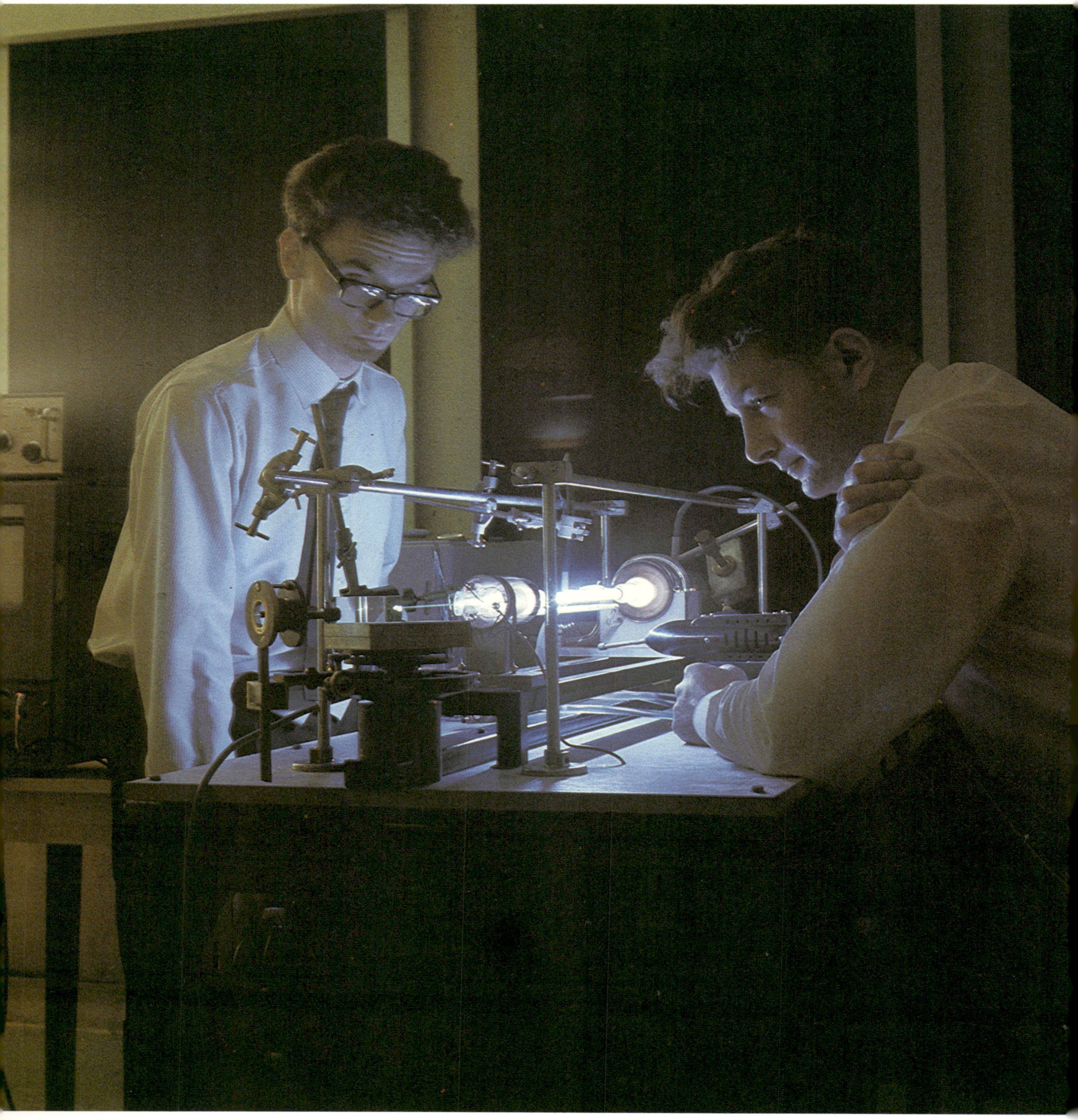

A hundred and fifty years later, in 1822, the eccentric English genius Charles Babbage made public his plans for an 'analytical engine', which was the true ancestor of the modern computer, and had features like the use of punched cards (a spin-off from Jacquard's control system for weaving) for programming the machine. Yet again, technology was too far behind the mind of the inventor – because the parts he wanted could not be machined to the precision he had specified.

In the early twentieth century it became obvious that the key would lie in the use of electronics, and after several attempts at semi-electronic machines, the first fully electronic calculator was demonstrated at the University of Pennsylvania. It was the work of J. Presper Eckert and John W. Mauchly. Acronym-happy again, they called it the 'Eniac', short for 'electronic numerical integrator and calculator'.

If at times our lives seem ruled by computers, it is also the case that Leibniz was absolutely right: they *do* save an awful lot of

LEFT *Working with a laser.*
ABOVE *Computers are everywhere – in this case Poland.*

time. One example will show how *much* time. Every schoolboy knows that the Greek letter 'pi' is used to stand for a mathematical relationship which always exists between circles and spheres, and their diameters. It is, very roughly, 3·142. But mathematicians have always been curious to see how far they could go in getting an exact figure for pi.

In the mid-eighteenth century, Leonhard Euler, a Swiss mathematician, calculated it to 660 decimal places (only guaranteeing that the first 600 were accurate!). It took him two years. Then in 1947 Eniac, whose first task the year before had been to calculate the trajectory of artillery shells, was given the pi problem. It took two days to do the calculation, this time, though, to 2000 places of decimals.

Today's largest computers can do that in two seconds. That they can do so is due to one of the great inventions of the twentieth century: the transistor. It arrived in December 1947, the brainchild of three American physicists, William Shockley, John Bardeen and Walter Brattain.

It had been known for forty years that there were certain sorts of crystals which had peculiar electrical properties; they would

The power to destroy everything – a hydrogen explosion.

not conduct an electrical current, but on the other hand they wouldn't resist it, or insulate it. They became known as semi-conductors, and almost from the beginnings of radio it was known that they would act as detectors of radio waves. Indeed, the old 'cat's-whisker' crystal sets made use of that property.

What they could not do was to act as amplifiers, until Shockley and his team discovered ways of modifying them to enable them to do just that, winning themselves a Nobel prize in the process. The transistor could do, in the space occupied by a speck of dust, what a radio valve could do – and it was virtually shock-proof. It could be, and was, immediately put to a thousand uses in the various fields of electronics, of which its best known, in the tiny transistor radios, is only one, and a relatively unimportant one at that – except that, to that mythical figure, the man in the street, these are the products of invention that do matter. To him, it is the shape and size and colour of his nylon shirt that matter, not the amazing advances this century has seen in the production of plastics and artificial fibres from the by-products of coal and oil.

Again, he wants to know what is on at his local cinema, and who is acting in it, rather than the long series of inventions that began in 1895, when the brothers Lumière, Louis and Auguste, showed a Parisian audience a film of a train and a rowing-boat, and founded a vast industry.

The man in the street is probably right. Inventions and technologies are barren if they cannot in the end be used to benefit people. All the same, the inventors should be given their dues. Next time you use a zip-fastener, think of the American Whitcomb L. Judson, who first had the brainwave (it was, after all, a *radically* new way of doing things up), and the Swedish Gideon Sundback, who perfected it in 1913. Next time you press the nozzle of an aerosol spray, think of Lyle D. Goodhue, the American who invented it in 1941; again, a *radically* new way of dispensing liquids, from air-freshener to shoe polish.

But the two developments that may prove to have been the most significant of this, or any other, century were not the work of any one man. They were the work of huge teams of men, and the culmination of centuries of knowledge. The one ventured inward, to the world of the infinitely tiny constituents of matter; the other outward, to the realms of the unbelievably vast. They were the harnessing of nuclear energy, and the first steps in space-travel.

There is no simple way to explain what happens in a nuclear reaction. But it is based on the fact that at the centre of every atom is a thing called a nucleus. It is very small – the atom itself is about a hundred thousand times larger than the nucleus – but it is also very heavy, representing nearly the entire weight of the whole atom.

The reason the nucleus is so heavy is that it is composed of even smaller particles, called protons and neutrons, which are bound very tightly together by energy, making the nucleus as a whole extremely dense. Some nuclei have just one or two neutrons and protons, others have hundreds.

Nuclear fission was the principle involved in the 'atomic' bomb that was first exploded at Alamogordo, in the desert of New Mexico, on 16 July 1945, and subsequently dropped on Hiroshima and Nagasaki. In it, the nuclei of a heavy element (one that has a lot of neutrons and protons in each nucleus) – which in that case was uranium – are bombarded by neutrons from an outside source. This has the effect of splitting each nucleus in two. This splitting releases a great deal of energy, together with a number of 'spare' neutrons from the broken nuclei, which go on to split up other nuclei – which is why it is known as a 'chain' reaction.

In 1954 the Russians built a very small power station which harnessed these nuclear reactions in a controlled way to produce electricity, but the first major nuclear power station was opened two years later at Calder Hall, in Cumberland.

In principle, there is enough suitable fuel in the world for nuclear fission to keep us supplied with energy for millions of years. The trouble is that a lot of it is comparatively hard to get at, being locked up in tiny amounts in the granite rocks that form much of the earth's surface.

However, there is another possibility: nuclear fusion, which is the principle involved in the 'hydrogen' bomb. It is roughly the reverse of fission. Instead of a heavy nucleus being split, two very light nuclei are made to join together, or 'fuse'. The most suitable 'fuel' is deuterium, which is a variety of hydrogen (from which the bomb got its name).

The problem with fusion is that it requires enormous amounts of heat, similar to those released by an 'atomic' bomb, to make the fusion happen. And it is extremely difficult to contain that heat for long enough to be able to convert it into usable power.

By 'long enough' we mean fractions of seconds. Any longer, and it would simply melt everything around. The present thinking seems to be that the way to contain the reaction is to hold it inside a magnetic field. So far, the Russians and the Americans can do this for approximately one hundredth of a second. If they can do it for as long as a tenth of a second, our worries about sources of power are over – because deuterium exists in all water. Potentially, the deuterium contained in one cubic foot of water can provide the energy equivalent to ten tons of coal.

And then, there was Space. The fantasies of Jules Verne and H. G. Wells finally came true. In 1957, the Russians put up the first artificial satellite, the little 'bleeping' Sputnik. Four years later they put up the first astronaut, Yuri Gagarin, who circled the earth in eighty-nine minutes. On 20 July 1969, the Americans put Neil Armstrong and Edwin 'Buzz' Aldrin on to the surface of the moon. In 1976, they landed two unmanned 'Viking' spacecraft on the surface of Mars.

These have been the first critical steps in an exploration of whose end we can have no idea. But already, the use of space is proving of inestimable value to man. For example, there are the weather satellites. They sit 22,300 miles above the Equator, and travel at such a speed that they circle the earth in exactly the same time as it takes the earth to rotate. Thus they remain in a fixed position relative to the earth, and send pictures of the entire hemisphere that is visible to them – invaluable for weather-prediction. Other satellites, on a similar 'synchronous' orbit, are equally invaluable for communications, and can, for instance, beam TV programmes into isolated communities that could otherwise never receive them.

Perhaps the most dramatically useful of all the satellites is the one called 'Landsat'. It flies much lower than the weather satellites, at a height of 570 miles. And unlike them, its orbit takes it round the poles, or very near them, so that the earth rotates *within* the satellite's orbit. This means that every time the satellite 'comes round again', it is looking at a different strip, 115 miles wide, of the earth's surface. The strips it has 'missed out' are covered on succeeding orbits, and in this way it covers the entire face of the earth every eighteen days.

It is fitted with a multi-spectrum camera – that is, a camera which looks at the earth simultaneously through several different parts of the spectrum. By 'adding these pictures together' in

The Chapelcross nuclear power station in Scotland.

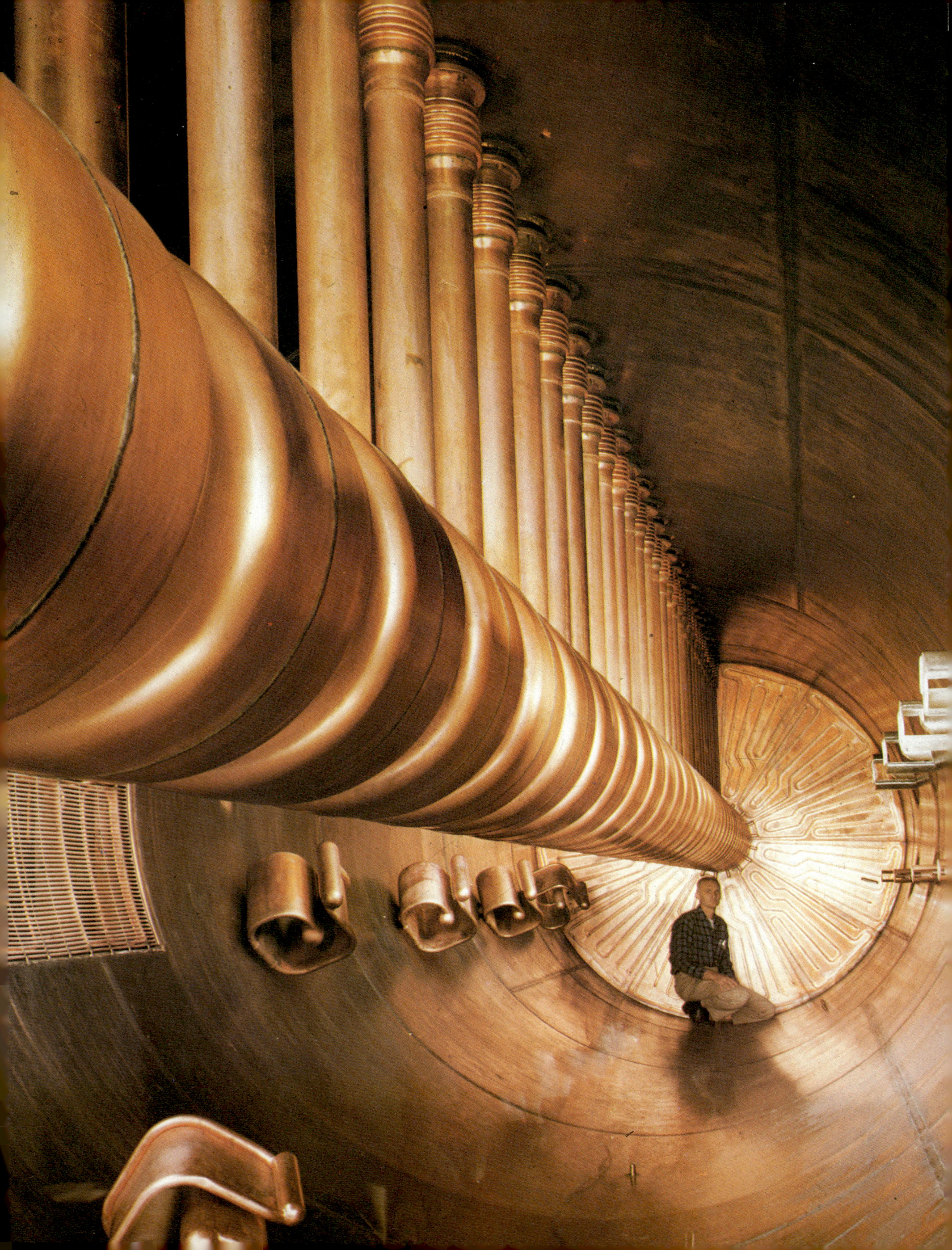

ABOVE *What Werner von Braun began with his Second World War rocket attacks on Britain ended with astronauts in space.*
BELOW *The Apollo command and service modules put the earth into perspective.*

LEFT *The tools of modern science come expensive. A linear accelerator of the University of California.*

different combinations, an unbelievable variety of information is gathered. It can tell a farmer, with a large acreage to care for, what part of his crops are affected by disease, or which are ready for harvest. It can show how floods are building up, or sand dunes are 'creeping'. It can tell you where to look for valuable mineral deposits that were previously unknown. It can warn you of pollution build-up, and it can tell you what harbours are going to need dredging. It can point trawlermen to the best fishing grounds, and it can tell the managers of large forests how much timber there is available. Its uses are virtually limitless, and in the long run it may well prove to be space's greatest gift to earth.

As I have said, the great advances today seem to be exclusively the work of huge, co-ordinated teams of highly skilled scientists. Since that seems to spell a bleak future for individual genius and the sudden flash of inspiration, let me end with the story of Percy Shaw.

One night in 1933, Mr Shaw was driving along a dangerous road between Queensbury and Halifax in Yorkshire. It was a foggy night, and he was about to drive through a fence and over a sheer drop when he was saved by seeing, reflected in his lights, the eyes of a cat which was sitting on the fence. He put that idea together with the reflecting studs that he had seen on advertising posters, and he invented the 'cat's-eye' road stud, which since that day must have saved thousands of lives. It was almost the perfect invention. It was comparatively cheap to install; it required no power to operate, since it only worked by reflection; it was virtually indestructible; and it was self-cleaning.

It made a fortune for Percy Shaw, who was the son of a poor labourer. More importantly, it proved that the world still has need of the inventive brainwave, which can only come from where it has always come from, and where it always will come from – the bright spark of a man's lonely intuition.

Acknowledgments

Illustrations are reproduced by kind permission of the following:

Alinari: 70–1
Bernisches Historisches Museum: 50 below
Bibliothèque Nationale: 60
British Museum: 13 above, 49 above, 53, 56–7
British Museum (Michael Holford Library): 10, 14, 15, 18, 23 above
   left and below, 27, 31
British Museum (Eileen Tweedy): 96–7
Camera Press: 12, 120–1, 135
Department of the Environment: 17
Mary Evans Picture Library: 118
John Freeman: 20
Germanisches Nationalmuseum: 58–9
Giraudon: 62
David Harris: 8
Harvester Company of Great Britain: 112
Hirmer Fotoarchiv, Munich: 24
Michael Holford Library: 22 above and below, 42, 73, 117
Mansell Collection: 29 below, 39, 40–1, 48, 64, 87, 89, 101, 102, 103, 104–5, 115, 122 left and right, 123 large and inset, 126, 128 above
Metropolitan Museum of Art, New York: 29, 32

Musee Cernuschi, Paris (Michael Holford Library): 26
Museo Naval, Madrid: 61
NASA: 137 above
National Maritime Museum: 79, 80–1 (Michael Holford Library)
National Portrait Gallery: 86
Joseph Needham, *Science and Civilisation in China*: 54 right
Photomas Index: endpaper
Picturepoint: 2–3, 49 below, 109 above, 116 below, 128 below, 129, 130, 132, 133, 136–7, 137 below
Popperphoto: 109 below, 134
Ronan Picture Library: 6, 11 left and right, 16 above and below, 21, 29 above, 33, 34, 35, 36, 37 above and below, 38, 44 left and right, 50 above, 51, 52, 54 left, 55, 67, 72, 74, 75 left and right, 76, 77, 78, 90, 91, 92, 94–5, 96, 98, 99, 100, 108, 110, 111 left and right, 116 above, 124, 125, 131
Royal Institution (Michael Holford Library): 88, 93
Scala: 65, 66–7
Science Museum: 82, 106, 114, 130
Science Museum (Michael Holford Library): 68, 69, 113 left and right
Ronald Sheridan: 13 below, 23 above right, 30
Stiftsbibliothek St Gallen: 46
Eileen Tweedy: 84–5
York Archaeological Trust: 43 above and below

139

Index

aeolipile, 37, 89, 130
aerosol spray, 134
air-pump, 74–5
airship, 99, 124–7
Al-Biruni, 49
alembic, 49
Alhazen of Basra, 114
alphabet, 24
Ampère, André Marie, 89
Appert, Nicolas, 110
aqueduct, 28–9, 44
Archimedes, 33–5, 76
Arkwright, Richard, 101–2
Arlandes, Marquis de, 99
artillery (early), 41
assay, 30
astrolabe, 59, 77

Babbage, Charles, 133
Bacon, Roger, 50, 67
Baird, John Logie, 127
balance, 29–30
ballista, 41
balloon, 97–9
barbed-wire, 111
barometer, 73–4
basket, 13
battery, 89
Bell, Alexander Graham, 113
Benz, Karl, 123–4
Bessemer, Henry, 91–2
bicycle, 99
birth-control pill, 119
Blanchard, Jean Pierre, 99
boat, 17, 45; *see also* steamboat
Bosch, Robert, 124
bow, 10–11, 21
Braun, Karl Ferdinand, 128
brick, 25
bullet, 107

Callinicus, 48–50
cam, 54–5
camera, 114
cannon, 50–3, 63, 107
cartridge, 107–8

cathode-ray tube, 128–30
cat's-eye, 138
cement, 41
Charles, J. A. C., 99
chronometer, 81
clepsydra, *see* waterclock
clock, 35, 73, 79–81
coal, 64; as fuel, 83; coke smelting, 91; safety in mining, 92–4
collar, padded, 48
Colt, Samuel, 107
combine harvester, 111
compass, 58
computer, 122, 130–3
concrete, 41–3
Cooke, William, 113
Copernicus, 67
Cornu, Paul, 127
cotton-gin, 106
crane, 29
crank, 54
Crompton, Samuel, 102
crossbow, 39–40
Ctesibius, 33–7

Daguerre, Louis, 114
Daimler, Gottlieb, 123–4
Darby, Abraham (I, II, and III), 91
Davy, Humphrey, 92–5
Diesel, Rudolph, 124
dioptra, 38
distillation, 49
Dunlop, John Boyd, 99
dynamite, 108–10
dynamo, 89

Edison, Thomas, 117
Einstein, Albert, 128–30
electricity, 87–90
electric light bulb, 117, 130

Fahrenheit, Gabriel, 74
Faraday, Michael, 89, 127
fire; and prehistoric man, 9; methods of making, 9–12; use of heat, 15–16; artificial light, 16–17
Fleming, Alexander, 119

flying shuttle, 100–1
force pump, 36–7
Ford, Henry, 124
Forsyth, Alexander, 107
Fourneyron, Benoît, 89
Franklin, Benjamin, 87

Galileo, 68, 73–4, 79–80
Galvani, Luigi, 87
Gascoigne, William, 68
gastraphetes, *see* crossbow
Gatling, Richard Jordan, 107–8
Giffard, Henri, 99
glass, 25; in optical lenses, 67–8
Glidden, Joseph, 111
Goodhue, Lyle D., 134
gramophone, 114–17
Greek fire, 48–50
Guericke, Otto von, 74
gunpowder, 50
Gutenberg, Johann Gensfleisch zum, 58

Hadley, John, 77
Hargreaves, James, 101
Harrison, John, 81
Hero, 33, 37–9, 89–90
Hertz, Heinrich, 127
Hipparchus, 33, 59
horseshoe, 48
Houiller, 107
hovercraft, 17–19
Huygens, Christiaan, 73
hydraulic screw, 34

Jacquard, Joseph, 102–6, 133
Janssen, Zacharias, 67
Jeffries, Dr, 99
Jenner, Dr Edward, 119
jet engine, 38, 130
Jouffroy d'Abbans, Marquis de, 97
Judson, Whitcomb L., 134

Kay, John, 100–1
Keppler, Johannes, 67–8
Kuhnold, Dr Rudolph, 130

lamp, safety, 92–4
laser, 17, 130

141

Leeuwenhoek, Anton van, 67–8
Leibniz, Gottfried, 130–3
Lenoir, Etienne, 122
lenses, 67
lever, 11, 19, 24, 28, 61; principle of, 34–5
lighthouse, 45
Lippershey, Hans, 68
loom, 13; *see also* textile industry
Lumière, Louis and Auguste, 134

machine-gun, 107–8
Macmillan, Kirkpatrick, 99
Manby, Aaron, 97
maps, 58
Marconi, Guglielmo, 127
Mauchly, John W., 133
Maxwell, James Clerk, 127
Maybach, Wilhelm, 123–4
McCormick, Cyrus Hall, 111
mechanical reaper, 111
medicine, 66–7, 119
metallurgy, 9, 15–19, 65, 77, 91; copper, 15–16, 25–8; gold, 15–16; silver, 16; electrum, 16, 31; lead, 16; bronze, 25–8, 50; tin, 25; iron, 25–8, 50, 64, 91–2; steel, 25–8, 83, 91–2
Michelangelo, 63
micrometer, 68
microscope, 67–8
Minié, Claude, 107
money, 29–30, 63
Montgolfier, Jacques and Joseph, 97–9
Morse, Samuel, 113
motor-car, 122–4
motor-cycle, 123

needle, 13
Neilson, J. B., 91
Newcomen, Thomas, 76
Newton, Isaac, 37, 73
Niepce, Joseph Nicéphore, 114
Nipkow, Paul, 127
Nobel, Alfred, 108–10
nuclear energy, 119, 135

Oersted, Hans Christian, 89, 113
Ohain, Dr Hans von, 130
onager, 41
organ, 37
oscilloscope, 128
Otto, Nikolas August, 123

paper, 55
Papin, Denis, 75–6, 95
Paré, Ambroise, 66–7
Parsons, Charles, 90
Pascal, Blaise, 73, 130
Pasteur, Louis, 119

patent, origin of, 63
pendulum, 68, 73, 79–80
penicillin, 119
Perkins, Jacob, 110
Philo, 74
phonograph, 117
Pincus, Dr Gregory, 119
Pi Sheng, 55
piston, 36, 50
piston engine, 76
plough, 14, 47–8
plumb-line, 24
pneumatic tyre, 99
pottery, 15–16, 19
prefabrication, 25
Presper, Eckert J., 133
pressure cooker, 76, 95
printing, 55–8, 65, 85
prosthetics, 67
Puckle, James, 107
pulley, 24
pycnometer, 49
pyramids, 24–5

radar, 130
radio, 122, 127
railway, 95
refrigerator, 110–11
revolver, 107
road, 41–3
rocket, 50
Ronalds, Sir Francis, 111
Röntgen, Wilhelm, 119
Rosing, Professor Boris, 128
Rozier, Jean Pilâtre de, 99
rudder, 17, 61

sail, 17, 45, 61
Santorio, 74
Savery, Captain Thomas, 75
Scheiner, Christoph, 68
screw-press, 38–9
sextant, 59, 77
shaduf, 29
Shaw, Percy, 138
Shockley, William, 133–4
Sholes, Christopher Latham, 114
Smith, Horace, 107
space, 135–8
spindle, 13
spinning jenny, 101–2
spinning and weaving, *see* textile industry
steamboat, 95–7
steam-engines, 75–6, 85–7, 90, 94–5, 122–3
steel converter, 92
Stephenson, George and Robert, 95
Stevens, Colonel John, 97

stirrup, 47
stomach-bow, *see* crossbow
submarine, 108
Sundback, Gideon, 134
swingletree, *see* whippletree

Talbot, William Henry Fox, 114
telegraph, 111–13
telephone, 113
telescope, 68
television, 122, 127–8
textile industry, 13, 55, 83, 100–6
thermometer, 74
thermoscope, 74
tools; use of by prehistoric man, 9; stone tools, 12–13; for spinning and weaving, 13, 54; agricultural 14, 48; industrial, 15–16; and pyramids, 23
torpedo, 108
Torricelli, Evangelista, 73
transistor, 133–4
Trevithick, Richard, 95
trip-hammer, 55
Ts'ai Lun, 55
turbine, 89–90, 97
typewriter, 114

Vernier, Pierre, 108
Vinci, Leonardo da, 37, 47, 65–6, 127
Volta, Alessandro, 87–9

Wallis, Sir Barnes, 129
water; draining and irrigation, 28–31, 63, 74; transport, 17, 60; as power-source, 44, 51–4, 74, 89–90
water-clock, 35
water-frame, 101
water-wheel, 29, 44, 97; as power-source, 44–5, 51–5, 74, 89
Watson Watt, Robert, 130
Watt, James, 85–7
weapons, 10–11, 19, 39, 41, 47–53, 63, 107–10, 112, 128–30, 135
Wesson, Daniel B., 107
Wheatstone, Charles, 113
wheel, 17–19, 24
whippletree, 48
Whitehead, Robert, 108
Whitney, Eli, 106–7
Whittle, Frank, 130
windmill, 38, 74
Wright, Wilbur and Orville, 124
writing, 21–4

x-ray, 119

Zeppelin, Count Ferdinand von, 124
zip, 134
Zworykin, Vladimir, 128–9

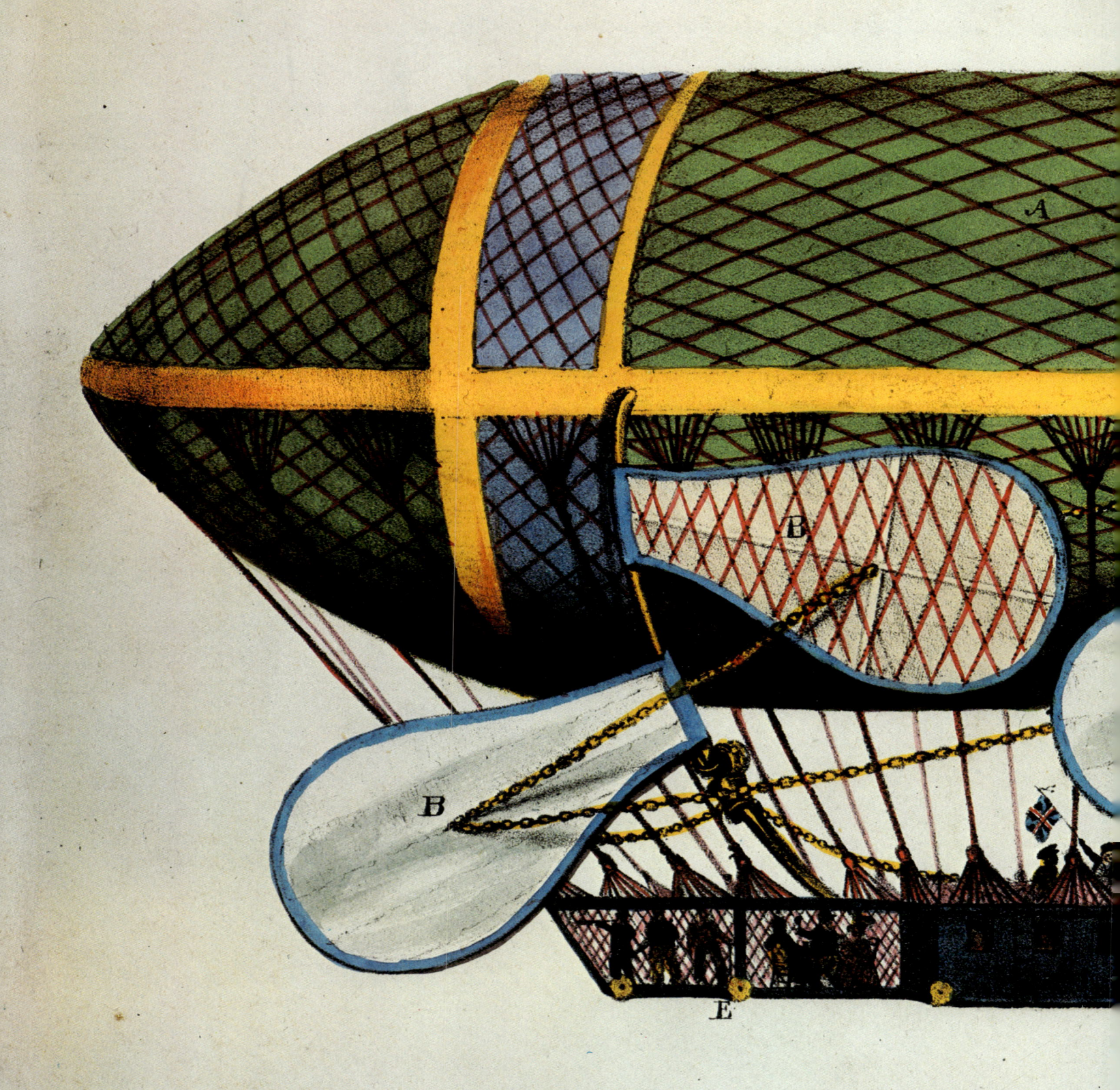

This stupendous machine of a circular form diverging to a line at its extremities is ⎯
of 2400 yards of oiled Lawn and contains about 7000 cubic feet of Gas. The frame ⎯
ing a cabin in the Centre 6 feet wide, is securely attached to the Balloon by ropes.
It is intended to leave London for Paris early in August which they expect to rea⎯

A. The body of the Vessel containing the Gas

B. 4 Wings with movable flaps made of Lawn with net work on one si⎯
ately by machinery contained in the Cabin.

C. The Cabin.

D. The Rudder to steer with, made also of Cane covered with Lawn

E. The extremities of the Car secured with netting for the purpose of walking o⎯